Imagination in the Western Psyche

Imagination in the Western Psyche: From Ancient Greece to Modern Neuroscience offers a comprehensive treatment of the human imagination by integrating the rich discourse on imagination in the humanities with modern neuroscientific research. This book is the first to offer an integrated understanding of imagination from both a humanistic (i.e., historical, philosophical, cultural, depth psychological) and scientific perspective.

The book presents neurobiological accounts that align with prominent theories in Jungian and archetypal psychology and offers a window into the many ways imagination can be understood. It elaborates on the discourse on imagination in Western civilization that goes back thousands of years. Chapters analyze how imagination has been considered throughout history and contrasts a modern neuroscientific approach that looks at imagination by studying its component parts without addressing the phenomenon in all its experiential richness and complexity. By bringing these two approaches together an account of the human imagination emerges that is grounded in scientific rigor without diminishing the fullness of human experience.

This book will appeal to academics, researchers, and post-graduate students in the fields of analytical psychology, depth psychology, Jungian studies, and psychotherapy.

Jonathan Erickson, a writer and educator, holds a BA in English literature from UC Berkeley and a PhD in depth psychology from Pacifica Graduate Institute, California, USA.

Research in Analytical Psychology and Jungian Studies Series

Series Advisor: Andrew Samuels

Professor of Analytical Psychology, Essex University, UK.

The *Research in Analytical Psychology and Jungian Studies* series features research-focused volumes involving qualitative and quantitative research, historical/archival research, theoretical developments, heuristic research, grounded theory, narrative approaches, collaborative research, practitioner-led research, and self-study. The series also includes focused works by clinical practitioners, and provides new research informed explorations of the work of C. G Jung that will appeal to researchers, academics, and scholars alike.

Books in this series:

Marian Apparitions in Cultural Contexts
Applying Jungian Concepts to Mass Visions of the Virgin Mary
Valeria Céspedes Musso

Jung's Psychoid Concept Contextualised
Ann Addison

Transcendent Writers in Stephen King's Fiction
A Post-Jungian Analysis of the Puer Aeternus
Joeri Pacolet

The Self and the Quintessence
A Jungian Perspective
Christine Driver

Imagination in the Western Psyche
From Ancient Greece to Modern Neuroscience
Jonathan Erickson

For more information about this series please visit: www.routledge.com/ Research-in-Analytical-Psychology-and-Jungian-Studies/book-series/ JUNGIANSTUDIES.

Imagination in the Western Psyche

From Ancient Greece to Modern Neuroscience

Jonathan Erickson

LONDON AND NEW YORK

First published 2020
by Routledge
2 Park Square, Milton Park, Abingdon, Oxon, OX14 4RN

and by Routledge
52 Vanderbilt Avenue, New York, NY 10017

Routledge is an imprint of the Taylor & Francis Group, an informa business

© 2020 Jonathan Erickson

British Library Cataloguing-in-Publication Data
A catalogue record for this book is available from the British Library

Library of Congress Cataloging-in-Publication Data
A catalog record has been requested for this book

ISBN: 978-0-367-20516-4 (hbk)
ISBN: 978-0-429-26197-8 (ebk)

Typeset in Sabon
by Wearset Ltd, Boldon, Tyne and Wear

Contents

Acknowledgments

Thanks to Elizabeth Nelson, Erik Goodwyn, Ruth Lanius, Yvonne Lefebvre, Elliot Berkman, Mindy Nettifee, Fabienne Abt, and Rae Johnson for their insight and support throughout the research and writing process.

Part I

Introduction

This initial section lays out the premise of the work: a deep investigation into the human imagination from both scientific and humanistic perspectives. These early chapters explore both the challenges of this approach and also make the case for why such an integrative perspective is both necessary and fruitful.

Chapter 1 offers an initial sketch of how imagination is treated in the laboratories of neuroscience and how this reductive approach contrasts with the rich discourse on imagination in the humanities stretching back millennia. Various definitions of imagination are considered and a working definition is given, along with some helpful psychological and methodological frameworks. Chapter 2 takes a deeper look at overarching philosophical issues around the production of knowledge through scientific versus humanistic means. Scientific method is distinguished from scientism and reductionism, and recent developments in complexity theory and neurophenomenology are presented as promising alternatives approaches to engaging the human imagination.

Chapter 1

Chasing imagination

The great physicist Albert Einstein is often attributed the celebrated aphorism that *imagination is more important than knowledge*. The full context of the quote, which comes from a published interview, offers a bit more nuance: "Imagination is more important than knowledge. For knowledge is limited, whereas imagination embraces the entire world, stimulating progress, giving birth to evolution. It is, strictly speaking, a real factor in scientific research" (2009/1931, p. 97). Despite Einstein's endorsement on the matter, nearly a century later *imagination* remains a challenging concept to reconcile with methods and understandings of quantitative science.

Imagination, after all, is a subjectively experienced phenomenon, complex and protean in its play of content and meaning; by its very nature, it resists reductive methods and understandings. Outside the sphere of science, a long humanist discourse on imagination extends from modern depth psychology backward through Romantic philosophy to find roots in Ancient Greece. The expansive imagination described in both depth psychology and Romantic philosophy speaks of the deep interior of personal meaning, the mystery of creative genius, and even reaches for visions of the cosmogonic. Meanwhile, modern neuroscience, widely recognized as a powerful authority on the human condition, has approached the subject of imagination haltingly (Richardson, 2011). Imagination in the laboratory of neuroscience, poked and prodded and reduced into measurable "objective" frameworks and methodologies, is understandably difficult to define and contain.

Nevertheless, the revolutionary explosion of neuroscientific knowledge in recent decades has not failed to probe into this tricky topic. As might be expected from a predominantly quantitative methodology, the neuroscience of imagination has largely been conducted by the study of its component parts. For example, "imagination" is the term often used to describe "mental time travel," the process of envisioning a potential future scenario (Debus, 2014). The data produced from such study contributes to the neuroscience of imagination, but this remains one small aspect of what depth psychology and Romantic philosophy understand by the term.

Likewise, studies of the way the visual cortex is recruited in forming mental images (Kosslyn, Ganis, & Thompson, 2001) offer another model for understanding imagination, through still only partial. Additional rich veins of data may be found in the neuroscience of dreams and the neuroscience of creativity, two broad fields in themselves that overlap with imagination without fully containing it. Each one of these areas holds a small piece of the puzzle, offering insight into how the brain and nervous system supports and interacts with imaginal experience.

One of the chief tasks of this book is to undertake a synthesis of the fragmented pieces of neurobiological research into imagination. But even with such a synthesis, I will argue that what neuroscience can tell us about imagination is only part of the story. Science, by most accounts, can only speak to that which can be consistently controlled and measured, and the full breadth and depth of human experience simply does not fit into these constraints. Imagination is emblematic of this fact: it is an experience of pure possibility, a protean matrix from which whole worlds can be born. To study the brain science of imagination is a worthy goal and doing so will teach us a great deal. But the phenomenon of imagination itself is a subject so large and complex that if we are to truly do it justice, we must equally draw from the rich discourse in the humanities that has existed for thousands of years. This book is an attempt to do just that: to address the complexity of imaginal phenomenon through an integration of scientific and humanistic perspectives.

Throughout this book, a number of disciplines will be woven into this narrative of imagination: historical, philosophical, psychological, and cultural. In doing so, the purpose is not to create a definitive fusion of all humanistic accounts of imagination—such an endeavor would be neither desirable nor entirely possible. Rather, the purpose is to weave together a sufficiently robust account that demonstrates how such humanistic understanding is constructed and to bring it into dialog with scientific discourse. The history of imagination presented here is but one such history, one version of the story, a piece of the larger truth that nevertheless gives some indication of the whole. Other histories may be written that emphasize different elements, or go into greater detail. It is in the nature of the humanities to welcome multiple perspectives, multiple acts of synthesis, which may then be brought into varying degrees of dialog and integration with scientific accounts. This particular project is about that latter step: an attempt at dialog and integration of scientific and humanistic understandings of imagination.

Defining imagination

Because the pages ahead will flesh out imagination as a dynamic, living phenomenon of consciousness, I hesitate to reduce it to a single linguistic

definition at the outset. Indeed, Chapters 3 and 4 will explore this phenomenon historically and etymologically, and my sincere hope is that the
more an unfamiliar reader engages with these evolving conceptions and
descriptions of imagination throughout history, the clearer it will become
that imagination is better *imagined* than defined. I am aware this seeming
tautology will be unsatisfying to those of a more rational persuasion, and
for that reason a working definition will be provided. But in doing so I
maintain that the imagination defined abstractly by language is not the
imagination as experienced in-the-world. That our linguistic labels can at
times occlude us from the non-linguistic reality they reference is summed
up in Alfred Korzybski's popular aphorism, "the map is not the territory,"
and later reformulated by philosopher Alan Watt's assertion that the
"menu is not the meal" (1957, p. ix). So it is with the phenomenon of
imagination—to restrict it to a narrow linguistic definition from the outset
may in fact obscure the dynamic lived experience that the word signifies.

Nevertheless, a provisional definition of the term, as it will be investigated in this book, is thus: *Imagination is the generation of meaningful,
coherent images and narratives arising in consciousness*. As such this definition excludes meaningless, incoherent images that may arise in phenomenological experience as "mental noise." It is true that what may appear
as "mental noise" initially may prove to have a meaningful and coherent
place in a larger imaginal pattern. But to whatever degree that is the case,
it is the eventual emergence of coherence in the imaginal field that is the
subject of investigation, regardless of whether it initially seemed meaningless or not. For example, the clearly perceived image of a powerful goddess
with bright eyes, flowing black hair, dressed in ornate gold armor and
holding a rune-etched broadsword can be understood as a coherent whole
from which multiple meaningful interpretations can be derived. By contrast
a "noisy" collection of scattered images of a woman, a sword, runes, celestial light in the sky, and developed biceps have potential coherence and
meaning, but remain largely incoherent and unintegrated, and thus unreal-
ized in this regard.

This working definition further raises the question of how "meaning" is
to be understood. Leaving aside the hall of mirrors that discourse on the
meaning of "meaning" portends, I suggest instead a broad and inclusive
understanding of the term. We can speak of a spectrum of meanings,
ranging from simple linguistic understanding to more holistic accounts as
found in the hermeneutic philosophies of Dilthey and Heidegger (i.e., living
a meaningful life). By way of example, imagine the image of a red bird in a
tree. If we can produce a simple linguistic meaning from the image (i.e., the
sentence: "a red bird in a tree") that will suffice as a bare minimum of
recognized meaning in the image. Beyond this, the image can contain any
number of additional meaningful factors: emotional, cultural, personal,
historical, spiritual, and so on. To whatever degree an individual is able to

produce meaning from engaging with the image, we can speak of it as a meaningful image. This is a highly subjective affair, and rightly so: from a humanistic perspective, meaning is multitudinous, not singular. The image might trigger a childhood memory with a strong emotional charge in one person. The red bird might have symbolic or cultural significance for another. Red might represent passion or vitality to an aesthetically minded pedestrian, or have a specific mythic connotation to a member of an indigenous culture. The specific form of the image matters as well: is the image fixed or moving? Is it photo-realistic or does it resemble a particular school of art? If the image is moving (as imagination is prone to do), what is the bird doing, what is its style and quality of movement, what does it seem to want? What else is happening around the bird? What happens next? Each of these factors contribute to a greater aggregate of complex meanings inhering in the experienced image. The more complexity and coherence the image exhibits, the more "meaningful" it becomes.

This approach to imagination is in sharp contrast to the cognitive–behavioral notion of "propositional imagination" that dominated psychological research in the twentieth century. Propositional imagination was understood as a cognitive process whereby the mind posits an as-if or what-if scenario as a matter of logic and reason, and as such does not necessarily involve any images at all (Moore, 2010). For example, the mind might posit: "if I go to the park, I might see a red bird," a possible scenario that can be understood entirely in conceptual, abstract linguistic terms—as data—without necessarily engaging mental images of the park or the red bird whatsoever. This sort of dry, linear conception of the human mind may seem quite foreign to depth psychologists, for whom image is primary. But to a generation of positivistic psychologists interested primarily in behavior and computer models of cognition, propositional imagination was adequate to their scope of research. Suffice to say, the notion of propositional imagination is ancillary to this book. It interests me only insofar as it is implicated in the working definition given above—that is, *the generation of meaningful, coherent images and narratives arising in consciousness.* With regards to imagining the red bird in the tree, this book is primarily concerned with the phenomenological experience of the imaginal red bird and tree, not the propositional logic that posits its possible occurrence.

It should further be clarified that to speak of images does not imply exclusively visual experience, although visual experience may prove an important point of departure. Image is here understood as a multisensory phenomenon, incorporating not only visual images, but also sound (as in "musical imagination"), smell, touch, taste—one can image the smell of a rose, or the caress of a lover. This understanding of image is born out in depth psychology (Hillman, 1979a) and is common in neuroscientific literature (see Agnati, Guidolin, Battistin, Pagnoni, & Fuxe, 2013; Damasio,

1999; Moore, 2010). Furthermore, imagination may involve a schema of multiple sensory forms, forming a complex aggregate of experience, as is often seen in dreams. In contrast to strictly linguistic experience, where multiple streams of data are reduced to an abstract word or linear syntax of multiple words, imaginal experience allows "data" to be experienced as complex, aggregate wholes expressed through multiple, simultaneously perceived channels of perception.

A further distinction is in order between the specific use of the terms *imagination*, *imaginary*, and *imaginal*. Where imagination is the phenomenon itself, we often use "imaginary" as an adjective to describe a thing as pertaining to or existing in imagination—for example, an "imaginary friend." The term imaginary is problematic, as it has come to have a strong connotation of "false" or "unreal." Henri Corbin (1972) has instead introduced the term "imaginal" as an alternative adjective that connotes something that is not unreal, but rather represents an ontological reality of a different order. James Hillman and others have since adopted the term to refer to the ontological ground of the psyche: the non-physical but phenomenologically real world of subjective experience. Philosophically speaking, this stance might be akin to "neutral monism" or "dual aspect monism" theories of consciousness (see Chalmers, 2002), though neither Corbin nor Hillman engaged those terminologies or philosophical debates explicitly. Rather, they described the imaginal as an intermediary experiential space between physical reality and mental abstraction.

To further flesh out the concept of the imaginal, recall the above example of the goddess with a sword: in the moment when this image arises in consciousness, the subjective experience of the image is phenomenologically real *as a content of consciousness*. That is, it is a real "inner" experience even if it has no external referent. Any emotional charge, cognitive interpretation, or psychological meanings that emerge along with this image are incorporated in the imaginal reality of the phenomenon. To assert that this imaginal experience of the goddess is ontologically real and psychologically meaningful is not necessarily to assert that the goddess exists as a metaphysical entity—that is another question entirely. Rather, we recognize that whatever else she may or may not be, she exists as an imaginal reality, real to consciousness and potentially significant to psyche. Of course, there is more to Corbin's formulation than this brief sketch allows, and there is evidence that he disapproved of Hillman's purely psychological adoption of the term. Corbin's contributions and their ontological implications will be explored further in Chapter 5 on imaginal psychology. (The ontological and epistemological considerations of the current research will be further discussed in Chapter 2 on method.)

Among the most important and powerful uses of the term "imagination" in common parlance is the function of imagination to open up possibilities. This is perhaps best exemplified in John Lennon's words, "imagine all the people living life in peace"—a song that invokes in the listener a vision of a better world. We find some sense of this in Einstein's "imagination is more important than knowledge," and a great many other places besides. Here "imagination" references a human capacity to go beyond limiting beliefs and rigid worldviews, to experience something new and more expansive, and thus to discover new solutions and avenues forward. This vital function of imagination is largely compatible with the working definition provided above: when we imagine new possibilities in all their fullness, they will very often come to us in the form of vivid, complex imagery. I will maintain, however, that this imagination of possibilities is not the only way imagination can be psychologically meaningful. In depth psychology, imagination is also a way to engage the present, to access the fullness of the human psyche, and to experience the self in a deeper way.

It should be noted that throughout this work, imagination is treated as an inherent and inborn psychological capacity, much like thinking or reasoning or empathy. There is considerable evidence that other intelligent non-human species have some degree of imaginative capacity—neuroscientist Rodolpho Llinas (2001) suggests that image-making is actually one of the primary functions of the nervous system of all animal life. Following this argument, I take the position that the basic capacity of imagination is something that all humans initially possess. It may be rightly objected that factors such as personal trauma or socio-economic conditions may interfere with these capacities. I certainly agree and would applaud more research done into these important areas. That said, an inquiry into factors that inhibit or interfere with imagination will not be the focus of the present work. Likewise, it should be clarified that although this book focuses on the story of imagination in Western civilization it in no way privileges Western conceptions of imagination as being exceptional or superior to conceptions of imagination that have arisen from other cultural traditions. Here, too, there is much fruitful research yet to be done.

Imagination and depth psychology

This book makes use of depth psychology as one of its primary frameworks for understanding and engaging the phenomenon of imagination. One good reason for doing so is that depth psychology is arguably the branch of psychology that has maintained the most focus on the importance of imagination historically. As such, it provides sophisticated theoretical frameworks for imagination as a psychological phenomenon that are lacking in more reductionist approaches. Depth psychology is also useful in that it integrates much of the philosophical discourse on imagination that preceded it. All of this will be outlined in detail in Chapter 5, but in the meantime a brief description of depth psychology may prove helpful.

For the unfamiliar reader, depth psychology is a field of theory and practice that began in the early twentieth century with Sigmund Freud and Carl Jung, chiefly characterized by a study of the dynamic relationship between the conscious mind and unconscious contents of the psyche. Modern depth psychology in general is profoundly interested in bringing phenomenology and qualitative methods back into the foreground of psychological research. Depth psychologists are also more prone to advocate for the use of metaphor and imagery when exploring the full spectrum of human experience. Both Freud and Jung drew on mythopoeic language to express their understanding of psyche ("soul," to return to the original Greek). Jung in particular followed this mythopoeic orientation toward a discourse on image as a primary conduit for meaning in psychology. While early depth psychology strove to express itself in medical and scientific terminology to conform to the intellectual culture of its day, modern depth psychologists have questioned and in some cases rejected the notion that depth psychology was ever really a natural science, and locate it instead as a legitimate field of knowledge and inquiry more suited to the humanities, akin to history, philosophy, and the study of literature (Paris, 2007, p. 86).

It may be shocking for some scientifically inclined readers to imagine a field of psychology that makes no attempts to prove itself a natural science (it certainly was for me). But such shock suggests a misunderstanding of the scope and purpose of the humanities as a legitimate sphere of research and knowledge. In fact, intellectual historian Richard Tarnas (1991) explicitly describes the early depth psychology of Freud and Jung as "a fruitful middle-ground between science and the humanities." Tarnas goes on to describe depth psychology as

> Sensitive to the many dimensions of human experience, concerned with art and religion and interior realities, with qualitative conditions and subjectively significant phenomena, yet striving for empirical rigor, for rational cogency, for practical, therapeutically effective knowledge in a context of collective scientific research.
>
> (p. 385)

Nor is the notion of psychology as a middle ground with roots in both spheres a purely historical conception. Clinical psychologist Michael Sipiora (2012) writes "psychology is unthinkable without the humanities.... A well-conceived psychology needs both calculation and imagination, both the natural sciences and the humanities" (p. 110). The great works of art and literature that survive the ages do so precisely because they provide lasting inspiration and insight into the human condition. Shakespeare was no scientist, but his works remain revered in Western culture because they contain a treasure trove of wisdom about the human soul. There is inherent psychological value in literature and the arts, history, philosophy, cultural studies—precisely because they explore and reflect our humanity back to us with a complexity and emotional resonance that quantitative scientific data, by its very nature, lacks.

Even Freud, who labored to express his insights into the psyche in scientific and medical terms, believed that a deep understanding of literature was essential to psychoanalysis (Hillman, 1994/1983). One of the great ironies surrounding Freud is that while modern scientific psychology has been inclined to dismiss his work as pseudo-science, literature departments have become increasingly enthusiastic about including his works in their curriculums. Christine Downing (2000) advocates beautifully that the greatest value in Freud's work may emerge when one is willing to read him poetically, to see him as a doctor of the soul rather than a technician of the brain. That is to say, his work takes on new humanistic value when we stop trying to frame it as science.

Freud and Jung did not have access to the brain-scanning technologies of today, but they were both dedicated empiricists, developing their theories through rigorous and engaged practice with their patients. Had these early researchers access to such technologies, they would have certainly used them in conjunction with their humanistic psychological approach. Indeed, it is ironic that many aspects of their theories, dismissed as "unscientific" in the late twentieth century, have actually found renewed support through twenty-first century scientific inquiry (see Cozolino, 2006; Goodwyn, 2012, Solms & Turnbull, 2002; Wilkinson, 2006). As such, it is my hope that depth psychology might remain that rare field of discourse that cannot be strictly confined as a humanistic or scientific project, but rather maintains a perspective and avenue of inquiry broad enough to integrate both approaches to understanding the human condition.

The phenomenon of imagination explicitly became a central concept in depth psychology through the work of Carl Jung, who asserted that "everything of which we are conscious is an image, and that image *is* psyche" (1967/1929, p. 50). In his seminal paper *On the nature of the psyche*, Jung argues that the "rational certainty" which constitutes experience "is, in its most simple form, an exceedingly complicated structure of mental images" (1960a/1947, p. 327). Engaging and working with images through fantasy, active imagination, creative arts, and dreams is instrumental to the practice of Jung's analytic psychology, in which the individual grows and develops through an ongoing encounter with these often emotionally charged imaginal contents. For Jung, these images were not mere phantasms, but rather expressed a soulful level of truth from the unconscious layers of the psyche. Although Jung labored extensively to express his ideas in conceptual language, the active engagement with images of the psyche was the foundation from which he worked (1989/1961, p. 199)

The continued commitment to the psychological primacy of image is among the most important ways archetypal psychologist James Hillman carried on Jung's legacy. In *Re-visioning psychology* (1976), Hillman states his goal: "Our desire is to save the phenomena of the imaginal psyche" (p. 3). He later elaborates this dedication in detail:

> All consciousness depends on these images. Everything else—ideas of the mind, sensations of the body, perceptions of the world around us, beliefs, feelings, hungers—must present themselves as images in order to become experienced.... In the beginning is the image; first imagination, then perception.... Man is primarily an imagemaker and our psychic substance consists of images, our being is an imaginal being, an existence in imagination.
>
> (1976, p. 23)

Hillman was an exceptional scholar in his own right, and these bold statements about the role of image in psychology were made with full knowledge of the technical and scientific language that had come to dominate mainstream psychological understandings. Hillman argued that something vital was lost when the human soul was laid bare in an exclusively mechanistic or functional understanding. He radically challenged this convention by advocating instead for "a psychology that assumes a poetic basis of mind" (1994/1983, p. 4). In this regard, Hillman was contributing to a wider intellectual movement against reductive materialism (see Chalmers, 2002; Kelly & Presti, 2015; Koons & Bealer, 2010; Nagel, 2015; Tallis, 2011 for a wide array of robust anti-materialist positions)—Hillman's particular means of doing so was to return to imagination as a foundation of human psychology.

I suspect this emphasis on imagination in psychology might seem radical to both mainstream psychology and the general public, which is precisely why an elaboration of the neurobiological correlates of imagination is called for. While I personally often prefer the language of poetry to the language of neuroscience in describing reality, I recognize that we live in an era where neuroscience is recognized as a voice of immense authority. Rather than simply criticize that authority and laud the phenomenological, the qualitative, and the poetic, I find inspiration in contributing to a bridge that allows these seemingly opposite worldviews an increased degree of dialog and integration. A deep exploration of imagination through the lens of neuroscience has the potential to both awaken and legitimize a broader appreciate of imagination in both academia and the general populace. Furthermore, such an endeavor can build alliance and understanding between the depth psychology and neuroscience communities, and between the sciences and humanities in general.

The great divide

Historian of science Lorraine Daston (2005) accounts for the suspicion (and even "loathing") of imagination that has been found within modern scientific culture as a relatively recent development. Prior to the mid-nineteenth century, imagination was widely recognized as essential to the practice of art and science equally, and was only dangerous in excess. "In Enlightenment art and science, the imagination was Janus-faced: on the one hand, it was essential to creative work in both realms; but on the other, it could betray the natural and the verisimilar by breeding monsters" (p. 22). Partnered with reason, imagination drove science forward; only when let to run wild was it a portal to madness. Daston cites several reasons for the divorce of science and imagination in the mid-nineteenth century: trends toward non-representative art meant science and art no longer shared the common dedication to naturalism; the emphasis in Romantic imagination on individual subjective experience clashed with the scientific culture's call for communal objectivity; eventually, the scientific call for a more extreme "mechanistic objectivity" sought to remove the human element altogether. Daston further suggests that as science aged into the twentieth century, the rate at which established scientific theories were replaced with new ones became a cause for alarm. If the lauded and unquestioned theories of Newton could be replaced with new models of physics, for example, the stable ground of objectivity seemed all the more tenuous, and thus the imagination looked all the more threatening.

But there is a larger divide at work here that has grown throughout the twentieth century: the rift between the sciences and humanities as fields of human knowledge. To better illuminate this gap, it may be helpful to review specifically how these two different branches of knowledge production function. Broadly generalized, while the sciences seek to discover the objective workings of the universe, the humanities are a collection of disciplines that seek to answer the question: "what does it mean to be human?" Traditional science works by careful quantitative experiment and measurement, while the humanities investigate both the richness of human experience, and the meanings humans have made of their condition. Predating modern science by millennia, what we now understand as the humanities began in Ancient Greece as a formal education for developing the character of Greek citizens, the participants in our world's first democracy. Susan Rowland (2012) points out that as late as the nineteenth century, the purpose of the humanities in academia was largely understood as a means for "developing a story for national and personal identity" (p. 27). Rowland further argues that it was only when the humanities began to diversify and give voice to heretofore under-represented demographics (women, the poor, the LGBT community, and so on) that public funding for their programs began to dry up. Indeed, the role of the humanities in the production of knowledge—and qualitative research in general—has become an increasingly politicized matter (see Denzin & Giardina, 2008).

I raise the issue of politics not to politicize my own research on imagination but to acknowledge that it inevitably occurs against a somewhat politicized background and cannot hope to completely escape that context. The questions of truth, where it comes from, and who gets to decide, are fundamental concerns for all human beings, and the conclusions drawn about the nature of truth have far-reaching consequences. To affirm that the lived human experience is a source of knowledge, different from but equally important as scientific data, not only empowers individuals, but empowers them equally. Honoring the qualitative gives voice to marginalized perspectives within a supposedly "objective" scientific Western worldview that prior to the late twentieth century was largely constructed by privileged white patriarchy. To be clear, this is in no way a disavowal of the validity, importance, or power of scientific knowledge, but rather a revaluation of its humanistic counterpart. These issues become entangled with the question of imagination because by investigating the roots of imaginal experience we will inevitably come to the question of what is real and what is imagined in the human experience. A further exploration of the kinds of knowledge produced by scientific and humanistic methods will be outlined in greater detail in the next chapter on methods.

Suffice to say that my own intention as a writer and researcher has been to seek harmony between these two spheres and their very different contributions to understanding imagination. Though they may seem intractably polarized at the outset, I maintain that a deeper investigation will open the way to a more inclusive integration of the truths they provide. Through this volume I have attempted to make a nuanced and even-handed exploration of these sometimes-contentious issues. In doing so, I meant to honor the incredible contributions of science to human understanding, and at the same time advocate for the liberation of the imaginal in conscious human experience.

Model agnosticism

To best understand the spirit in which this book will proceed, a few words are in order about my intellectual predispositions as a writer and researcher. In the field of depth psychology, researchers are often encouraged to unearth and keep an eye on their unconscious assumptions and motivations. In that vein, I would like to acknowledge my own worldview and theoretical stance in organizing the story of imagination in the chapters ahead, a position that might be best summarized by the term *model agnosticism*.

I first encountered the idea of model agnosticism in the works of polymath Robert Anton Wilson (1932–2007), although it has substantive roots in both physics and philosophy. I cite Wilson with some trepidation, as he is somewhat problematic from a scholarly perspective. Wilson was sometimes a serious philosopher and scholar, at other times an impassioned and inflammatory polemicist, and still at other times a comedian and self-proclaimed trickster. One of the things I find most valuable about Wilson is that his writing often seemed more concerned with encouraging his readers to think critically about their basic ontological assumptions, rather than presenting them with received objective truths. The result is that many of his assertions about "reality" are tongue-in-cheek, shocking, or simply bizarre. This "guerilla ontology" (as he humorously put it) makes for a thrilling reading experience, but it can also lead to misunderstanding if his texts are taken as a traditional transmission of unquestioned, literal truth. Wilson did not want his truths to go unquestioned—just the opposite: he opposed dogmatism and fundamentalism in all forms, and hated the idea that his own thinking might become systematized into just another dogma (2005, p. 245). Above all, he wanted his readers to think for themselves.

The basic idea of model agnosticism is that all systems of human knowledge, expressed symbolically or linguistically, are *models* of reality: maps constructed to help us make sense of a confusing world. These models are constructed in the sciences and the humanities, in religion and the arts, in cultural understandings and educated worldviews of all kinds. Scientific materialism, neopaganism, democratic socialism, Darwinian evolution, existentialism, post-modernism, general relativity, and model agnosticism itself can all be understood as linguistic–symbolic maps that organize human experience. So for example, Freud offered us one model of the human psyche ("psychoanalysis") that had a huge cultural influence with regards to self-knowledge, primal instincts, and sexuality. Jung took that model as a foundation but ultimately offered us another model ("analytical psychology") that was both more image-oriented and more rooted in the models of Kantian and Romantic philosophy. In much sharper contrast, materialists like Daniel Dennet and Patricia and Paul Churchland offer us a radically different model of the psyche (Blackmore, 2006)—and in fact may eschew the word "psyche" altogether when addressing the same basic concerns. These are but a few examples with regards to linguistic maps of the human mind, and diverse models are to be found in all fields and arenas of human knowledge and behavior, inside and outside of the academy.

To be a *model agnostic* it to acknowledge that: (1) Any given model is an approximation of reality, not reality itself, and (2) No model is completely true or completely false, but rather exists on a spectrum of *more or less useful* in understanding and engaging with the phenomena it maps.

At first glance this may look like a descent into the relativism of post-modern philosophy, but there are a few important differences. First, this approach is inherently pragmatic—it engages with models not as literal truths, but rather as constructive tools to be applied in helping us understand a highly complex universe. Models are applied where they fit, and discarded where they don't: the Freudian model may come in very handy to a young man who grew up in a sexually oppressive household, regardless of whether that model passes scientific muster in a laboratory. Likewise, the scientific model of "eliminative materialism" employed by Dennett and the Churchlands may indeed provide fresh insights in the scientific study of brain matter, while being less useful or even destructive if employed, as-is, in the practices of psychotherapy, creative arts, or community organizing. This move, then, is not a nihilistic resignation to the relativity of truth, but rather an acknowledgment that truth is complex, and that different models contain different aspects of the truth without ever containing the totality.

Using this approach, we can for example appreciate polarized thinkers such as Karl Marx and Ayn Rand together, recognizing the historical forces that shaped each body of thought, recognizing their respective insights into human nature while acknowledging that both perspectives have considerable flaws when applied too broadly. Wilson's approach, in his own words, is to "remain agnostic about all methods, although *willing to learn* from them in an open-minded way" (1997, p. 6). This final point is important because it requires humility: new and contrary models are opportunities for learning, not competing ideologies to be attacked and deconstructed. When one encounters an unfamiliar model, scientific, humanistic, religious, cultural, or otherwise, it is tempting to view it strictly through the lens of our favorite familiar model, collapsing the new model into the old—and thus misunderstanding it completely. Whereas to truly understand a new model requires the difficult work of coming to understand it on its own terms. Far from being "anything goes" relativism, this approach requires a serious commitment to careful study, learning, and a dialogical approach to the unfamiliar.

Furthermore, such an approach requires us to be very specific about the scope of a given model, what in particular it does and does not contain. Many Americans may, for example, hold the common belief that "Christianity is opposed to homosexuality." But as a model for Christianity as a whole, this statement is easily demonstrated to be inaccurate: the Episcopalian and Lutheran churches, among many others, have endorsed gay marriage. We might speak more meaningfully about the Episcopalian model of marriage versus the Southern Baptist model of marriage—though even this is likely to be overly abstract and in need of more specific modeling: it is likely that some conservative Episcopalian churches are against gay marriage, and some progressive Baptist congregations are open to it. Models thus are not static categories—they are linguistic and symbolic systems making their way through culture, sometimes evolving, other times remaining fixed for hundreds or thousands of years. We know a model only by carefully studying it, trying to understand it on its own terms; otherwise we merely project. In the increasingly specialized world of academia, an acknowledgment of this point alone would likely clear up much misunderstanding. In that spirit, I readily admit my casual reference to "the relativism of post-modern philosophy" above is itself an overly simplified abstraction, as post-modern thought is revealed to be both diverse and quite nuanced when carefully examined on its own terms. Brevity may require that we summarize, but our summaries must not be mistaken for substantive judgments.

Nor is there anything in a model agnostic approach that precludes consensus: rather, it contains an injunction to arrive at that consensus more carefully and rigorously. Taking for example the crucial topic of climate change now facing the planet, a purely relativistic approach would have little traction engaging with this issue, because the consensus of climate science would be viewed as just one perspective among many. But from a pragmatic standpoint, if a majority of scientists are providing us with robust model of human-created climate change with potentially catastrophic consequences, and the opposition cannot provide an equally compelling model for taking no action, there is every reason to take a stand for the best model we have. That said, rather than simply attacking the opposition, a more thorough investigation of the premises and nuances of their oppositional models would likely help to foster more constructive dialog.

The idea of model agnosticism as employed by Wilson has roots and parallels across several disciplines. Wilson (1990) cites developments in physics in the early twentieth century: the certitude of Newtonian mechanics (model 1) gave way to the relativity theories of Einstein (model 2) on the one hand and quantum mechanics (model 3) on the other. Each of the new theories proved accurate in themselves, but they have yet to be integrated and remain essentially two different ways of understanding the universe, each empirically verified. To make matters more complicated, Newtonian mechanics still holds as a valid model on the level of gross motion (i.e., in common, everyday experience). In another example, within quantum mechanics came the shocking discovery that light sometimes behaves as a particle (model 1), and sometimes behaves as a wave (model 2), depending on how it is measured. Barring a unifying theory that has yet to emerge, physics was forced to accept a pragmatic system of multiple models to describe the universe. Wilson suspects this differentiation of models in the sciences is indicative of human perception and understanding in a fundamental sense, and argues that multiple models can be applied to all linguistic–symbolic constructs of reality.

In the humanities, Wilson traces this mode of thinking through the existentialism of Nietzsche and Kierkegaard, the pragmatism of William James, the instrumentalism of John Dewey, and perhaps most controversially, the general semantics of Alfred Korzybski. Korzybski was a complex thinker, a contemporary of Jung and Freud who, like them, was perhaps overly generous in applying the word "science" to his own interdisciplinary model. Nevertheless, Korzybski offered valuable insight into the ways the misuse of language can create pervasive and sometimes destructive category errors in human experience. His famous proclamation: "A map is not the territory it represents, but, if correct, has a similar structure to the territory which accounts for its usefulness" (2010/1948, p. 24), refers to the human tendency to confuse abstract verbal thoughts with non-verbal concrete realities, sometimes with disastrous effects. This is obvious in the case of such statements as "Mexicans are rapists," "America is evil," "atheists are immoral," "spiritual practice is useless" in each case, something concrete has been linguistically identified with an idea that exists on a higher level of abstraction, thus leading to vague and potentially bigoted thinking. Korzybski asserted that this kind of linguistic identification of concrete things with abstract thoughts creates a fundamentally skewed experience of reality, a state he likened to insanity.

Korzybski's attempts to frame his system of general semantics as a "science" has garnered some criticism (see Gardner, 1957, p. 280 and Putnam, 1990, p. 120), and the colloquial use of his aphorism "the map is not the territory" have led some to dismiss him out of hand as a linguistic relativist. But I think these criticisms miss the essential point, as summed up in the second half of the maxim: that if the map is *correct*, it has similar enough structure to the territory to be *useful*. Korzybski is not taking a relativistic stance about language, but rather *demanding far greater accuracy in its usage*. Language makes a map of reality; it constructs a model that allows us to make better sense of the complexity and chaos of the life-world. To acknowledge the use of linguistic maps and models makes us more aware of our potential blind spots, and more flexible in our thinking when encountering the unknown.

The constructive outcome of all this is that when examining claims of truth, we do well to remember that words are always partial descriptors of a more complex reality. In a very pragmatic sense, models of reality can be both true and useful in a particular context without being universally applicable in all contexts. Application—the usefulness of a given model—is the key. We can find agreement on usefulness through relational methods of constructive dialog, good faith attempts at communication and understanding. Alternately, we can engage in a power struggle where "truth" becomes a matter of rhetorical force and social domination. Theory aside, these dialogs and power struggles underlie human peace and conflict on all levels, and as such are a deeply human issue, even (and sometimes especially) when the truth in question is purported to be "objective." "Certitude is seized by some minds not because there is any philosophical justification for it, but because such minds have an emotional need for certitude" (Wilson, 1997, p. 6). By acknowledging the inherent human messiness of discovering and communicating truth, we can approach it with greater depth and humility.

The concept of model agnosticism will be significant in at least two ways going forward. Most immediately, the question of "universally applicable truths" remains a topic at hand, because establishing such universality is arguably one of the chief aims of scientific method. How do we honor the validity of carefully researched and verified scientific models while at the same time honoring the humanistic contexts in which they appear? Second, the notion of models of reality ties readily into the broader topic of worldviews and how they are produced and maintained by the human mind. When one is confronted with a radically different model of reality, what is the first task if not to try to *imagine* it? Imagination in this context becomes a tool for understanding, an essential starting point for navigating a complex and multifaceted world.

Overview

The basic premise of this book is to present an integrated understanding of imagination that includes both humanistic–historical and contemporary scientific perspectives. With regards to the latter, the central task is to explicate the neurobiological models that correlate with the phenomenon of imagination. But a comprehensive examination of the topic must not stop there. To simply research the "neuroscience of imagination," however fruitful its results, would do violence to the phenomenon of imagination by reducing it to a mechanistic shadow of itself. From the perspectives of history, phenomenology, and depth psychology, the phenomenon of imagination exists prior to any scientific measurement or reduction.

The basic assumption of materialism holds that the brain somehow generates imagination and that discovering the mechanisms of that process is the end of the story. But a more comprehensive and holistic account must be willing to explore the reverse: the ways in which our understanding of the brain, and even neuroscience itself, are shaped by our imaginative faculties. Thus while the central task may be an investigation of the neurobiological correlates of imagination, this endeavor will be balanced by an honest inquiry into the ways in which imagination shapes neuroscientific knowledge to begin with.

Rather than reducing the phenomenological to the quantitative or the quantitative to the phenomenological, these two aspects of being will be approached as a reciprocal pair. A comprehensive inquiry into the dynamic relationship between imagination and neuroscience must be grounded in an understanding of both fields of discourse. This is tricky theoretical territory, and the next chapter on methods will dig in a bit deeper regarding how we understand knowledge and the production of truth in the sciences and the humanities alike.

The remainder of the book will follow three basic moves. Part II, *Imagination as phenomenon*, takes a deep dive into imagination as a humanistic phenomenon, prior to applying a scientific lens, with particular emphasis on the history of Western ideas and culture, beginning in Ancient Greece. From these early beginnings, the human understanding of imagination will be tracked through the Renaissance and into modernity. Because depth psychology is the academic discipline outside of the arts that has most honored imagination going throughout the twenty-first century, Chapter 5 will focus specifically on the imaginal psychology that has emerged from that tradition.

Part III, *The neuroscience of imagination*, examines what neuroscience currently has to tell us about the human phenomenon of imagination as detailed in the previous section. Because no comprehensive scientific study of imagination exists (at least not one that begins to approach the richness of the phenomenon as understood in humanistic discourse) this inquiry proceeds by looking at how neuroscience has approached imagination through its component parts. Chapter 6 focuses on mental imagery and the blurred relationship between sensation, perception, and imagination. Chapter 7 looks at the link between narrative formation, memory, imagining the future, and recently discovered default mode network of the brain. Chapter 8 focuses on creativity and dreams, and argues that these two seemingly separate phenomena may have more in common than meets the eye.

Part IV, *The imagination of neuroscience*, resumes a humanistic stance to look at the role human imagination plays in the production of neuroscientific knowledge. Chapter 9 details the perhaps surprising role that imagination plays in scientific progress in general, both in day-to-day scientific enterprise and in scientific revolutions. Chapter 10 takes a more provocative stance and examines the way neuroscientific data is converted and transmitted as story and myth, both in the popular culture and even between scientists in the laboratory.

The book concludes with treatise on the myth of the ancient sea god and archetypal shapeshifter Proteus. Indeed, Proteus is a figure who will appear from time to time throughout this book. In the classical myth as told by Homer, Proteus is an oracle and a truth-teller, a God who would provide answers to those who came seeking—but only if they were able to hold him as he changed form. The image of Proteus evokes both the fluidity and the unity of the ocean, the "sea-change" of profound transformation. This capacity for manifold change could be taken as a metaphor for imagination itself, fluid and formless in one moment, vividly detailed and meaningful the next. And with the discovery of neuroplasticity—the ability of the brain to reshape itself over time—the archetype of the shapeshifter now reaches into the realm of neuroscience as well.

Though his many forms might suggest a missing essence or vacant core of being, the same myths proclaim Proteus as a keeper of hidden truth. It is only by holding the many forms as they shift that the heroes of these tales find the answers they seek. Imagination will take many shapes in the pages ahead, and the world itself may seem to shift as we come to view it from a variety of perspectives, both humanistic and scientific. The myth suggests that despite the flux and seeming chaos, holding focus through these shifting forms will eventually lead us to the answers we seek.

Daunting as that task may be, the surviving myths tell us that with perseverance it can be done. Proteus reminds us that the labor to bridge imagination and neuroscience is not so much a battle as an injunction: to hold the tension of manifold forms, in search of a deeper truth.

Chapter 2

Measuring the imaginal

The term *methodology* may, for many readers, conjure phantoms of the dry and technical. It references the study of method in research, the sets of rules and procedures by which new knowledge is produced. Certainly, there are a great many methodologies to choose from, both scientific and humanistic, quantitative and qualitative (see Denzin & Lincoln, 2011). But I contend that, far from being a banal technicality, method is always a topic of vital importance. In all research, method is the specific means by which we try to arrive at the truth, and proclamations of truth can have real impact on human life, effecting public policy, physical and mental health, and spiritual wellbeing, among other things. Nor can we fully separate our methods from our worldview, for implicit in any methodology are a series of hidden premises about the nature of reality (ontology) and the nature of human knowing (epistemology). Sometimes, the method we use tells us as much about the results as the results themselves. And in an information age where knowledge is power, and contrary worldviews are multitudinous (the so-called "postmodern" era), a critical examination of the methods by which knowledge and truth are produced should be a vigorous and ongoing process.

To best build a foundation for understanding the tricky relationship between neuroscience and imagination, this chapter undertakes a foundational examination of scientific method, the kind of truth that it produces, and evaluates its strengths and weaknesses in approaching a protean subjective phenomenon such as imagination. Neuroscience is of course contained within the larger enterprise of scientific method, and scientific method itself exists in the context of both a rich cultural history and an ongoing debate with regards to its scope and limitations. At the same time, researching imagination qualitatively as an experiential phenomenon necessarily means a departure from the precise measurement and objectivity found in traditional scientific method. This brings us into the realm of phenomenology, the study of first-person "subjective" lived experience, which requires methodological considerations all its own.

This book was produced through a third distinct research approach, known as dialectical hermeneutics. In short, hermeneutics is concerned with the interpretation and understanding of texts of all kinds, from philosophical monographs to first-person statements, published scientific studies to cultural artifacts and works of art. The term hermeneutics is not widely known outside of graduate programs in the humanities, and yet it remains one of the basic ways human beings discover truths and produce knowledge across many spheres of life.

As divergent as scientific and humanistic methods may first appear, one thing they share is the production of texts to communicate the knowledge they produce. Whether these texts purport to an analysis of "objective" data or an account of "subjective" lived experience—or a philosophical discourse on what it all means—these texts are inevitably bound by the language, symbolism, history, and culture in which they occur. A robust understanding of these texts thus requires an understanding of their *contexts*. To be clear, emphasizing the importance of context does *not* equate to a position of absolute relativism, whereby truth is completely dependent on its linguistic and cultural milieu. Rather, it is an acknowledgment that culture and language are inevitably intertwined with how we understand the truths of a given text. Even science must rely on the intricacies of language and meaning for its transmission. To ignore such interpretive factors may be provisionally possible within the confines of a very specialized field of discourse and research (for example, molecular cell biology or Romantic poetry), but any sort of multidisciplinary, integrative, or holistic approach to knowledge must take a broader interpretive perspective in order to succeed. And this brings us back to the necessary practice of hermeneutics: the art of interpretation and understanding.

Scientific method

Given the air of certainty that surrounds science in the intellectual and popular cultures of the twenty-first century, I initially assumed, in preparing to write on this topic, that science and scientific method would be relatively easy to define. Instead I found another rabbit hole: centuries of debate over what science is and is not, how it should and should not proceed, philosophical discourse on its ultimate meaning, its scope, and its limitations. On the one hand the magnitude of perspectives underscores the need for a hermeneutic approach for more nuanced understanding. But on the other hand, the dizzying array also awakens greater sympathy within me for the project of settling on a simple definition, an Archimedean truth point from whence science can proceed.

A popular lay understanding of science might be something along the lines of: "science is the careful and systematic study of something." This sort of understanding is closer to what Dilthey had in mind when he spoke of law, philosophy, and history as "human sciences" as opposed to "natural sciences" (see Oakes, 2005). But for most modern scientists, this lay definition would likely seem far too broad and far too vague, lacking stipulations of precise measurement, empirical observation, replicable results, and the quest for a purely objective truth. Positivist philosophy, which rose to prominence in the early twentieth century, helped cement a vision of science as rigorously committed to a realist worldview determined by measurable quantities and the slow accumulation of objective and absolute truth (Nickles, 2005). And although positivist philosophy is now widely recognized as untenable (Howe, 2008; Wilson, 1998), if not "dead ... as dead as a philosophical movement ever becomes" (Passmore, 1967), its influence in modern scientific method lives on (Madill, 2008; Okasha, 2002).

Some of the most influential and groundbreaking philosophers of science in the twentieth century remain some of the most controversial. Paul Feyerabend's contentious book *Against method* (2010/1975), criticizes the prevalence of rationalism in the sciences and argues that no single methodology can account for the full spectrum of scientific discovery, essentially arguing for an anarchistic, "anything goes" approach to science. Even more influential, Thomas Kuhn's *The structure of scientific revolutions* (1996/1962) argues that historically science has proceeded by revolutionary *paradigm shifts*, radical reorganizations of worldview which are not necessarily cumulative or commensurable. But while Feyerabend and Kuhn's ideas are widely discussed and lauded by many, they have also sparked backlash. In a famous 1987 issue of *Nature*, physicists Theocharis and Psimopoulos argued that Kuhn, Feyerabend, and others had undermined the entire scientific enterprise by casting doubt upon the universal and absolute nature of objective scientific truth. Don Ihde (2009) sums up the debate within the scientific community: "the 'war' was over whether science is to be understood as ahistorical, acultural, universal, and absolute in its knowledge, or whether it is embedded in human history and culture and thus inclusive of the usual human fallibilities of other practices" (p. 6). This issue of the "humanness" of the natural sciences is far from settled, and the debate over the nature and scope of scientific truth continues to this day.

But as Kuhn pointed out, "scientists have not generally needed or wanted to be philosophers" (p. 88). These philosophical considerations are important for sussing out the nature of truth, but the actual practice of science proceeds regardless. Thus, while keeping an eye on philosophical implications, it is quite possible to return to a more grounded discussion of scientific *method* as it is actually practiced today.

Perhaps the most widely recognized form of modern scientific method is the *hypothetico-deductive method* (Haig, 2010). Generally speaking, this method proceeds through the following phases: (1) The formulation of a testable hypothesis, (2) The testing of that hypothesis through controlled experimentation, (3) The analysis of the data produced by the experiment, and (4) The replication of the results. This model emphasizes controlled experimentation, quantitative measurement, and replicability as the hall-marks of scientific truth. Phenomena that cannot be controlled or discretely measured are excluded from the scientific cannon, and in general experiments must be repeated, ideally by multiple scientists, in order for the results to be considered objectively valid. Part of the beauty, power, and efficacy of science comes from the fact that these standards set the bar quite high as to what is and is not considered scientific. It can take years of hard labor to produce a new piece of scientifically valid knowledge, and the hard-working humans who undertake this labor can be understandably hostile to casual claims of scientific truth that have not been rigorously tested.

Indeed, the rigor with which a scientific study achieves the most objectively valid data, the degree to which it can demonstrate freedom from human subjectivity, has been a hallmark of the scientific enterprise. One of the gold standards for studies involving human subjects is the "randomized, double-blind controlled trial" whereby not even the scientists know which humans are receiving experimental treatment, as opposed to placebo (Kradin, 2008). These studies take every measure to remove completely the human element, presumably leaving only raw objective truth as the result. But while this practice remains the standard for medical science, Dr. Kradin also points out its limitations: "many interventions—including surgeries and a host of alternative and complementary therapies and psychotherapies—are not amenable to either randomization or blinding" (p. 68). This is an important point, because it means that more holistic models of health—those that integrate psychology and physiology, for example, cannot be evaluated via randomized double-blind control trial. This poses a challenge for traditional Western medicine, especially in light of increasing evidence that psychological factors, including human relationships, play a significant role in health outcomes (see Horrigan, 2003; Sternberg, 2009).

Leaving holistic concerns aside for the moment, we need not go far to find examples of science operating outside the hypothetico-deductive method altogether. Astronomy, for example, is the systematic study of distant heavenly bodies that cannot be experimented on. Rather, astronomy relies on the invention and calibration of tools for careful observation of the cosmos, derives theory from the data collected, and then seeks new data to confirm and expand its theories. This must also be the case in the scientific study of wild animal populations in their natural habits, and the project of ecology in general—one cannot put an entire ecosystem inside a lab for a controlled experiment. Philosopher of science Samir Okasha (2002) elaborates: "no one has ever seen one species evolve from another, or a single continent split into two, or the universe getting bigger ... scientists arrived at these beliefs by a process of reasoning or inference" (p. 18). While inductive reasoning can certainly sometimes lead to false conclusions, it is hard to imagine the scientific enterprise moving forward without it. "Scientists use inductive reasoning whenever they move from limited data to a more general conclusion, which they do all the time" (p. 22). Where science proceeds by induction but lacks hard proof, there is sometimes discussion of "inference to the best solution" (IBS), whereby the simplest and most reasonable explanation for the data is taken as a tentative conclusion. But Okasha also points out that there is no consensus among philosophers of science that defaulting to the simpler explanation is necessarily the best course, however much we may want it to be. The question of simplicity will be taken up further in the discussion of reductionism and complexity theory below.

Whether a given scientific discipline proceeds more by hypothetico-deductive or inductive means, they share the practice of empirical investigation with the aim of discovering objective truth. The principle of replicability (or reproducibility) in science aims at finding consistency in natural phenomena regardless of the humans making the study. Multiple astronomers must observe Neptune before science declares it a planet, multiple zoologists must observe multiple elephants gestating for 21 months before that gestation term is taken as a scientific fact. In the field of neuroscience, multiple brain scans must show increased activity in multiple amygdalas in correlation with fear response before the amygdala is accepted as a part of the brain that supports the process of fear. In sharp contrast to humanistic research concerned with experience and meaning, quantitative science seeks to establish objective facts that transcend individual human experience. It is precisely the continuity of the observed truth across multiple observers that qualify it as objective.

Philosophically, "objectivity" is a contentious issue, and the debates between "objectivists" on the one hand, and "relativists" on the other, can be traced back at least as far as Plato's criticism of Protagoras in Ancient Greece (Bernstein, 1985). But on close examination, these are largely philosophical debates over metaphysics and worldview, rather than methodological disagreements. From a pragmatic standpoint, it is no great challenge to accept that elephants usually gestate for 21 months: there are neither advocates nor evidence to the contrary. We can classify this as a fact without too much trouble. On issues of larger scale, objections to established scientific truths do appear—for example, a minority of religious believers deny Darwin's theory of natural selection, and to this day members of the Flat Earth Society contend that the earth is indeed flat. But these extreme examples aside, the debates over truth become much trickier when it comes to more complex issues such as public health and education—issues that have real impact on millions of lives. From a social perspective, these debates are of vital importance, and both the objectivist and relativist camps have much to contribute toward finding the best solutions. But prior to the political moment of power struggle, before "objective truth" becomes a question of influencing perception, it is perhaps not so contentious to point out that everyone in the above debate would probably, for example, agree that most humans are born with ten fingers and ten toes. Not all humans are born this way, of course, but most are. This is a far less controversial starting point for acknowledging objectivity in the world: that which we can all see together.

Max Velmans (1999) has gone so far as to assert that what is called *objectivity* in science might be better understood as *intersubjectivity*—the agreement on observations among multiple subjects. According to Velmans, intersubjectivity requires

> a shared language, shared cognitive structures, a shared worldview or scientific paradigm, shared training and expertise and so on. To the extent that an experience or an observation can be generally shared (by a community of observers), it can form part of the database of communal science.
>
> (p. 304)

We need not necessarily adopt Velman's terminology to recognize the communal experience he references as the basis for all claims of objectivity. That is to say, objectivity in scientific method represents a consensus among humans who have carefully observed the phenomenon in question. This may be upsetting to those who want to retain literal objective truth as an absolute description of the universe outside of human experience. But as Kant's *Critique of pure reason* demonstrated back in 1781 (1958/1781), the case for a human capacity to directly perceive ultimate and unmediated reality "in-itself," beyond the human sphere, is at the very least uncertain. I would even go further to argue that Kant's notion of "a priori categories" (pre-existing human modes of perception structuring human experience) has only been strengthened by modern neuroscience allocating various perceptual functions to particular brain regions. We are neurobiologically wired to perceive reality in a uniquely human way.

Recognition of the intersubjectivity underlying objective science emphasizes the social element in both scientific method and the progression of scientific knowledge. Acknowledging that science must take place within the context of a human community need not necessarily diminish the weight of its validity. Indeed, historian of science Lorraine Daston (2005) traces Kant's notion of "objectivity as communicability" as an essential driving force in establishing a global scientific community in the nineteenth century (p. 23). It was precisely because scientific results could accumulate across different European cultures and languages that science rose to prominence as a source of authoritative truth.

Thomas Kuhn's (1996/1962) work on scientific revolutions also places heavy emphasis on the social aspect of scientific progress. In Kuhn's historical analysis, young scientists are educated via received knowledge about the current scientific paradigm—that is, they are given a theoretical set of ideas as received truth, rather than deriving and observing these truths for themselves. Consequently, the work of "normal science" is to clarify and elaborate the tenets of the given paradigm in which they received this education. But over time, careful scientific study begins to produce data that does not fit the given paradigm ("anomalies"), and the scientific community is eventually brought to the point of crisis about their basic assumptions. At this point, creativity comes into play, new theories begin to circulate, and after much debate, an entirely different scientific paradigm emerges. This paradigm shift often requires a radical revision of worldview, but once complete, it becomes the new organizing principle for the field, and "normal science" resumes, sometimes with a fundamentally different understanding of what is true. One of the consequences of this process is that "normal science" is always theory-laden and thus contains pre-judgments about the world that complicates its claims to objectivity. At the same time, Kuhn points out that it is precisely the theory-laden organizing principles provided by the paradigm that allows minute elaboration and examination of phenomena to take place. Furthermore, without this minute and careful elaboration engender by the theory-laden paradigm, the "anomalies" would likely never be discovered to begin with.

Kuhn's model of scientific progress suggests a complex social phenomenon that cycles through alternating periods of rigid, received knowledge and radical restructuring. Philosophical questions abound about the ultimate objectivity of the knowledge produced according to Kuhn's model. As mentioned above, some scientists are quite hostile toward Kuhn for suggesting that knowledge produced by science may not be as objective as it seems. My own reading of Kuhn is that he does support the notion of objectivity, and the scientific mission to uncover it—but he also recognizes that arriving at such objective truth is much more complicated than popular science had heretofore assumed. Despite the ongoing controversy, Kuhn's work has impacted the practice of contemporary scientific method. As summed up by Harper and Schulte (2005), "Modern methodologists aim to avoid both the extremes of a context-free universal scientific logic on the one hand, and an entirely context-specific study of particular historical episodes on the other" (p. 682). Thus, although there remain strong traditionalist elements that eschew consideration of the social and historical dimensions of scientific knowledge, there is also a growing awareness of contextual considerations and openness to a more integrative approach within the global scientific community as a whole.

But a model agnostic approach to scientific method demands that we consider even the traditionalist model on its own terms. That is to say, while it may be tempting to reduce all accounts of universal objectivity into a humanistic understanding of socio-historical context, I believe it is also essential to remain open and curious about the traditionalist perspective that believes in a universal, ahistorical truth. By understanding such a belief to be a model—a linguistic and conceptual tool or map to be applied selectively in understanding reality—we can pragmatically enjoy the experience and implications of "objectivity" while dispensing with the larger metaphysical debate. We can consider, for example, the degree to which a belief in absolute and ahistorical objective reality may be necessary for the sciences to proceed. The capacity to imagine an absolute, objective world that can be discovered and measured through careful study may be as necessary to scientists as a belief in aesthetic beauty is to artists. For that reason, I will continue to use the term *objective* to refer to data received from rigorous scientific measurement. While this will no doubt fail to satisfy the staunchest of objectivists, it nevertheless leaves a conceptual door open to the intricacies of their world.

Science and scientism

A clear distinction must be made between scientific methods and the philosophical beliefs and worldviews that have arisen in conjunction with those methods. We can recognize the methods of science (and the knowledge produced by those methods) as valid, while simultaneously holding them as distinct from the many philosophical, ideological, and cultural beliefs that claim to be science-based. A multitude of humanistic scholars have voiced criticisms of the worldviews that arose in conjunction with science (Okasha 2002). Morris (1981) and Tarnas (1991), for example, both argue that the historic triumph of science also resulted in a reductive and culturally devastating "disenchantment" of the world. One of the harshest attacks comes from feminist philosopher Carolyn Merchant (1980) who asserts that the Scientific Revolution resulted in a dismal mechanistic worldview, the domination and exploitation of the natural world, and the subjugation of women. A fair evaluation of these claims is well beyond the scope of the present work. I only wish to note that even if these criticisms of the prevalent science-based worldview are shown to be true, they are not in themselves critiques of scientific *method*. Rather they criticized the cultural and ideological forces that have used scientific method as a justification for their power. We can recognize the misapplication of scientific knowledge while still honoring the method that produced it.

When such criticisms arise, they are usually referring not to science per se, but to the collection of beliefs generally referred to as *scientism*. This term is usually understood to indicate a belief that science is the ultimate, perhaps even the only, source of truth. Okasha defines scientism as a pejorative label for describing "science-worship—the over-reverential attitude toward science found in many intellectual circles" (2002, p. 121), and notes that this accusation is often levied against the analytical philosophy tradition in particular. Nickles (2005) defines scientism as a belief system with roots in positivist philosophy: "the view that empirical science is the primary cultural institution, the only one that produces clear, objective, reliable knowledge claims about nature and society that accumulate over time and thereby the only enterprise that escapes the contingencies of history" (p. 1852). Most striking in this description is the claim to exclusion: not that science is a great source of knowledge, or even the best source of knowledge—but that it is the only source of knowledge.

This worldview is prevalent among some of the most accomplished scientists of our day. Evolutionary biologist Richard Dawkins, in a recent book written for a lay audience, asserts that we can only know what is "real" in three ways: direct sense data, instruments that augment sense data, and creating predictive models which are then measured against reality using sense data; in short, "it always comes back to our senses, one way or another" (2012, p. 18). In one fell swoop, Dawkins decimates the truths of philosophy, hermeneutics, somatics, phenomenology, spiritual experience, religion, imagination, and cultural narrative as fundamentally unreal. Cognitive scientist Steven Pinker makes an even more explicit claim. In an article written for *the New Republic*, Pinker defends scientism outright:

> The findings of science entail that the belief systems of all the world's traditional religions and cultures—their theories of the origins of life, humans, and societies—are factually mistaken..... We know that the laws governing the physical world ... have no goals that pertain to human well-being. There is no such thing as fate, providence, karma, spells, curses, augury, divine retribution, or answered prayers ... the beloved convictions of every time and culture may be decisively falsified.... In other words, the worldview that guides the moral and spiritual values of an educated person today is the worldview given to us by science.
>
> (Pinker, 2013, para. 14)

In fairness to Pinker, the first part of his statement refers to the fact that historically pre-scientific and non-Western cultures do not have access to scientific data supporting the theory of evolution, the heliocentric solar system, and so on. But as the statement continues Pinker tears down the capacity of other cultures to accurately apprehend reality in any way other than what Western science has measured. Like Dawkins, he refuses to hold open any possibility that other cultures—or other methods of knowing within Western culture—could possibly produce any kind of meaningful truth about reality. Furthermore, he asserts that anyone who is "educated" must accept these philosophical premises: that only what science has measured is real. It is precisely this sort of dismissive, reductionistic, and exclusive belief system that is being criticized when scientism is described as a destructive form of cultural imperialism. I hope that the discourse on method so far has at the very least demonstrated that scientism is hardly a forgone conclusion among the "educated persons" of today.

Does scientific method, in itself, have any means of pointing beyond itself to make objective statements about phenomena it cannot measure? Is there anything in the method itself that suggests nothing can exist beyond sense data, simply because sense data is necessary for scientific method to proceed? I contend that any such assertion is essentially a metaphysical proposition and a cultural narrative, a belief system in itself unverifiable by scientific means. Scientism is a perfectly valid belief system in all its forms (scientific materialism, naturalism, realism, etc. ...), in the same way that Marxism or Idealism or Catholicism or Zoroastrianism is a perfectly valid belief system. It is a collection of stories and beliefs that make meaning of the world, but which cannot in themselves be objectively measured. Despite being ostensibly based on scientific findings, scientism cannot be considered scientific knowledge per se, because it cannot pass muster by the very method it lauds—it is not verifiable. To put this another way, the ultimate measurability of the universe cannot itself be measured. To recognize such is not a descent into relativism nor an attack on science, but rather a simple exercise in epistemic humility. When Carolyn Merchant speaks of the devastation to our planet in the wake of the Scientific Revolution, she is not speaking of the method or of the knowledge produced by that method—but of the authoritarian, bullying, colonizing scientism that would impose its mythos everywhere.

I suspect part of the reason this sort of criticism can cause distress among the scientific community is that it has the potential to undercut their very important contributions. A team of scientists may labor for decades to produce concrete evidence that humans are dangerously accelerating climate change, and they understandably don't want their hard-fought truth held as equal to a politician who makes the opposite claim merely as a matter of opinion (or worse, political and financial interests). If the post-modern era is a time of competing narratives, many scientists see great danger in relativizing science to "just another narrative"—as if technology hasn't radically transformed the world; as if penicillin hasn't saved countless lives. And so some dig in their heels and proclaim that science is exceptional, privileged, and superior to all other methods in the carefully collected knowledge it produces. But if we take a step back from the extreme polarization of science as "absolute truth" on the one hand and as "just another narrative" on the other, perhaps more fruitful ground will be found. Beyond the tension of these opposites, we may begin to work toward a nuanced articulation of the unique and important role that science plays, both in history and in our future.

In this spirit, I will suggest that scientific knowledge is exceptional in at least two ways. First, scientific method is exceptional in the extremely high standards it holds for rigorous and careful research. While those standards are no foolproof measure against error, they nevertheless demand a level of precision and careful analysis that clearly demarcates what is scientific knowledge and what is not. We can thus trust that when science is operating well, it is offering us information well worth serious consideration. Indeed, the rigor of this method encourages researchers employing and developing qualitative methodologies to continuously evaluate, articulate, and improve their own standards for knowledge production, to better match the standards their scientific neighbors have set. The second way that science is clearly exceptional is also a potential source for criticism: there is no question that the technologies produced by science have radically transformed our planet, both for good and for ill. Western medicine, industry, pollution, Internet, transportation, carbon emissions, climate science, nuclear weapons: all the fruits of scientific method, all tangible and transformative in a way that few other fields of study have matched. Whatever our stance on these technologies, the power that created them deserves our respect, even when we question the extent of our allegiance.

Perils of reduction and promise of complexity

The discussion of scientific method thus far has been concerned with the principles, premises, and techniques that guide the scientific enterprise as a whole. For the purpose of narrowing the focus toward brain science in particular, some discussion of reductionism and complexity is necessary. The brain is after all one of the most complex objects known to exist in nature, and this raises the question of how science approaches complexity itself. Historically, natural science has proceeded by reductionism—that is, understanding the whole by reducing it to the functioning of its parts. And certainly there is no contest that this approach was a monumental success in the realms of physics and chemistry. But with the science of biology bridging the marvels of chemistry with the mysteries of life, consciousness, and culture, the ultimate efficacy of reductionism becomes contentious. Intellectual historian Richard Tarnas (1991) elaborates: "As reductionism was successfully employed to analyze nature, and then human nature as well, man himself was reduced ... consciousness itself became a mere epiphenomenon of matter, a secretion of the brain, a function of electrochemical circuitry serving biological imperatives" (pp. 331–332). This reductionistic model became a dominant aspect of the scientific worldview of the twentieth century: humans were nothing more than biology, biology nothing more than chemistry, chemistry nothing more than physics. From a humanistic perspective, it is not hard to see how this might resemble a wildly destructive descent into nihilism.

A more balanced perspective comes from Steven Pinker (2002), who differentiates between two kinds of reductionism, one destructive and the other useful. Destructive, or "greedy" reductionism is that which I have just described—the attempt to explain an aspect of the human sphere by reducing it solely to its constituent parts, as when we attempt to explain depression exclusively in terms of biochemistry, disregarding all other psychological, developmental, social, and environmental factors (among others). In contrast, Pinker's "useful" form of reductionism does not try to replace one field of knowledge with another, but is rather a matter of "connecting and unifying them" (p. 70). Thus we do not reduce the musician to the firing of her neurons, but mapping the firing of her neurons may enrich our understanding of her performance. I appreciate this formulation, which on the surface shares much in common with recent attempts at finding "consilience" between the sciences and the humanities (see Slingerland & Collard, 2011). But I wonder if this deferral toward an integrated understanding does not somewhat avoid the problematic "-ism" of worldview present in reductionism.

Pinker claims that destructive reductionism is no longer a majority opinion, but philosopher Thomas Nagel (2015) starkly disagrees: "Among the scientists and philosophers who express views about the natural order as a whole, reductive materialism is widely assumed to be the only serious possibility" (p. 4). Nagel is taking up the question from a more ontological perspective, analyzing how modern science has come to understand the cosmos. The fact that his criticism strikes so broadly at this reductionistic "assumption" indicates a deeply entrenched cultural belief system about both science and the world. Nagel further states: "Almost everyone in our secular culture has been browbeaten into regarding the reductive research program as sacrosanct, on the ground that anything else would not be science" (p. 7). In this view, science and reductionism have become largely synonymous in the popular understanding.

Richard Tarnas offers a more optimistic view, suggesting that after the revolutionary advent of relativity and quantum theory in physics, many scientists began to rethink some of their deeply held beliefs:

> Increasing numbers of scientists began to question modern science's pervasive, if often unconscious, assumption that the intellectual effort to reduce all reality to the smallest measureable components of the physical world would eventually reveal that which was most fundamental in the universe. The reductionist program dominant since Descartes, now appeared to many to be myopically selective, and likely to miss that which was most significant in the nature of things.
>
> (1991, p. 357)

But even if segments of the scientific community began to recognize inherent limitations in the reductionist program, it remained a powerful force both in scientific and popular culture. Part of the problem, perhaps, is that even as cracks began to appear in the old paradigm, a viable scientific alternative had yet to emerge.

Toward the end of the twentieth century, the intimations of a new scientific worldview began to take shape in the science of complex systems, or complexity theory. Physicist Mitchel Waldrop (1992) chronicles the rise of this interdisciplinary field in the 1980s at the Santa Fe Institute. There, diverse minds from the fields of biology, physics, mathematics, economics, and computer science converged to study the properties of naturally occurring complex systems. Their collective aim was "forging the first rigorous alternative to the kind of linear, reductionistic thinking that has dominated science since the time of Newton" (p. 13). Perhaps the most extraordinary thing about these complex systems is that they display properties that cannot be accounted for by the study of individual components. Rather, through the interaction of these components, the system becomes *measurably* more than the sum of its parts.

Computer scientist Melanie Mitchell (2009), a faculty member at the Santa Fe Institute, offers five common examples of complex systems: economics, the world wide web, insect colonies, the human immune system, and the human brain. In each case, the simple interactions of component parts give rise to complex phenomena and behavior that would be completely unpredictable in a reductionist model that isolates the parts from each other. The measurable occurrence of these higher-order phenomena is commonly referred to as *emergence*, and it is widely considered to be one of the most compelling and mysterious problems of twenty-first century science. Mitchell offers two complementary definitions for complex system:

> [1.] A system in which larger networks of components with no central control and simple rules of operation give rise to complex collective behavior, sophisticated information processing, and adaptation via learning or evolution…. [2.] A system that exhibits nontrivial emergent and self-organizing behaviors.
>
> (p. 13)

One of the most striking things about this account is that such systems appear to self-organize, process information, and adapt to changing conditions in the environment, without any sort of central control. A favorite example is army ants: a hundred ants on a flat surface will wander randomly until they die, but a million ants becomes a kind of super-organism exhibiting sophisticated behaviors that the study of any individual ant could never predict (Franks, 1989).

It is important to bear in mind that the occurrence of self-organization and emergence in nature are not speculation or theory: they represent actual objective measurement. With the use of computers, information in these systems can be tracked and observed at a level that was unthinkable in Newton's time. The applications of these models are only beginning to be explored: Lewin (1999) details the growing interest in applying complexity theory to sociocultural systems of all kinds. Depth psychologists Helene Shulman (1997) and Joseph Cambray (2009) explore what it would mean to understand psychological healing and transformation as a process of emergence. Shulman writes: "The old concept of 'matter' treats the natural world as a closed or frozen system ... In the new paradigm, both soma [living tissue] and psyche are evolving information processing systems that depend on feedback from the environment" (p. 119). Thus brain, psyche, and body are modeled via complex interactions rather than simple causality, and non-linear relationships are emphasized over simple reductive explanations. As summed up by Witherington (2011): "Taking emergence seriously entails a strong commitment to circular causality and the reciprocal nature of structure-function relations through the adoption of a pluralistic model of causality, one that recognizes both local-to-global processes of construction and global-to-local processes of constraint" (p. 66). In circular causality, the whole emerges from the interaction of its parts, and that whole in turn influences the interactions of those parts, which in turn further transform the whole.

Mitchell explicitly names the brain as a complex system of note, whereby 100 billion neurons interact to produce myriad cognitive functions and contents of consciousness. Neuroscience has carefully mapped the electric and chemical mechanisms through which neurons exchange signals, but the question of how conscious experience could arise from the sum of these signals remains a daunting puzzle. Nevertheless, complexity science has become a promising model for future explorations of brain and consciousness, and this will be important to keep in mind when investigating the neurobiological correlates of imagination. Though cultural bias may push for a reductive explanation, locating imagination in a single brain region or network, complexity and emergence offer another, potentially more accurate starting point. Freeman (2000) for example, shows how the experience of "meaning" appears to correlate with global high-order distribution patterns of neural activity. Thus, meaning emerges not through a local region of the brain, but through the complex interaction of multiple parts.

At the same time, we should remember that science did not invent complexity. In a telling passage from 1976, H. P. Rickman summarizes Dilthey's nineteenth century views:

> [Dilthey rejected the] approach which starts from simple elements and attempts to reconstruct more complex entities from them.... Human life as we know it cannot be accounted for by a hypothetical combination of elementary responses, instincts observed in animals or children,

and artificially elicited laboratory responses. Complex structures can and should be analyzed so as to reveal the elements they consist of but, if we begin with these, we cannot easily recapture the richness of experience which gives human life its distinctive qualities.

(p. 6)

In this sense, it has always been the task of the humanities to work with the complex wholes of human experience. Nor should we assume that the breakthrough of objectively measured complexity means that science will now somehow fully account for the humanistic project. Rather, these breakthroughs open up a new space for rapprochement, meaningful dialog, and mutual enrichment. I am reminded of the recent groundbreaking scientific discovery that meditation creates measurable benefits in the brain (Begley, 2007). This scientific affirmation of meditation does not alter the fact that meditation was improving lives for thousands of years before the brain scientists came to study it. What those meditation brain studies did was create greater respect and understanding among two different spheres of culture and practice. In a similar fashion, complexity theory may provide a similar bridge between science and the humanities.

Phenomenology and neuroscience

An especially promising area of methodological integration between scientific and humanistic research, particularly with regard to depth psychology, is the recent effort to integrate phenomenology into neuroscience. In the philosophical tradition, phenomenology begins with the work of Edmund Husserl (1859–1948) who undertook an investigation of the lived experience of phenomena as they arise in consciousness. Gadamer (1977/1966) notes that this project was an attempt to chart a course apart from the positivist scientism taking hold in Husserl's day. The intention was to "go back behind the scientific experience to the simple phenomenological data, like sense perception or practical experience ... the life-world claims its own phenomenal legitimacy" (p. 183). Particularly as phenomenology has moved forward, this return to the "life-world" means apprehension of the complex whole of human experience, prior to theory-laden ideals of objectivity and other methodological constraints. In modern qualitative research, phenomenological inquiry has evolved into a valid methodology for investigating human behavior and experience (Denzin & Lincoln, 2011).

Now phenomenology has also begun to find its way into neuroscience. The desire to integrate the conscious experience of subjects whose brains are being studied objectively has given rise to the new field of neurophenomenology. Doctors Frewen and Lanius (2015), for example, demonstrate that neurophenomenology is particularly well suited to the study of trauma and post-traumatic stress disorder, in which victims experience marked changes in their conscious experience of time, body, thought, and emotion. In their words: "neurophenomenology, the branch of phenomenology that addresses mind-body-brain correlation and mutual causation, involves examining both first person subjective experience and third-person objective brain-body functions simultaneously so as to understand both better" (p. 48). This mixed-method approach allows for the integration of quantitative and qualitative data, and thus presents a far more nuanced and complete picture of the phenomena in question. Furthermore, Frewen and Lanius utilize a model of bidirectional causality to understand mind-brain interactions: "experience and neurophysiology are intercausal; experience causes neurophysiological change, and neurophysiology causes experiential change" (p. 57). The beauty of this approach—in addition to being more thorough in the data it produces—is that it invites a full breadth of both scientific rigor and humanistic wisdom to bear on the very human problem it faces.

One of the early pioneers of integrating phenomenology into quantitative science was Chilean neuroscientist Francisco Varela. In *The view from within*, Varela and Shear (1999) call for a more robust methodology for the inclusion of subjective experience as data in scientific studies. Moving away from the age-old debate about subject/object, Varela and Shear instead frame the question in the familiar literary terms of "first-person" and "third-person" perspectives on the phenomenon being studied. The point here is not to somehow privilege the first-person experiential account from the third-person quantitative measurement, but rather to recognize it as a rich source of data for a more complete picture. In order to facilitate this integration, a "second-person" perspective is necessary, one that emphasizes communication and empathy in the pursuit of mutual understanding. Developing methods for working with these "second-person" considerations opens the door to the validation of intersubjective experiences—that is, "first-person" subjective experiences that share similar structures across individuals.

Facing Proteus

The hermeneutic philosopher Hans-George Gadamer makes a place of imagination in the pursuit of truth: "It is imagination [*Phantasie*] that is the decisive function of the scholar. Imagination naturally has a hermeneutical function and serves the sense for what is questionable. It serves the ability to expose real, productive questions" (1977/1966, p. 12). Such a move underscores the challenge of the present multidisciplinary inquiry: using the quantitative data of neuroscience to understand imagination, even while exploring the phenomenological role of imagination in neuroscience. It invites an ongoing hermeneutic spiral not only between researcher and texts, but also between disciplines and methods.

With this constant shifting of figures and grounds, becoming lost in the flux is a legitimate concern. Gadamer writes: "It is necessary to keep one's gaze fixed on the thing throughout all the constant distractions that originate in the interpreter himself" (2004/1975, p. 269). This formulation of the "fixed gaze" amid distraction recalls again the myth of the shapeshifter Proteus. Homer tells us that when Menalaus and his men were stranded, their only hope was to seek guidance from the Old Man of the Sea, but in order to obtain oracular counsel, they would have to hold him as he transformed into all manner of elements and beasts. But this is not merely a myth of wrestling with a shapeshifter—it is also a tale of finding deeper truth in the face of complexity and change. Though his challenge is great, Proteus is ultimately an ally in the pursuit of truth. So too, we hope, shall be the case with imagination.

Part II

Imagination as phenomenon

This section explores the phenomenon of imagination through humanistic perspectives, prior to applying any scientific lens. By examining imagination through the lenses of history, philosophy, and depth psychology, I mean to offer an account of how the phenomenon has been understood and what it has come to mean to humanity in all its richness. The intention here is not to prove causal claims about how ideas developed, but rather to trace conceptual and imaginative threads as they appear in various forms across the centuries. It is likely impossible in a work of this length to attempt to address every historical conception of imagination through Western civilization. Nevertheless, by following broad trends, a meaningful portrait of imagination across the centuries emerges.

Oftentimes when imagination is evoked with reference to a specific era, it is used to mean "the sorts of things that people were imagining" during that time, which might include arts and literature, cultural and religious ideas, mythology, as well as a general worldview. Books on "the imagination of the Renaissance," for example, are often more concerned with the art history and cultural beliefs of the Renaissance era, rather than how imagination itself was understood and viewed during that period. Likewise, the "the imagination of Ancient Greece" could readily indicate a treatise on its mythology: Olympian Gods and heroes, centaurs and satyrs and nymphs and whatnot. These are all fair uses of the term imagination, but they will not be the central focus in the following chapters. Rather, I am interested in how the people in Ancient Greece, the Renaissance, and beyond recognized and talked about the phenomenon of imagination itself—what they thought it was, what it meant to them, how they engaged with it.

Given the vast scope of ground covered—thousands of years of human history—this account necessarily presents a broad overview. To focus the material, I adopt the teleological aim of tracing conceptions of the imagination as they eventually culminated in twentieth-century depth psychology. In doing so, I maintain a healthy skepticism toward the notion of historical progress—that imagination conceived in the twenty-first century is inherently superior to those of earlier eras and cultures. No doubt we *homo sapiens* have made much progress in our short time on this planet— but it is also quite likely that in our mad dash forward, we have lost a thing or two along the way. Thus, I leave the matter of hierarchies of ideas to others, and tell the story of human imagination as a tale of love, found and lost and found again, as our species struggles to understand what we are.

Chapter 3

A brief history of imagination

From prehistory to the Renaissance

> *The lunatic, the lover, and the poet*
> *Are of imagination all compact.*
>
> A Midsummer Night's Dream

How old is imagination? Depending on how the term is defined, we will find different answers. The archeological record shows the first signs of aesthetic adornment and representative art beginning between 30,000 and 50,000 years ago (Pagel, 2014). Paleolithic cave painting and sculpted figures are clear artifacts of imaginative activity, but they don't necessarily mark the beginning of imagination itself. Particularly if we assume some kind of imagination at work in innovative problem solving, we would have to consider that many non-human animals exhibit these behaviors. Such innovative multi-step problem solving is well documented in highly intelligent species, such as apes, cetaceans, corvids, and elephants, most notably in their use of basic tools (see Bekoff, 2010; Bradshaw, 2009; Griffin, 1981). I am inclined to agree with the hypothesis put forth by Temple Grandin (Grandin & Johnson, 2005), that although animals may lack our capacity for abstract thought, they nevertheless are capable of thinking in images. Furthermore, the rapid eye movement (REM) sleep state that correlates with vivid dreaming has long been observed in all mammals, and in 2016 evidence emerged that reptiles also exhibit something similar to a REM sleep cycle (Shein-Idelson, Ondracek, Liaw, Reiter, & Laurent, 2016). If this is true, we can posit some form of primordial imagination existing on planet earth for hundreds of millions of years before humans came on the scene.

Nevertheless, our focus here will be humans. Historian Yuval Harari's *Sapiens* (2016) offers a compelling and provocative model for the role imagination played in the development of civilization. Harari notes that for most of the time *homo sapiens* existed, there was not much to distinguish us from other highly intelligent animals (apes, cetaceans, elephants). Then, about 40,000 years ago, a "cognitive revolution" occurred. This was a move beyond the basic language, emotional-social bonds, and tool-use of other intelligent animals to a capacity for mutually imagining *fictions*. In Harari's model, these imaginative fictions include absolutely everything that is not given by material reality: myths, cultural codes and rituals (like marriage), religion, laws, human rights, money, and more recently, multinational corporations. None of these things are given by biological reality per se—each exists only in the shared imagination of humans—we collaboratively imagine them and believe in them, sometimes to our detriment. If we all stopped believing in money, for example, it would be worthless—it has value because we collectively imagine that value. Individuals and small groups who refuse to believe in the consensus imagination of their culture are marginalized, punished, or even killed. Once these "imagined orders" began structuring human life and interactions, massive populations were able to gather where before small social bands of less than a hundred members had been the social norm (i.e., our very long history as hunter–gatherers). It should be noted that Harari is applying a specific definition of imagination: his idea of "imagined order" is wrapped up in the *literal belief* in whatever is being collectively imagined. In the historical investigation undertaken in this chapter and the next, imagination and belief are not always so necessarily bound. Nevertheless, Harari makes a compelling argument that stories and other imagined aspect of culture have always structured civilization on a fundamental level.

Harari is not the first to suggest that imagination played a vital role in the development of the human species. Written language is after all only some 5000 years old. Writing was preceded by a long prehistory—tens if not hundreds of thousands of years—of oral transmission of knowledge, often through storytelling, ritual, and song. Educational philosopher Kieren Egan argues that tribal storytelling encoded vital information that the tribe needed to function and thrive:

> Imaginative vividness was stimulated by the need to remember. In oral cultures, people know only what they can remember. The lore that binds a tribe together, and helps to establish each individual's social roles and very sense of identity, is coded into the myths.
>
> (n.d., p. 2)

Not only social structures, but also information about the land, cycles of seasons and weather, behaviors of animals, and properties of plants lived from one generation to the next through oral storytelling. Phenomenologist David Abram concurs: "the more lively the story—the more vital or stirring the encounters within it—the more readily it will be re-incorporated" (1996, p. 120). By this argument, emotionally charged and vivid narratives and images are more easily recalled and transmitted than dry lists of facts, so that the survival of prehistoric tribes was very much wrapped up in their storytelling abilities. Furthermore, Abram argues that by personifying plants and animals into animate, active agents in the story—in essence, non-human persons—the more vivid and personal the story becomes. "That which we literates misconstrue as a naïve attempt at causal explanation may be recognized as a sophisticated mnemonic method whereby precise knowledge is preserved and passed on from generation to generation" (p. 212). Storytelling was thus for the majority of homo sapiens existence not merely a matter of entertainment; it had evolved as a way of life.

At what point did *homo sapiens* begin talking about imagination as a distinct phenomenon? We can never know what sorts of conversations took place within hunter–gatherer tribes over their long and diverse prehistoric existence. For Western civilization, the written records of such discussions began earnestly in two places: the Hebrew tribes, and Ancient Greece. But in turning to these ancient cultural roots, it is important to bear in mind that our twenty-first century conceptions of imagination are likely quite different from those in antiquity. To understand history of imagination, we must be willing to set aside even the word itself. Prior to the English *imagination* we find the Latin *imaginatio* and *imago* of medieval Christianity. To trace the roots further still, we step outside the Roman alphabet altogether, we come to הַרֵצ [*yetzer*] of Hebraic tradition, entangled with issues of creation, obedience, and ethics. And as we turn to the burgeoning philosophical tradition of Ancient Greece, the starting point for a historical discourse on imagination begins in the debates over φαντασία.

Phantasies of Ancient Greece

Plato and Aristotle both articulated theories of **φαντασία** [*phantasia*] that would reverberate for millennia to come. Although casual summaries often depict these conceptions as diametrically opposed, a deeper look suggests a more nuanced set of distinctions. The fundamental difference between the Platonic and Aristotelian imagination is an inevitable extension of their respective idealist and realist metaphysics. "For Plato, the particular was less real, a derivative of the universal; for Aristotle, the universal was less real, a derivative of the particular" (Tarnas, 1991, p. 57). Plato distrusted the senses and thus the world of appearances, and taught instead that truth comes from the realm of archetypal ideas. Goodness, Beauty, and Truth could not be apprehended through the senses alone, only through the intellect and the light of reason. His rebellious pupil Aristotle grounded his own worldview firmly in the empirical, and like modern materialists, found truth primarily through the measurable world of the senses. That this divide in the Ancient Greek worldview continues in many respects into the contemporary debates of today will be traced throughout this chapter and the next. But for now, noting this extreme epistemological divergence between master and pupil, it is no surprise that their respective conceptions of φαντασία would appear to fit a general mold of polarization.

Though both εικασια [*image-making*] and **φαντασία** [*phantasia*] are terms often translated as imagination, it is the latter which received the more complex treatment in Greek philosophy. Historian Murray Wright Bundy (1927) traces the etymology of **φαντασία** to **φαινω** "to appear," "to be apparent," or "to come to light." Thus, phantasia was from the beginning concerned with the notion of "appearances"—the way phenomena appear to humans. The arguments about phantasia were arguments about appearances of phenomenon and how they should be understood. This goes to the heart of the difference between Plato's and Aristotle's treatment of the subject. For Plato, "appearances" as given by the senses were mere shadows of the real, while for Aristotle, "appearances" were the window to empirical truth.

The platonic imagination

Many accounts interpret Plato as condemning imagination outright as a source of falsehood, owing largely to his scathing criticism of art and artists in the *Republic* (~380 BCE). But a more discerning analysis shows that Plato was specifically criticizing **μίμησις** [*mimesis*] or imitation—the imagination that imitates the world of the senses. He was criticizing the process of producing images as reproductions or copies of the sensate, material world—a world that for Plato was, by its nature, a mere shadow of the divine–archetypal realm of ideas. The human world of appearances was an illusion that the philosopher must overcome, and thus any reproduction of this world through images was a road to ignorance. In Book VI of the *Republic* (511 d–e), Plato uses the term **εικασια** [*image-making*] to declare imagination as the lowest of the four faculties of the soul (Plato, trans. 1968, p. 192). The carpenter who makes a table is making a worldly reflection of the archetypal table, but the artist who paints that worldly table is making a copy of a copy. For Plato, this process of mimesis moves progressively away from a realization of archetypal truth, condemning humanity to live in "the cave" of false appearances instead. The aim of the philosopher, then, was to "emerge from the cave of ephemeral shadows and bring his darkened mind back into the archetypal light, the true source of being" (Tarnas, 1991, p. 42).

Thus, the condemnation of imagination in the *Republic* is at heart a condemnation of that kind of image-making that imitates the material world of appearances. His treatment of **φαντασία** [*phantasia*] on the other hand, was far more ambiguous. Historian Murray Wright Bundy (1927) offers this analysis:

> It is unfortunate that, just as the term "imagination" [εικασια] was in Plato's mind bound up with the theory of realistic art, so "phantasy"

[φαντασία] should have been connected with a false standard of sub-jectivity. The necessity for attacking false standards meant also attack-ing the terms through which they are expressed.

(p. 33)

Plato's rhetoric of imagination in the *Republic* and the *Sophist* was in part a push back against the relativistic Sophist school of philosophy, whose "false standards" Plato strongly opposed. Where the Sophists saw truth as relative, Plato argued exhaustively for the primacy of reason as a means to grasp universal truth. Because he condemned both dependence on the senses and relativistic subjectivism, he condemned imagination wherever it seemed to serve those purposes.

But Plato's treatment of imagination does not end with his criticisms of mimesis, and a careful reading of the full body of Platonic thought demonstrates a more nuanced conception of imagination with a consider-able positive aspect. Richard Kearney (1988) points out that even in the *Republic*, Plato "concedes that knowledge (*episteme*) may have recourse to what he calls 'thought-images' in order to enable our human under-standing (*dianoia*) to give figurative expression to its abstract ideas" (p. 99). In Kearney's analysis, these "thought-images" are never viewed as ends in themselves, but rather serve a *mediating function between the material and transcendental realms*. Turning to Plato's *Sophist*, Kearney further details this mediating imagination as an "ontological paradox" where the images "both are and are not" and "possess a sort of quasi-existence" (p. 102). Rather than being total falsehoods, images are a midway point between ultimate being and mere appearance. Thus, while reason remains the ultimate path to truth for Plato, human imagination can indeed offer necessary support along the way. This context helps to illuminate Plato's seemingly contradictory statement at the end of the *Republic*: that poetry might be admitted to the city so long it takes the form of "hymns to gods or celebrations of good men" (Plato, trans. 1968, p. 607a). That is, poetry is welcome where it serves divine–archetypal, rather than sensate–material, truth.

Elsewhere in the platonic cannon are passages where imagination is implicated with direct relationship to the divine. *The Timaeus* describes how divine visions from the gods are sent in the form of "images and phantasms" (Plato, trans. 2000, 70e–72b). In Bundy's (1927) analysis:

Here a divine power of creating impressions acts through a compar-able and complementary function in man's lower nature.... This object of vision is not the abstraction of discursive thought, or even the image of an idea; but the idea itself made intelligible through its perfect embodiment, its expression in sensible terms.

(p. 53)

That is to say, the transcendent is transmitted directly to the faculties of lower human nature in the form of concrete images. Kearney (1988) offers a similar assessment:

> Divine images may enable visionaries to come upon truth immediately, thereby dispensing with the arduous dialectical ascent to the ideas through philosophical argumentation.... In such moments of ecstatic vision, the imagination becomes the privileged recipient of divine inspiration.
>
> (p. 104)

This conception of divine imagination is a complete reversal of the polemic against mimesis found in the *Republic*. Whereas the mimetic imagination was described as the lowest faculty of the soul, here a higher imagination is seen as medium for directly apprehending the highest truth. The essential difference, according to Kearney, is that this transcendental imagination is "beyond the control of man," something that is not produced by human creativity, but granted as a gift from a divine source (p. 105). In addition, Bundy argues that Plato's *Phaedrus* "clearly defines the inspired madness of the poet as a process of contemplating Heavenly Beauty, and connecting the lower with the higher as image and universal type" (p. 57). Again, imagination is conceived as a mediator between archetypal divinity and the imperfect world of the senses. While the lower imagination of mimesis occludes the truth by endlessly copying appearances, the higher imagination is a servant and conduit of the transcendent. This idea that imagination might access a divine, higher, or ultimate aspect of reality is one that humanity would come upon again and again as the centuries passed.

The Aristotelian imagination

In stark contrast to Plato's idealism, Aristotle was a dedicated realist. Tarnas summarizes: "Aristotle's intellectual temperament was one that took the empirical world on its own terms as fully real.... True reality, he believed, was the perceptible world of concrete objects" (1991, pp. 55–56). Thus, it is no surprise that Aristotle's treatment of φαντασία dispensed with both Plato's hostility toward mimesis and his penchant for divine vision. Accordingly, Kearney (1998) notes that Aristotle shifted imagination from metaphysical to psychological terrain: he emphasized the mental nature of images, whereas Plato's discussion of mimesis had been more concerned with extrenal works of art. (p. 106). It is telling that Aristotle's *Poetics* focuses on a new evaluation of art and μίμησις [*mimesis*], while avoiding the terms εικασια [*image-making*] and φαντασία [*phantasia*] in his discussion of aesthetics (Bundy, 1927, p. 65).

For Aristotle's psychological conception of **φαντασία** we must turn instead to *De Anima*, a treatise on the nature of soul. There he writes: "Unless one perceives things one would not learn or understand anything, and when one contemplates one must simultaneously contemplate an image; for images are like sense perceptions (*aisthemata*), except that they are without matter" (trans. 1968, 432a3). Here is a theory of mental images (*phantasmata*) that is intimately bound to both perceiving the world and thinking about those perceptions. Kearney elaborates: "The image serves as the internal representation of sensation to reason ... Without the transitional services of the imagination, reason would be unable to make contact with the sensible world of reality" (1988, pp. 108–109). Again, we see imagination given the role of mediator, this time between sense perception and the intellect. The appearances of these mental *phantasmata* may ultimately be seen as accurate or inaccurate in their representation of the world, but without them, humans would not be able to think about the world at all!

Aristotle also recognized that imagination was implicated in memory, an idea that modern neuroscience would not "discover" for thousands of years hence. "As regards to the question of which part of the soul memory belongs, it is, then, clear that it belongs to the same part as the imagination; and those things that are essentially the objects of memory are also such of which there is imagination" (Aristotle, trans. 2007, p. 450a). Given its essential role in both thought and memory, the Aristotelian imagination appears integral to the human condition and a necessary component of all human understanding. Nevertheless, Kearney is quick to point out that "this admission does not mean that imagination is itself the origin of meaning. At best, it may be enlisted in the service of higher truths: truths which exist beyond our images of them" (p. 112). Though this model gives imagination a central role to play in human consciousness, it continues to be a role of subservience to the reasoning intellect. It is also decidedly more mundane than Plato's archetypal imagination; Aristotle rejected the Platonic account of divinely inspired dreams. "The phantasy of the dreamer is the same power which is operative in the waking state, merely functioning under other conditions," and furthermore, Aristotle's "discussion of dreams ridicules, and his discussion of memory explains away, Plato's notion of phantasy as the mystic's power of vision" (Bundy, 1927, p. 80). Thus, the first great champion of empiricism gave us a realist imagination, integral to both the material world and human psychology, but decidedly earthbound.

These two ancient Western models of imagination also share a few key qualities in common. Just as Plato articulated a lower mimetic imagination that led humanity astray and a higher archetypal imagination that revealed universal truth, Aristotle agreed that phantasy had both a lower and higher function for the human soul. The phantasy of the lower soul was driven by appetite and desire: "So powerful are these simple phantasies in their influence upon action that often in obedience to them men act contrary to their better knowledge; phantasy rules reason" (Bundy, 1927, p. 70). Contrast this with Kearney's account of Artistotle's higher form: "the rational imagination is capable of uniting and combining our empirical sensations in terms of a 'common sense,' which is in turn representable to reason" (1988, p. 111). Though their metaphysics differ, both of these ancient philosophers recognize positive and negative versions of imagination, those that lead minds astray, and those that serve greater clarity and truth. Likewise, we see in both systems of thought a conception of imagination in a mediating role, an imagistic faculty of transmission and translation that, like Hermes, transmits meaning to the perceiving mind.

The Greek legacy

Plato's and Aristotle's philosophical systems would go on to influence the West throughout the medieval period and beyond. Though there were other models of phantasy throughout the long span of Ancient Greek culture, the works of Aristotle and Plato in particular would be elaborated and debated for millennia to come, and have lasting impact on the Western psyche. Indeed, much of what followed even in subsequent Greek thought were reactions and elaborations to Platonic and Aristotelian thought. The Stoics, for example, drew on both traditions in their assertions that "the great ethical problem is the right use of phantasies" (Bundy, 1927, p. 92). In the Stoic worldview, it was an ethical imperative for humans to control their phantasies, which might otherwise lead to trouble. This ethical framing would influence similar Christian conceptions of imagination in the centuries to come. Another tradition worthy of mention is the Asklepieia, the healing temples of the god Asklepios, who remained among the most popular gods of antiquity for over 1000 years (600 BCE–499 CE) (Patton, 2009). Pilgrims suffering afflictions of all kinds would make a pilgrimage to the Asklepieia in hopes of a healing dream from the god, a vision that would either offer a prescription, or heal them outright. Here we see a longstanding practice of the kind of divinely inspired dreaming that Plato discussed in his philosophical works.

While the empirical realism of Aristotle arguably had the greater influence on the development of Western thought through its early intimations of science and psychology, Plato's system would also powerfully influence future generations, particularly in the form of Neoplatonism. In the Neoplatonists, particularly Plotinus, we find a third influential model for Ancient Greek imagination. Tarnas (1991) describes Neoplatonism as an attempt build a bridge between "the rational philosophies and the mystery religions" of the antiquity; an integration of Platonic thought with both explicit mysticism and Aristotelian psychology (p. 84). In this system, the highest transcendental principle was called "the One," and from this One an "overflow of sheer perfection produces 'the other'—the created cosmos in all its glory—in a hierarchal series of gradations moving away from the ontological center to the extreme limits of the possible" (p. 85). From the One emanated the Divine Mind or Intellect (*Nous*), which contained the archetypal ideas; from *Nous* emanated the World Soul (*Anima Mundi*) that animates nature; and at farthest remove from the indescribable purity of the One is the world of matter, generally seen as a realm of restriction and darkness.

Plotinus provides a unique metaphysics of "image" to explain these relationships: the lower level is always an image of the higher. "Being, the image of the One, is unknowable ... Mind (Nous) or cosmic mind is the image of being; the soul is the image of Mind; and nature is the image of the soul" (Bundy, 1927, p. 118). This framework suggests a kind of meta-physical imagination, working in the very structure of the universe itself— a universe that emanates through and from the divine–archetypal Mind. These metaphysical "images" are always less than the higher reality they point to, but still a mediating point of connection between the levels. If we understand imagination to be the generation of meaningful images, then the Neoplatonic model makes imagination something not merely psycho-logical, but a phenomenon in and of the world, expressed through the World Soul as an emanation from the Divine Mind.

That said, some of the Neoplatonists after Plotinus were prone to dismiss "*phantasy*" as a shadow of ultimate reality, and thus a potential danger to reason. Bundy notes that there is no uniform agreement about the nature of "*phantasy*" among subsequent Neoplatonic thinkers:

> This paradoxical nature of Neoplatonic thought concerning φαντασία can hardly be overemphasized: its idealism taught it to despise phanta-sies, its dualism found a place for them, it's psychology, largely Aristo-telian, taught it to study them, and it passion for the *Timaeus* led it to recognize them as God-given.
>
> (p. 146)

On the whole, Bundy concludes that the Neoplatonists regarded phantasy with suspicion, and this would in turn add to the general hostility toward imagination among Christian thinkers throughout the medieval era.

But Tarnas (1991), perhaps taking a longer view of history that con-siders the Renaissance and beyond, offers a more positive summation of the Neoplatonic position:

> Because all things emanate from the One through the Intellect and the World Soul, and because human imagination at its highest participates in the primal divinity, man's rational soul can imaginatively reflect the

transcendent Forms and thus, through insight into the ultimate order of things, move toward spiritual emancipation.

(pp. 85–86)

In this view, the Neoplatonic imagination is a means to direct participation in the divinity of the One, and thus a force for spiritual liberation. Anne Shepard's (2014) more recent study of Greek *phantasia* concurs that the Neoplatonic imagination goes beyond imitation "to reflect the loftiest heights of metaphysics accessed by the innermost depths of the human soul" (p. 104). Douglas Hedley (2016) further argues that the Neoplatonic model of divine emanation overcomes dualistic thinking by allowing images to "participate in what they express," not merely pointing to a higher truth, but manifesting as an aspect of that truth (p. xvii). Images then become the carriers of a "non-propositional truth," leaving behind allegory and signs that merely point to abstract concepts, and allowing the concrete particularity of the image to speak for itself as an emanation of the archetypal.

While largely quieted throughout the Middle Ages, this conception of a participatory, divine imagination would eventually reassert itself in early humanist thinkers of the Renaissance. Perhaps most surprisingly, the Neoplatonic worldview would eventually come to play an important role in bringing about the Scientific Revolution, a topic that will be addressed in Chapter 9. For now, we depart briefly from the Greeks and turn to the other great tap-root of Western civilization, the Judeo-Christian tradition.

The Judeo-Christian imagination: from הַרַע to Imaginatio

Kearney (1988) gives the primary Hebrew term for imagination as הַרַע [*yetzer*], and notes the etymological root *yzr* and its cognates *yetsirah* (creation), *yoster* (creator), and *yatsar* (create), deeply implicating the Hebrew notion of imagination with divine creation and authority. "The *yetzer*, understood accordingly as man's creative impulse to imitate God's own creation, was arguably first realized when Adam and Eve ate the forbidden fruit of the Tree of Knowledge" (p. 39). This creation story claims that God made man "in his own image," implying that man, while a creation, also contains the seed of divine creativity. This early myth depicts humanity exercising its own creative power in the decision to defy authority and eat the forbidden fruit. "The sin of imagination leads to the fall of Adam and Eve into historical time.… Imagination enables man to think in terms of *opposites*—good and evil, past and future, God and man" (p. 40). From the very beginning, then, the Ancient Hebrew imagination is connected to serious questions about ethics, authority, free will, and temptation. The common term *yetzer hara* or "evil imagination" is translated literally as "the inclination to do evil," the dark impulse within humanity that tempts one away from God and into ruin (Kraemer, 2005). This came to be particularly associated with carnal desire, and in response "contemplation of death, self-denial and other ascetic practices are recommended as curbs to the erotic impulses of the imagination" (Kearney, 1998, p. 44). Add to this the third commandment of Moses, "Thou shalt not make unto thee a graven image, nor any manner of likeness, of any thing that is in heaven above" (Exodus 20:4, King James Bible), and it would be easy to conclude that imagination in the Ancient Hebrew tradition was seen as entirely negative.

But the Talmud also states "God created man with two *yetzers*, the good and the evil" (Berach, 61a), so the evil inclination toward carnal desire and sin is matched by a good inclination to act in accordance with God. "The good imagination ('*yetzer hatov*') opens up history to an I–Thou dialog between man and his creator" (Kearney, 1988, p. 47). In this relationship, humanity is able to participate in the realization of God's plan by aligning the human *yetzer* with the will of the creator. "Though contaminated by the original sin of Adam, imagination might yet serve as the midwife to an ultimately good end" (p. 50). This becomes a free will and human choice: "The *yezser* is neither good nor bad until man makes it so" (p. 48,) which foregrounds again the essential questions of ethics and obedience to divine authority. Kearney concludes this emphasis on the ethical rather than the ontological dimensions of imagination is one of the principle differences between Hebraic and Ancient Greek conceptions of the idea.

Ethical considerations aside, it must also be noted that visions and dreams were long considered to be potential messages from God in Hebrew scripture. In Numbers 12:5–8, God says that he will speak to prophets in visions and in dreams, and only Moses would be spoken to directly. Thus, all the prophets that follow Moses might expect dream and vision to be the medium through which God sends his messages. Throughout the scriptures are accounts of the prophets Isaiah, Amos, and Ezekiel all being visited by visions from God (Wieland-Robbescheuten, 2006, p. 355). In addition, we find accounts of prophetic dreams occurring for Joseph (Gen 37:5–11), pagan rulers like the Pharaoh (Gen: 41) and King Nebuchadnezzar of Babylon (Daniel: 2), and ordinary men like Daniel (Daniel: 7) and Laban (Gen: 31:24). Taken in sum, dreams and visions have a clear capacity for divine inspiration and communication within the Judaic tradition. As with Plato, divinely inspired images arising in consciousness are considered God-given rather than man-made. From the beginning of human civilization, then, imagination and divinity went hand in hand.

The Ancient Greek and Hebrew traditions described thus far were both significant contributors to the emerging Christian worldview that dominated the West throughout the 1000 years of the medieval period. The first great synthesis of these streams of thought was undertaken in the fourth century by Augustine of Hippo, who forged "a sustained and systematic concordance between Judeo-Christian theology and Greek ontology" (Kearney, 1998, p. 116). In Augustine we also find the first sustained and systematic use of the Latin *imaginatio*. *Imaginatio* derives from *imago* (image) with roots in *imitari* (to imitate) thus linking back to the Greek μίμησις (*mimesis*) or "imitation." The suffix *–atio* ("-ation" in English) indicates action or doing, as in the English words *generation* (the action of generating), *vacation* (the action of vacating), *improvisation* (the action of improvising). So the Latin *imaginatio* and the English *imagination* can be read as either "the action of making images" or simply "the action of images," depending on whether we conceive of them as actively created by individuals, or as an autonomous phenomenon of consciousness. According to Bundy (1927) Augustine introduced the new term *imaginatio* in conscious distinction to *phantasia*. *Imaginatio* is used by Augustine as a term for the phenomenon of imagination in its broadest sense, including the basic sense-impressions of Aristotle. *Phantasia* is used as a specific kind of *imaginatio*: those recombined or novel mental images beyond immediate sense-impressions, and thus also those images deliberately employed or created in the service of reason (p. 161).

Beyond this elaboration of Aristotelian psychology, Augustine adopted many of the more negative formulations of imagination left by his Greek and Hebrew philosophical forbearers. His summation combines "a) the biblical condemnation of imagination as a transgression of the divine order of creation ... and b) the [Greek] metaphysical critique of imagination as a counterfeit to the original truth of Being" (Kearney, 1988, p. 116). Thus, by its very nature, human imagination is distrusted by Augustine as both an ethical and an epistemological threat. "He observes that this play of phantasy becomes dangerous," Bundy writes, "the work of imagination can only with difficulty be restrained by reason" (1927, p. 160). That Augustine sees the willful control of the imagination as an ethical imperative draws on both the Stoic philosophy of Greece and the two *yetzers* of the Old Testament. Drawing also from the more dualistic stream of the Neoplatonic tradition, Augustine "recognizes imagination as a means to insight, [but] not insight itself" (p. 168). Eternity is beyond any image representing it, and though God may grant dreams and visions, it is the intellect of interpretation that marks the true prophet, not the visiting images.

Just as Augustine is credited with the first great intellectual synthesis of the medieval era, Thomas Aquinas is often credited with the last. And yet in the 800-odd years that passed between these men, the medieval conception of the imagination changed little. In Aquinas' seminal *Summa Theologica*, which uses *imaginatio* and *phantasy* synonymously, "all uses of imagination are subordinate to the superior claims of reality and reason" and must be "controlled by the rational intellect" (Kearney, 1998, p. 129).

Not only does untethered imagination drive the individual toward unreality and sin—it is also a faculty vulnerable to malevolent entities: "a demon can work on man's imagination and even on his corporeal senses, so that something seems otherwise than it is" (Aquinas, 1945/1265–1274, p. 1052). Similar to the *yetzer hara*, the medieval Christian imagination was feared as a source of discord, carnal desires, evil impulses, and even supernatural attack. Divine vision was possible, but only by means of the intellect: "An angel causing an imaginative vision, sometimes enlightens the intellect at the same time, so that it knows what these images signify; then there is not deception" (p. 1027). In these regards, Bundy reads Aquinas as emblematic of an age that incorporated "Platonism, Aristotelianism, and Stoicism, subordinated the imagination and the emotions to reason and intelligence, and poetry and dreams to theology and metaphysics" (1927, p. 224). Not entirely surprising for an authoritarian era ruled by monarchs and priests, imagination was at its best a humble servant, tolerated only when firmly under control.

Perhaps the best example of the positive use of imagination under this pretext is to be found in the work of Bonaventure (1221–1274), a contemporary of Aquinas. Michelle Karnes (2011) has written extensively about Bonaventure's use of imagination as a cognitive tool in contemplative Christian meditation. Whereas the tradition of divine visions was a matter of passive reception, Bonaventure used imagination in meditation deliberately as a means to knowing God. Drawing in part on Aristotle psychology, "whereby imagination enabled a transition from sensible to intelligible apprehension, imagining the life of Christ used the imagination to impel the meditant from Christ's humanity to his divinity" (p. 5). Bonaventure thus established himself as an authority on the use of imagination to actively engage scripture as a means to deeper insight and moral improvement. Although the symbolic and narrative content was largely proscribed, the active cultivation of vivid and meaningful mental images was nevertheless recognized as a powerful cognitive tool for spiritual development.

We should be wary to assume that the medieval imagination can be entirely summed up in the writings of a few Christian Patriarchs, even if they did largely dominate the worldview of their era. The church fathers may have sought to control imagination in themselves and others, but that does not mean they always succeeded. One such outlier is the life and work of Hildegard of Bingen, a woman who was visited by visions from an early age, and in following them became perhaps the most prolific woman of her generation: an abbess, a composer, and a writer of theological, medicinal, and botanical texts. Hildegarde's writings emphasized harmony with nature and often had a sensuous quality; she described her visions as coming to her through all five senses, and was regarded by many as a prophet, even in her own lifetime (Schipperges, 1995). Though Christian dogma proscribed the form and structure of her imagination, Hildegarde of Bingen brought to those forms a holistic perspective far ahead of her time.

Outside the Christian church, a discourse on imagination continued among the Rabbis and Imams of the other monotheistic religions, which would intermittently meet and cross-pollinate with the European West. The Jewish tradition continued its own theological development throughout the Middle Ages, producing a complex understanding of divine vision that coincided with the development of the mystical kabbalah (Wolfson, 1994). In sharp contrast to our contemporary stereotypes, medieval Islam was generally far more tolerant than medieval Christianity and thus, John Cocking argues, "their speculation was freer, less haunted by the dangers of heretical thinking" (1991, p. 103). The medieval Arab world was likewise influenced by the works of Aristotle, Plato, and the Neoplatonists, and Muslim philosophers al-F r bi (870–950) and Avicenna (980–1037) both articulated theories of imagination that integrated Greek philosophy with the Qu'ran, establishing "imagination as a link between perception, the reason of *nous*, and theophanic vision" (p. 133). Of particular interest is the sufi Ibn 'Arab (1165–1240), whose writings on imagination would come to profoundly impact twentieth-century depth psychology through the work of French Islamic scholar Henry Corbin. This relationship between depth psychology and Islamic mysticism will be discussed further in Chapter 5.

And what of common men and women of medieval Europe? Jacques Le Goff's (1985) study of the medieval imagination argues that Augustine's warnings on the dangers of imagination grew out of a culture where the distinctions between "real" and "imaginary" were not so clearly defined as they are today. In the context of this more fluid boundary between mental image and the empirical, Le Goff outlines the primary division in medieval culture between marvels (*mirabilis*), magic (*magicus*), and miracles (*miraculosus*). Whereas in pre-Christian times, magic could serve either good or evil, in the Christian era the church cast all magic as the work of Satan. Miracles, on the other hand, were understood as acts of God, though distinguishing *miraculosus* from *magicus* was not always easy. Marvels held an intermediate position as phenomena not fully comprehended by the human mind, but understood as part of the natural order. This demonization of *magicus* in an era hostile toward imagination raises the question if there might not be some etymological link between the Latin *imago* (image) and the Greek *magos* (magician, learned priest). Other than Morosini's (2010) conjecture that both words might have roots in the Avestan root *magh* (power), this line of thought appears largely unexplored. Such a connection would certainly be in keeping with biblical implication of *yester* as humanity's primal creative power.

The medieval times were largely an era marked by obedience rather than creativity, and thus imagination tended to be understood in the sense of received visions and dreams. Furthermore, Le Goff points out that even passively received dreams were an occasion for great moral tension: "In the middle ages the dream was one of the primary battlegrounds on which God contended with the Devil for possession of Man's soul" (1985 p. 16). Oneiromancy (divination through dreams) was condemned as magic, and where it survived, like the rest of the folk imagination of the time, it did so underground and out of sight from church authority.

We should also bear in mind that our firm, contemporary boundaries about imagination as being solely "in our heads" was not so clearly defined prior to modernity. Writing in the late sixteenth century, French philosopher Michel de Montaigne (the creator of "the essay") expresses in his writings many common cultural beliefs about Imagination as they had evolved in over the past centuries. In his *Essays* (1993/1580), Montaigne discusses the imagination as a contagious force with the power to spread emotion, health, or illness—even the power to kill. Stranger still, there was a sense that imagination could act as an active and transformative power in the world, transforming bodies and genders and manifesting strange happenings.

A final area where the questions of imagination, divinity, and magic were entangled was the controversy over holy images. Daniel Boorstin (1992) writes that beginning in the sixth century:

> Christian images played a magical role in the chronicles of pilgrims. Cures and miracles multiplied from sacred images in Christian households.... Even the candles lit before images would perform miracles and cure illness ... stories multiplied of the use of images as palladia, or magic shields.
>
> (p. 185)

In a distant echo of the Greek Asklepieia, where the afflicted sought healing through the images of dreams, the folk culture of the medieval era came to believe that Christian images in themselves had the power to heal. "Legends grew of images not made by human hands that brought their message direct from God....Such images were common enough to acquire a name of their own—*achieropoietoi* ... which suggested that such an image somehow perpetuated the incarnation" (p. 186). Such beliefs were eventually met by a violent counter-movement of iconoclasm, where religious authorities destroyed images and brutally suppressed image worship. In the eighth century, Constantine V executed priests "on mere suspicion of being image-worshipers" (p. 190). But belief in the power of holy images had its defenders within the church. Most notably Dionysos the Areopagite and John of Damascus each employed a Neoplatonic framework to argue that images engaged the senses in order to point to a transcendental reality beyond themselves. Such debates spanned centuries and became one of the great historical conflicts within the Christian church.

The Renaissance

There is much disagreement among modern historians about how the Renaissance ("the rebirth") should be defined, or if it is helpful to speak of a distinct historical "renaissance" at all. I use the term specifically to discuss the psychological and cultural transformations that bridged the medieval and modern worldviews in the West, regardless of the exact timeframes in which those transformations took place. In particular, the rise of humanism, the resurgence of interest in classical Greek philosophy and literature, and the flowering of the creative arts during this period have particular bearing on the history of imagination. In Carl Jung's psychological reading, the Renaissance was a return of the repressed: "the ideal of spirituality striving for the heights was doomed to clash with the material, earthbound passion," a clash that resulted in a pagan transformation of "the spirit of medieval Christianity ... exchanging the heavenly goal for an earthly one" (1968/1951, p. 43 [para. 78]). In the context of the present discourse, this means imagination would no longer be so strictly confined to the proscribed frameworks of Christian dogma. After 1000 years of suspicion, repression and authoritarian rule, imagination was at last beginning to break free from its chains.

Precursors to the Renaissance imagination

The people of the Middle Ages of course imagined themselves as living in the current age, late in the history of God's world, and subsequently relegated the Greeks and Romans to ancient times, a period of darkness before the light of Christ. It was Petrarch (1304–1374) who first looked back over the sweep of history and suggested the opposite: that following the decline of Rome, humanity had on the contrary entered an age of "darkness" with diminished cultural and intellectual development (Graziosi, 2013). This poetic characterization of the "dark ages" remains evocative to the present day, though most scholars and historians now reject that term and view the Middle Ages as an era of slow but steady innovation (Ingham, 2015). Nevertheless, Petrarch's stark revision of history gives some indication of how the thinkers of the Renaissance began to imagine themselves. Rather than living through the final age before the end times and apocalypse, there was a possibility of rebirth, an opportunity to grow into something greater.

Petrarch viewed the lost Greco–Roman civilization as a golden age, a time of creativity and high culture, whose literary fruits provided not just "scientific knowledge and rules for logical discourse, but for the deepening enrichment of the human spirit" (Tarnas, 1991, p. 209). Thus Petrarch called for a scholarly re-collection and integration of the great literary works of antiquity, not merely for historical interest, but as a living resource for a deeper appreciation of humanity. This marked the birth of the "humanities" in Western discourse. Human literature could now be recognized as "a source of spiritual insight and moral development ... learning that would better reflect the conflicts and vagaries of man's emotional and imaginative depths.... Rather than spiritual and scientific system building, [Petrarch's] focus was psychological, humanist, and aesthetic" (p. 210). This movement quickly spread beyond its origins in Florence, and ushered in new era of scholarship, discourse, and new ideas. In the *History of Western philosophy* (1945), Bertrand Russell credits the Renaissance as a time that promoted "independent thought" in the renewed debates on the merits of Plato versus Aristotle, and "more important still, it encouraged the habit of regarding intellectual activity as a delightful social adventure, not a cloistered meditation aiming at the preservation of a predetermined orthodoxy" (p. 521). In short, the culture was shifting toward a greater capacity for intellectual diversity, and at the same time developing a new appreciation for literature and art.

Tarnas lists a number of factors that fostered or accompanied this shift in worldview; the invention of the clock not only quantified time but also introduced to the human mind the possibility of human-created machines; the printing press, with its potential to democratize learning; the magnetic compass and the new frontiers for exploration that it opened; the subsequent making of new geographical maps, revealing the limitations of received geographical knowledge; and ultimately contact with new countries, new economies, new cultures, new religions—all of which fostered a new skepticism toward the accuracy of the traditional Medieval European worldview (1991, pp. 226–227). As the movement grew, Renaissance thinkers also began to have their metaphysical imaginations exercised through exposure to mystical systems outside of Christian dogma: kabbalah, sufism, hermeticism, astrology, alchemy, and other esoteric systems (Kearny, 1988; Russell, 1945; Steiner, 1911; Tarnas, 1991). It was a time of possibility, exploration, a new heroic image of humanity re-discovering the world, and a flourishing of the arts. In writing about the historical forces at work in the Renaissance, Dilthey states:

> Wherever a conceptual framework has perished and another is about to emerge we see that a new openness to experience and imagination dominate mental life ... the Medieval world of ideas had lost its dominance and mathematical science, which was to become the basis of modern thought, had not yet developed.
>
> (1976b/n.d., p. 83)

And yet as we shall see, this was not merely a burst of creativity between shifting paradigms—it was a time of unprecedented celebration of the human imagination.

Proteus in the gardens of the World Soul

The upwelling of imagination in the Renaissance was largely ignited through the humanism movement initiated by Petrarch. Not to be confused with the secular humanism of today, Renaissance humanism became a re-centering of intellectual interest from strictly theological matters to renewed focus on the human being. In *An intellectual history of psychology*, Daniel Robinson (1976) argues that if there is one central idea to be born from the Renaissance, it was the *dignity of man*, "with the associated insistence that the world was made for human beings" (p. 120). Indeed, Renaissance theologian Marsilio Ficino went so far as to declare that man "acts as the vicar of God," and is even a god in his own right: "[Man] is, finally, the god of all materials, since he handles all, and forms and changes them" (quoted in Trinkaus, 1986). This dignified vision of humanity enabled a new sense of individualism, not necessarily in the sense of selfish-ness, but rather in the sense of self-cultivation through the study of the humanities. Though the term *Renaissance Man* is a more recent invention, it is modeled on the notion of gifted polymaths such as Michelangelo and Leonardo da Vinci who excelled themselves across multiple fields. The human imagination that had been so long feared and repressed by the church now had the potential to be viewed as a vital asset instead.

Archetypal psychologist James Hillman (1976) suggests that the most prevalent mythic image to express the imaginative spirit of the times was Greece's archetypal shapeshifter: "Perhaps the Renaissance's most popular figure from myth was Proteus. His ceaselessly changing image that could take on any shape or nature represented the multiple and ambiguous forms of the soul" (p. 203). Renaissance scholar A. Bartlett Giamatti (1968) tracks how the figure of Proteus was elaborated in many directions during this period: "not only is Proteus appropriate to figure the multiple glories of man, but man's protean abilities to adapt and to act many roles is the source of the power that enables him to assume the burdens of civiliza-tion" (p. 439). In this way, "Renaissance man" was imagined as "protean man," containing a multitude of diverse human potentials.

Giamatti discusses Pico della Mirandola's famous *Oratio de Hominis Dignitate* (1486), viewed by many as a manifesto for the Renaissance, and notes that Proteus serves as a unifying theme. There, "Protean man [is] set forth at the outset … revealing the way in which, through the forms of the many, Pico is able to arrive at the One" (1968, p. 440). The "One" here is a return to Neoplatonic philosophy, for which Proteus becomes the new personification: the many forms of Proteus express the animate multitude of the World Soul, while at once emanating from the deeper unity of the Divine Mind.

The Greek myth of Proteus is after all not only about shapeshifting, but also about a prophet, a speaker of deep truth. As imagined in the Renaissance, Proteus comes to represent a union of opposites—the one and the many, unity and diversity, now playing out in the humanist psyche. Perhaps this version of Proteus expresses the Renaissance desire to unify the old gods with the new, Greek polytheism with Christian monotheism, imagination, and logos. But the original myth also reminds us that it is no easy unity to achieve. Struggle is par for the course, and Giamatti is clear that not all Renaissance depictions of Proteus were about actualized human potential—others implied chaos, melancholy, and even deceit and demonic powers. These multiple faces of Renaissance Proteus are appropriate both to a mythic shapeshifter, and to the spirit of the time, when new possibilities were opening in the human imagination, both for good and for ill. Among his many faces, Proteus came to be seen as an archetypal poet, a figure whose inherent creativity can express both good and evil, love and loss, darkness and light.

Amid the ambiguities of the newly possible, the resurgence of Platonic and Neoplatonic thought provided a novel container for the expanding role of imagination. The Renaissance Platonists viewed human creativity itself as being in the likeness of God, and the works of artists and poets could thus be seen as extensions of the creation, a participation in God's divinity (Renaissance Platonism, 2005). The ancient possibility first intimated by the *yetser hatov*—imagination in service to God—now became linked to art and artists in a tremendous outpouring of aesthetic activity. Tarnas elaborates: "Platonism offered a richly textured tapestry of imaginative depth and spiritual exaltation. The notion that beauty was an essential component in the search for the ultimate reality ... held much attraction for the growing sensibility in Europe" (1991, p. 212). Plato's famous trinity of transcendental ideas—the Good, the True, and the Beautiful—had been dissociated by the medieval church fathers. Their dualistic perspective honored Truth and Goodness, but was inclined to dismiss Beauty as an earthly matter. The Renaissance rediscovery of Beauty as an archetypal idea, a transcendent link between the human and the divine, elevated creative art making to a potential act of exultation. The Neoplatonic framework of emanation from the Divine Mind further strengthened this link. "Possessing a divine spark, man was capable of discovering within himself the image of the infinite deity" (p. 214). Indeed, God was now spoken of as an "Artist" by Pico Della Mirandola (1945/1519, p. 31) and the Christian mystic and humanist Nicholas of Cusa wrote "Christ is the Word of the omnipotent God and is the Creative Art" (Tarnes, 1978/1460, p. 103).

Under Cosimo de Medici's patronage, Marsilio Ficino (1433–1499) founded the Platonic Academy of Florence in 1462, and henceforth undertook the translation of numerous Platonic and Neoplatonic texts (Kristeller, 2006). Ficino pioneered a synthesis of Christian, Platonic, and Neoplatonic thought whereby the individual, through contemplation, might be elevated to know the divine. Although Ficino was ordained as a Catholic Priest in 1473, he also developed a surprising synthesis of imagination and magic. In John Cocking's (1991) account, for Ficino "magic is the power of imagination, the *vis imaginativa*, captured by the mind, brought under control, and re-directed upwards" (p. 178). While the lower imagination still had the power to lead humans astray, the rites of magic could contain and transform the imagination, making it a vehicle to experience the godhead. In these esoteric explorations, Ficino certainly courted heresy; that he did not call down the wrath of the church is evidence of his accommodating diplomacy and the great respect given by his contemporaries to the corpus of his philosophical and theological works (Ficino, 2005). A century later, the less diplomatic Giordano Bruno would proclaim a similar line of thought, suggesting imagination as the privileged vehicle of the Holy Spirit, and that the *vis imaginativa* was given to man to transform the world. For this and other heresies, Bruno was burned at the stake in the year 1600 (Kearney, 1988, p. 160).

But in the meantime, for Renaissance thinkers, "the garden of the world was again enchanted" (Tarnas, 1991, p. 214). Into this new zeitgeist of aesthetic appreciation came a new love for the Neoplatonic *Anima Mundi* ("World Soul"), the divine emanation that animates the natural world. "Stars and planets, light, plants, even stones possessed a numinous dimension. Neoplatonic Humanists declared the light of the sun to be the light of God ... with all of creation thereby bathed in divinity" (p. 213). The entire natural world took on qualities of aesthetic beauty and grace, a masterwork by a master artist. Dilthey writes "the philosophic background to this age of imagination was a faith that the world was completely permeated by mental processes ... everything which is inanimate to us had, for the man of that time, power and soul" (1976b/n.d., p. 79). This worldview of enchantment and ensoulment, Dilthey argues, was the backdrop for the great minds of that age, fostering poetry not only in the literary minds of Shakespeare, Spenser and Cervantes but also the theological writings of Luther and the scientific stirrings of Bacon and Kepler.

> The power of their imagination confronts modern man as something totally incomprehensible—as if it were the product of an extinct race of giants. Their works become a little more comprehensible if one sees them as the highest expression of an imagination which naturally dominated the world-view, the prose style, even the every day speech of the time.
>
> (pp. 80–81)

Tarnas makes an even stronger claim, that the Renaissance was not only a time of abundant creativity, but a time when imagination became viewed as a philosophical source of truth: "Imagination now rose to the highest position on the epistemological scale spectrum, unrivaled in its capacity to render metaphysical truth. Through disciplined imagination man could bring to his consciousness those transcendent living forms that ordered the universe" (1991, p. 215). Not only man, but the gods too regained their dignity, and ancient myth became a source of wisdom. Marsilio Ficino, himself critical of fortune-tellers, came to write astrological treatises as imaginative maps of the human soul, a discourse that Thomas Moore (1982) argues should be read as a kind early archetypal psychology. It was in this abundant and chaotic soil of ideas, images, and possibilities that the first seeds of the Scientific Revolution would take root.

Alas, this springtime of imagination would not last long. In its wake came the Protestant reformation, followed by the Catholic counter-reformation, each of which contained a strong "conservative religious backlash against the Renaissance's pagan Hellenism, naturalism, and secularism" (Tarnas, 1991, p. 238). The ensoulment of the world was dismissed as pagan fallacy, and replaced once more with the doctrine of man's dominion over the fallen natural world. Iconoclasm was revived among Protestants, and the Catholics mounted the Roman Inquisition, much to Giordano Bruno's misfortune.

Beyond the church walls, a new and greater threat to imagination was stirring. How should we understand that the seminal intellectual histories by Bertrand Russell (1945) and Daniel Robinson (1976) make scarcely any mention of "imagination" with regards to the Renaissance at all? These are men writing from a point in history where imagination is no longer a serious matter for intellectual discourse. Their brief treatments of the Neoplatonic resurgence and the multicultural confluence of other esoteric schools ultimately dismiss these movements as outdated superstition, if not outright nonsense. Both men seem to agree that the Renaissance had nothing to offer the progress of philosophy. These remarks by such distinguished learned men are telling signs of the dominant culture that would eventually emerge in modernity. Even as the absolute authority of the church began its long decline, a new set of masters would soon be at work fashioning an iron cage to keep imagination at bay.

Chapter 4

Imagination in modernity

From enlightenment to disenchantment

> *This spiritual Love acts not nor can exist*
> *Without Imagination, which, in truth,*
> *Is but another name for absolute power*
> *And clearest insight, amplitude of mind*
> *And Reason in her most exalted mood.*
> William Wordsworth, *The Prelude*, 1926/1850

The great flowering of human imagination that was the Renaissance paved the way for the Scientific Revolution. But with these new possibilities opened, the awakened imagination was once more cut back, and went to seed. As the modern era took shape, it was not only a resurgent religious conservatism that sought dominion over imagination, but also the birth of rationalism in philosophy, culminating in the Enlightenment of the eighteenth century. At the same time, the Age of Enlightenment would offer unique contributions to the understanding of imagination, largely through the works of Immanuel Kant, for whom imagination was vital to human understanding. Equally important, the over-abundance of reason in the eighteenth century would foment the counter-revolution of Romanticism in the nineteenth century. And in Romantic philosophy, the seeds of the Renaissance would bloom into even greater fruition, and imagination would appear in its most expansive articulation yet. It would be in the rich philosophical and aesthetic terrain between Kant, the Romantics, and the early existentialism of Nietzsche that the imagination of depth psychology would emerge.

The ascendance of reason

To understand the forms imagination would take in the modern era, we will first consider them in context of the larger intellectual movement toward empiricism and rationalism that accompanied the Scientific Revolution. As Tarnas puts it, "philosophy now commenced its momentous transfer from religion to science" (p. 272). This radical shift in worldview began a re-centering of power and knowledge from God and Church to the observational and reasoning powers of human beings. Renaissance human-ism did not only awaken the possibility of the creative powers of humanity—it also gave rise to a pioneering and even domineering spirit whereby humanity could master the natural world. This progression would occur over many centuries and encompassed many thinkers; among the most emblematic figures of this movement was philosopher and scientist Francis Bacon (1561–1626).

Bertrand Russell (1945) credits Bacon with the popularization of the phrase "knowledge is power," and notes that Bacon's aim was to "give mankind mastery over the forces of nature by means of scientific dis-coveries and inventions" (p. 564). Likewise, Robinson (1976) credits Bacon as the true father of modern empiricism for his renewed and vigorous emphasis on methodology to examine the direct experience given by the senses. This empiricism "stipulates that knowledge cannot exist unless this evidence has first been gathered, that all subsequent intellectual processes must use this evidence and only this evidence in framing valid propositions about the real world" (p. 152). In a broad sense, this was an echo of Aristotle's sensory realism, but with a renewed methodological rigor less tethered to metaphysical frameworks. Murray (1991) points out that Bacon also adopted the Aristotelian position on imagination as a mediating function between sense and intellect, while retaining the Chris-tian wariness that imagination could "usurp" its proper place as the servant of reason.

It was the philosophical rationalism initiated by Rene Descartes (1596–1650) that would explicitly provide imagination with a powerful new foe in the modern era. Descartes is much maligned in many con-temporary circles for suggesting a philosophical split between mind and body (one that neurophenomenology is still attempting to mend), but his philosophical contributions go far beyond that particular sticking point. Bertrand Russell (1945) considers Descartes the founder of modern philo-sophy, a thinker who put forth an entirely new philosophical system. "This had not happened since Aristotle, and is a sign of the new self-confidence that resulted from the progress of science" (p. 580). With science increas-ingly demonstrating an ability to quantify and map the natural world, rationality became a means to mastery. As Tarnas puts it, "with quant-itative mechanics ruling the world, an absolute faith in human reason was justified" (1991, p. 279). So profoundly did Descartes come to value rationality, he asserted that non-human animals were unconscious "autom-atons," because they lacked the rational faculties with which to interpret stimulation (Robinson, 1976, p. 202). Without reason, there could be no consciousness at all. This fundamental coupling of rational cognition to consciousness may seem absurd to twentieth-century thinkers who recognize all sorts of irrational, non-linguistic, and embodied forms of consciousness (to name but a few). Nevertheless, the notion that consciousness was synonymous with reason and rationality would have a strong influence on the intellectual development of the West for centuries to come.

Perhaps not surprisingly, this new exultation of reason came with a fresh debasement of the faculty of imagination. With Descartes, "disciplined critical rationality would overcome the untrustworthy information about the world given by the senses or imagination" (Robinson, 1976, p. 276). And yet some have remarked that this was not simply a lack of trust, but outright hostility. In his classic *Aesthetic*, Benedetto Croce (1972/1902) writes that Descartes "abhorred imagination, the outcome, according to him, of the agitation of the animal spirits; and though not condemning poetry, he allowed it to exist only as guided by the intellect" (p. 204). Kearney references Rousseau's famous quote, "the philosophy of Descartes has cut the throat of poetry," and goes on to trace this new philosophical hostility toward imagination through the work of Leibnitz, Spinoza, and beyond:

> The Cambridge idealist, John Smith, denounced imagination as a "deforming lens"; Gravina called it a "witch" and Muratori a "drunkard"; and even the intellectual aesthetic theories of Wolff and Baumgarten in the eighteenth century disregarded its creative potential.
>
> (1988, p. 163)

Likewise, the tendency in the revived Platonic tradition of communicating truth through symbolic and narrative means was attacked for its imprecision. Samuel Parker, Bishop of Oxford, wrote a scathing critique of the Platonists in 1666: "Emblems, fables, symbols, allegories, though they are pretty Poetick Fancies, are infinitely unfit to express Philosophical Notions and discoveries of the Natures of Things ... they unavoidably leave us fluctuating in meer uncertainties [*sic*]" (cited in Hedley, 2016 p. xiii). Empiricism and rationalism were rapidly becoming not just a means to truth, but the only means to truth. The empiricist John Locke became so wary of imagination that in his 1693 treatise on education, he encouraged parents who notice a "poetic vein" in their children to "stifle and suppress it as much as may be" [section 173]. It was in this cultural context, following a millennium of Christian suspicion and a fresh disdain from rationalist philosophy, that Immanuel Kant would offer a new conception of imagination altogether.

The synthetic imagination of Kant

The philosophy of Immanuel Kant (1724–1804) is important to the present discourse both for its reconceptualization of imagination and because of the influence it would later have on the development of depth psychology.

Kant's seminal work, the *Critique of pure reason*, has often been framed as a philosophical answer to the radical skepticism of David Hume (1711–1776), a thinker who influenced Kant profoundly (Robinson, 1976, p. 220). Hume was an empiricist whose inquiry into the nature of human knowledge ultimately resulted in a kind of epistemic crisis. Essentially, Hume concluded that the play of phenomenal sense data presented information to the mind, but could never point beyond itself to an ultimate cause outside the mind's perception. As summarized by Tarnas, "the apparent causal necessity in phenomena is the necessity only of subjective conviction, of human imagination controlled by its regular association of ideas. It has no objective basis" (1991, p. 339). From this perspective, there was no ontic Archimedean measuring point to hold up against the phenomenal play of sensation, and thus no ground to claim with certainty that sense data was accurately mapping reality. What's worse, in this void of uncertainty, reason becomes more a matter of habit and association rather than a ground of truth. In Kearney's analysis,

> The worlds of reason and reality, it seems, are both fictions of imagi-nation. The mimetic image no longer refers to some transcendent origin of truth; it becomes an end in itself … the only truth we can know is our image-representations. And this means no truth at all.
>
> (1988, p. 165)

Hume was well aware of the implications of these conclusions, but could not seem to find his way out of them, and advocated instead for human life to proceed "as if" certainty were possible. "We have therefor, no choice but betwixt a false reason and none at all," he lamented, and left it an open question to his colleagues how this dilemma of human knowledge might be resolved (Hume, 1978/1888, pp. 267–268).

Thus, one of Kant's chief aims in undertaking the *Critique of pure reason* was to reconcile the radical empirical skepticism of Hume with the extraordinary recent discoveries of science, and those of Newton in par-ticular. Kant believed that science could effectively map the natural world, but needed a solution as to how the chaos of phenomenal sensory experi-ence could meaningfully correspond to a reality beyond itself. Tarnas sum-marizes the revolutionary new perspective that emerged:

> In Kant's view, the nature of the human mind is such that it does not passively receive sense-data. Rather, it actively digests and structures them, and man therefor knows objective reality precisely to the extent that reality conforms to the fundamental structures of the mind.... In the act of human cognition, the mind does not conform to things; rather, things conform to the mind.
>
> (1991, p. 343)

In short, Kant proposed the human mind is structured with "a priori" categories for experiencing the world, and that we can only know the world by means of those categories. These a priori forms include the perception of space and time, cause and effect, relation, quantity, quality, modality—all the basic structures for comprehending sense data within a meaningful schema of experience. We may never know the *noumenon* ("the thing-in-itself"), beyond human perception, the apple on the table as it exists beyond our limited sensory impression of it. But we can know the structures of the mind by which the *phenomena* of sense data are organized into human perception. In essence, Kant balanced the uncertain nature of the world beyond the senses with a greater certainty about the structure of the mind that receives those senses. This radical shift in epistemology from world-structure to mind-structure is often referred to as the "Copernican Revolution" of philosophy (a phrase Kant himself originated) because it effectively shifted the center of knowledge from an external given to an internal subjective synthesis. The question of what might exist beyond the structures of human perception (i.e., metaphysics) became a matter of increasing skepticism, while the project of science was preserved within the shared field of empirical human experience.

In Kant's system, imagination plays a crucial role in the mind's synthesis of reality: "the schema is in itself always a product of imagination" (Kant, 1958/1781, p. 110 [para. B180]). Imagination becomes for Kant the synthesizing and structuring agent that both makes understanding out of sense impression, and gives form to abstract understanding through the use of images. In Mary Warnock's (1976) analysis, imagination both "operates in the presentation to us of objects of the world" (p. 27) and generates schema that are then applied to our experience of the world "in order to render it intelligible to the understanding" (p. 31). In the first regard, this is a complex elaboration of Aristotle's psychological imagination, which served as an intermediary between sense and intellect. But Kant takes this a step further, recognizing not only a reproductive imagination that presents sensory impressions to the intellect, but also a *constructive* imagination that applies imaginative schemata to the raw sensory experience of the world in order to organize and understand it. Rather than merely reflecting an established truth, Kant introduces the idea of truth being synthesized and projected onto the world from the understanding mind. Such a process was not foolproof, the mind might fail in its synthesis, particularly if working with poor information, and "a failing imagination could cause some forms of madness, including hypochondria" (Berrios, 2010, p. xxi). But whether faulty or successful, imagination was nevertheless made essential to the human process of understanding the world at all. Kearney argues that "Kant rescued imagination from its servile role as an intermediary between our sensible and intelligible experience, declaring it to be the indispensable precondition of all knowledge" (1988, p. 156). In the end, nothing could be known about the world except through imagination's ongoing synthesis of sense data and understanding.

Kearney further argues that with this move, Kant initiated the "modern conviction" that Being itself is a "product of man's own transcendental imagination" (1988, p. 158). It is important to clarify that Kant's use of "transcendental" in this context is in stark contrast to its previous metaphysical meaning. In Kant's own words "I entitle *transcendental* all knowledge which is occupied not so much with objects as with the mode of our knowledge of objects in so far as this mode of knowledge is a *priori*" (1958/1781, pp. 37–38 [para. A11]). The transcendental is thus relocated to the unconscious structures of the human mind, the underlying organizational factors of human consciousness that make knowledge possible.

Kearney views this as a pivotal turning point in the Western conception of imagination. The longstanding mimetic or "mirroring" model of imagination, in which the human mind could only reproduce or reflect mundane or divine reality, now gave way to a "transcendental model of formation" whereby the human imagination actively produced meaning, rather than merely reflecting it (1988, p. 168). This echoes the celebrated metaphor of M. H. Abrams' *The mirror and the lamp* (1953), which treats Romantic theory specifically as move from "mirror" to "lamp" as a model for the human mind. Whereas throughout the majority of human history the mind was seen as reflecting a fixed and given reality, in the Romantic period this conception was replaced with the metaphor of the lamp, "a radiant projector which makes a contribution to the object it perceives" (p. viii). Abrams notes that the conception of mind-as-projector is not strictly an invention of Kant, and has a clear metaphysical precedent in Neoplatonic thought. In Plotinus we find "the basic figure of creation as emanation, in which the One and the Good are habitually analogized to such objects as an overflowing fountain, or a radiating sun or (in a combination of the two images) to an overflowing fountain of light" (p. 58). Abrams cites several examples of Neoplatonic thinkers who connected this metaphor to the human mind prior to Kant's critique. Nevertheless, Kant was the first to articulate such a view within the modern philosophical discourse of rationalism and empiricism. In so doing, he firmly established the possibility of a distinctly human imagination as constant illuminator of the mundane world.

Though his genius is widely recognized, there is some debate as to where Kant should be located on the philosophical family tree. Robinson (1976) and Tarnas (1991) credit him as a synthesizer who was finally able to bridge the divide between empiricism and rationalism; Kearney (1988) views his work as the pivotal epistemic shift that underlies Romantic, existential, and ultimately post-modern thought; while Bertrand Russell (1945) questions the consensus that Kant is "the greatest of modern philosophers" (p. 731) and suggests instead that he should be viewed as the first in the tradition of German Idealists. To follow this latter argument, consider the idealist Johann Fichte (1762–1814), who transformed Kant's basic premises into a philosophy of "subjectivism" whereby the ego is "the only ultimate reality" (p. 744). This move to idealism was an attempt to further recognize the mind as primary, dispensing with the "thing-in-itself" by which Kant maintained fealty to the objective world. Though Russell (and many others) would come to view Fichte's extreme subjectivism as "a kind of insanity," it nevertheless opened up heretofore unseen possibilities for the power of human imagination.

In Fichte's case, this meant "all the synthesis of subjectivity, including those of reason, are rendered possible by the productive imagination" (Kearney, 1988, p. 178). In a complete reversal of the medieval conviction that imagination must be the servant to reason, imagination for the Idealists was not merely an equal partner, but perhaps the greater of the pair, responsible for apprehending the world. Following Fichte, Friedrich Schelling (1775–1954) argued that the inward, reflective contemplation of the philosopher is ultimately an aesthetic act of imagination. As translated by Peter Heath, "the philosophy of art is the true organon of philosophy" (1978/1800, p. 14); Kearney translates the same passage as "productive and synthetic imagination is the organon and pinnacle of all philosophy" (1988, p. 178). This monumental ascent of the role of imagination in human consciousness was hinted at in Kant's 1781 first edition of *Critique of pure reason*, but considerably toned down in the 1787 second edition. Kearney suggests that Kant recognized he was playing with fire and deliberately tried to pull his philosophical system back toward epistemic humility, and away from the mysticism that had grown up around imagination during the Renaissance. The more conservative productive imagination of the second edition of the *Critique* may well reflect Kant's "rationalist antipathy towards the enthusiastic claims for imagination made by the hermetic traditions" (Kearney, 1998, p. 425). Nevertheless, where Kant refused to go, Fichte and Schelling were eager to proceed. In so doing, the German Idealists helped to birth the Romantic period of the early nineteenth century. The Romantics would give the world a conception of *creative imagination* that in many ways remains a force in Western culture to the present day.

The creative imagination of the Romantics

The Romantic period has functioned as a teleological apex for the present historical narrative both because of its formative influence on contemporary ideas about imagination, and because of the influence it had on the development of depth psychology in the years following its decline. To the latter point, Ellenberger (1970) writes in his history of depth psychology that "Freud and Jung can be identified as late epigones of Romanticism" (p. 199), and outlines these connections in great detail. To the former point, James Engell opens his history of the *Creative imagination* (1981) with the assertion that the idea of imagination that took root in the seventeenth century and came to fruition in the eighteenth-century Romantic period is the imagination "as we still understand it today ... a critical survey of the entire creative process" (p. vii). But whereas our modern conception of imagination is more inclined to view imagination as an entre into the unreal, or at best as an entirely artistic enterprise, for the Romantics imagination held the promise of something far greater, an entre into the depths of reality itself. The transformation of this real realm of imagination into the unreality of the "imaginary" will be dealt with later in this chapter. First let us explore what this expanded worldview of imagination-as-reality entailed, and how it came to be.

Among the features that make the Romantic period unique is the degree to which the lines between philosophy, literature, and art became blurred. As Richard Gray puts it, "Imagination became the way to grasp truth" (2011, p. 4). As the human faculty of creative imagination came to be seen as a means to truth, great art then took on the power to express reality on par with, or even in excess of, the more intellectual philosophical tradition. There is little philosophical discourse on the Romantics that does not make reference to the poetry and literature of the time. Art was implicated in their philosophy, and philosophy in their art. As Dilthey writes of the great poet and scientist Johann Wolfgang von Goethe, "Art was for him the highest workings of nature" (1976a/1877, p. 103). For the tradition of analytical philosophy that dominated in the twentieth century, systems of thought based on imagination rather than reason and logic may not seem like real philosophy at all. But to a certain extent this is precisely the point—in an age increasingly ruled by reason, the Romantics offered an alternative worldview that elevated the imagination as a primary means of engaging the world. And while they may not have won the battle of ideas going into the twentieth century, nor was their worldview completely excised from the Western culture of today.

Roots of Romanticism

In German Idealism, mind became primary and imagination took on new power. What had been for Kant the "transcendental imagination" for Schelling became "unconscious poetry," a decidedly creative force underlying all human experience. "Schelling leaves us in no doubt that imagination creates *both nature and art* ... [an artistic genius] only differs from ordinary men insofar as he has realized the unity of unconscious and conscious imagination" (Kearney, 1988, p. 180). That is to say, the creative genius of the artist is simply that which taps into the great unconscious poetry of the universe. This idea of conscious union with an inherently poetic cosmos was one of several streams feeding the creative imagination eventually articulated by the Romantics. The Romantic imagination was bolstered further by a more mundane philosophical discourse coming out of the Enlightenment that maintained a fascination with imagination as human faculty, even when it could not be trusted. At the same time, the Neoplatonic and mystical currents from the Renaissance also experienced resurgence, and arguably came to their greatest fruition.

John Cocking (1991) locates the rise of Romanticism amid an Enlightenment discourse around primary and secondary qualities of objects as humans perceive them. Primary qualities were identified as the quantitative properties of an object, those properties that could be consistently measured. Secondary qualities included the unmeasurables of human experience: color, taste, warmth, etc.—what are in contemporary discourse sometimes called the *qualia* of experience. It was asserted by Galileo and others that secondary qualities were not "in" the object itself, but were rather created by the mind of the observer. Today we have the means to quantitatively measure far more properties of objects than we did in those days, but the issue of secondary, experiential qualities remains—and in fact continues to be hotly debated in the contemporary field of consciousness studies (see Blackmore, 2006). Scientists in the eighteenth century already had divergent views on whether science would ever be able to adequately explain secondary qualities. "Pre-Romantics" like Joseph Addison advocated for the importance of secondary qualities in the human sphere regardless of quantitative measurability, and claimed that "imagination is as important to cultivate as reason" (Cocking, 1991, p. 273). Parallel to this Enlightenment discourse, Cocking identifies a Neoplatonic current that ultimately "finds it's outlet in the Romantic Revolution. Imagination was then claimed as direct, personal contact with some kind of metaphysical truth" (p. 273). In the worldview of the Romantics, the centuries-old relationship between the quantitative and qualitative aspects of reality was reversed. The qualitative human experience became primary, and imagination was understood as an organ of perception for deeper truths.

Engell emphasizes that the Romantics were not necessarily objecting to reason or the Enlightenment in itself, which had after all fostered a grand new spirit of open inquiry and discovery. Rather they rebelled against certain aspects of eighteenth-century thought: "neoclassical formalism, materialistic theories of mind and body, and atomistic philosophy ... the narrowly sterile and mechanistic side of previous generations" (1981, p. 5). They were not against reason so much as rigidity of thought, and they recognized imagination as a means to opening up an increasingly mechanical worldview. Nor was this merely a descent into daydreams and fantasy—it was seen as a legitimate means to expand human potential. Richard Gray (2011) writes:

Theories of imagination were prominent on the intellectual agenda. By the end of the 18th century, an insistence on reason as the predominant human faculty had run its course and the imagination began to emerge as another force whose contributions to human intellectual existence and productivity had to be calculated and constantly recalibrated.

(p. 4)

Thus, Romanticism was not only a movement whereby imagination was more highly valued, but also one where it was actively re-theorized and re-imagined. Engell argues that what eventually crystalized as Romanticism in the late eighteenth century was ultimately the result of an interdisciplinary discourse on imagination that began with the Enlightenment. "The understanding of genius, poetic power, and originality, of sympathy, individuality, knowledge, and even ethics grew and took lifesblood from the idea of imagination" (1981, p. 1). The great Romantic poets who articulated theirs views on imagination with such sublimity are themselves part of greater shift in the Western psyche that had been emerging for some time.

This pre-Romantic spirit is perhaps best exemplified by Johann Wolfgang von Goethe (1749–1842), who as both a poet and a scientist brought an invigorated view of imagination to bear on both spheres. Goethe's early literary work, *The sorrows of young Werther*, would inspire the Romantics with its tragic tale of a young man intoxicated and tragically consumed by his passions. Goethe's late masterpiece *Faust* is considered among the great literary works of Germany. But Goethe was also a dedicated natural scientist. In Zweig's (2006/1967) analysis, Goethe felt the imagination had a vital role to play in intuiting the greater wholes of existence out of the piecemeal data provided by the senses. Empiricism and imagination thus worked together to reveal the hidden laws of the natural order. Dilthey writes of Goethe that "nature revealed itself to him when he experienced the creative power of his own imagination" and that he viewed nature as a lawful and active power that expressed itself "in metamorphosis, in development, in the systematic arrangement of typical forms and the harmony of the whole" (1976a/1877, p. 103). Rather than being an impediment to empiricism, imagination had the power to immerse the scientist more fully in the world and thus grasp its hidden connections. "Goethe sought to experience the archetypal form or essence of each plant and animal by saturating the objective perception with his own imagination" (Tarnas, 1991, p. 369). In this way, imagination was a viable path to knowledge, though also one that could be easily abused if not paired with rigorous empiricism and healthy skepticism. It should be noted that Goethe was far more conservative than the Romantics that followed him, and warned that imagination, where driven by unbalanced passion, could project falsehood. In Engell's (1981) summation of Goethe's thought:

A delicate balance must be maintained between awesome psychic forces, for the imagination deals with the inevitable, the probable, the possible, and the improbable, and it must fuse these into a picture of reality that is the only basis for happiness. The imagination becomes "errant" in all sense of the word: adventuresome, bold, wandering lost, thoroughgoing, treacherous, low and noble.

(p. 282)

Here is a vision of imagination which can both reveal and occlude, a force that can invigorate the mind or drive it to madness. It is a power that lived in the scientist and poet alike, a source of genius and a dangerous precipice.

The Romantic imagination

C. M. Bowra writes that among the five major poets of the Romantic movement (Blake, Coleridge, Wordsworth, Shelley, and Keats), "the creative imagination is closely connected with a peculiar insight into an unseen order behind visible things" (1950, p. 271). But while this unseen order is widely recognized as an important theme in Romantic thought, it would be a mistake to view the Romantic imagination as something that can be monolithically defined. Richard Gray (2011) points out that "insistent re-theorization of the imagination as a distinct human faculty is especially prominent during the Romantic Period" (p. 3), meaning even among the Romantics, the articulation and elaboration of "imagination" was an important *ongoing project*. Furthermore, there was a notion among them that the human imagination could be plural rather than singular, a manifold phenomenon taking many forms. Hegel's unpublished notebooks include the assertion that "what is needed today is a monotheism of reason and the heart, polytheism of the imagination and art" (cited in Gray, 2011, p. 4). This "polytheism of imagination" suggests many gods, many loci of power, form, and being, each influencing life and culture in myriad ways. Given that imagination now held the potential of underlying and enabling reason itself, it becomes more understandable to assert that imagination was not only being redefined, but also newly and actively *imagined*.

Samuel Taylor Coleridge (1772–1834), for example, is often taken as emblematic of the Romantic struggle to understand imagination within the language of philosophy. Warnock (1976) details how Coleridge borrowed widely from other thinkers in order to "find a theory … a higher-order language, in which to state his practical analysis of imagination, and by means of which to fit it into a much wider theory of human nature and of nature as a whole" (p. 72). Although an analytical approach to the Romantics might demand a precise taxonomy of definitions, I contend that the more important point is to recognize the degree to which imagination was lifted up, celebrated, enlivened, and lived-into during this time. These philosopher–poets were not simply theorizing about imagination from a distance, they were engaging with it as living power.

Coleridge, in any case, did offer a series of definitions that are often cited as being emblematic of the period, though both Warnock (1976) and Engell (1981) demonstrate that most of his ideas are derived from the century of discourse that preceded him. In the first place he famously argued for a distinction between *imagination* and *fancy*. *Fancy*, for Coleridge "is indeed no other than a memory emancipated from the order of time and space ... blended with and modified by that empirical phenomenon of the will" (1906/1817, p. 167). *Fancy* thus entails a somewhat mechanical putting together of established images or ideas, like combining a horse and wings to make a Pegasus—it requires only association and recombination of parts, nothing complex or creative. This formulation of *fancy* is reminiscent of Aristotle's psychological imagination, which mediates between sense, intellect, and memory without creating anything essentially new. On the other hand, *imagination* proper was for Coleridge a force of near cosmic proportions. He describes first a non-personal *primary imagination*: "the living power and prime agent of all human perception ... a representation in the finite mind of the eternal act of creation in the infinite I AM." This has clear parallels both to the Divine Mind of Neoplatonism and the universal "unconscious poetry" of Schelling. Coleridge contrasts this cosmic imagination with the *secondary imagination*, the human creative faculty that echoes the cosmic power, struggling to "idealize and to unify," and "coexisting with the conscious will" (p. 167). The *primary imagination* is essentially an unconscious force, underlying the human mind and presumably present in the universe itself, similar to the Neoplatonic model. The *secondary imagination*, by contrast, is the human will consciously engaging with that primary force not only to create art, but also to actively unify the world in human consciousness. Thus, from the psychological to the creative to the cosmic, imagination was both many-faced and essential.

Echoing the Renaissance, the Romantic writers often used the mythical figure of Proteus to personify the creative forces of imagination. Engell (1981) argues that this is fitting not only because of the many shapes that imagination might produce, but also because it was in the nature of imagination that each thinker would come to it a little differently. Precisely because no final definition was possible, each unique articulation of imagination kept it alive. As long as imagination was being imagined anew, imagination itself would not become a dead idea—and indeed, it has not. Finally, Engell suggests that the protean archetype is especially fitting for the Romantic imagination, because in the biographies of the Romantics, we see that their encounters with the imagination were truly transformative. "They exemplify, as Shakespeare exemplified to them, that imagination can free us from a self-centered world. Each mind, as it exercises and acts out its particular faith in the imaginative power, becomes protean" (p. 9). So by engaging fully and deeply with the phenomenon of creative imagination, the individual could become liberated, empowered, and consciousness could be transformed.

Despite this protean quality, there are several consistent and essential themes to be found beneath the shifting formulations of Romantic thought. Chief among them is the notion that imagination is absolutely essential to the human experience. Tarnas (1991) writes that "for many Romantics, imagination was in some sense the whole of existence, the true ground of being, the medium of all realities. It both pervaded consciousness and constituted the world" (p. 369). While this may seem like a descent into solipsism, it might be helpful instead to instead view it as a new kind of Western animism, a resurgence of the Neoplatonic *Anima Mundi*, or World Soul. By seeing imagination as a creative force in-the-world and not just in the mind, there was a new possibility of humanity being reunited with a natural world from which it was becoming increasingly alienated.

> Many gifted individuals saw in the imagination a power that could bridge the gulf between man and nature and knit the two together again.... It could overcome the alienation between man and nature by establishing a power of knowledge and creation common to nature and to the mind.
>
> (Engell, 1981, p. 7)

In short, it was seen as a solution to the growing dualism in modern thought, a way to bridge the transcendental and the empirical. In stark contrast to reductionistic positivism that was soon to follow, this nineteenth-century world overflowed with meaning: "For the Romantic, reality was symbolically resonant through and through, and was therefore fundamentally multivalent, a constantly changing complex of many-leveled meanings" (Tarnas, 1991, p. 368). It followed that the best way to make sense of the world was not to reduce it scientifically, but to capture this complex abundance in creative works of art.

Going well beyond our contemporary notion of "self-expression" the creative genius of art here had the power to make the world whole again within the realm of human experience. Creative imagination could express

> the aesthetic play or balance, and the final unity, between ideal and real, sensuous and transcendental, subjective and objective, the magic by which we perceive and create, and even the miracle by which the cosmos first took and is continuing to take shape.
>
> (Engell, 1981 p. 7)

The human truths arrived at by these methods were argued to be as legitimate as any other. "The Romantics were aggressive in asserting that the imaginative artist could help us to reach truth and reality no less than could the scientist: Beauty, as Keats compactly puts it, is Truth" (Egan, n.d., p. 11). Going even further, Shelley (1965/1840) declared in his *Defense of poetry* that "Poetry is indeed something divine, it is the centre and circumference of knowledge; it is that which comprehends all science, and that to which all science must be referred" (p. 70). This is not to say that poetry could somehow replace science, but that the poetic mind is essential in *assigning meaning and value* to what science discovers. Arts and literature were thus elevated to a lofty position as the expectation grew that they might not only mirror reality but actually give humanity a window into deeper truths. This essential notion, that art can express profound truth beyond dry reason, is still alive and well today.

But while our contemporary conception of artistic truth is far more metaphysically reserved, for the Romantics it took on an almost religious character. Tarnas (1991) writes:

> The artistic enterprise was elevated to an exalted spiritual role, whether as poetic epiphany or aesthetic rapture, as divine afflatus or revelation of eternal realities, as creative quest, imaginative discipline, devotion to the muses, existential imperative, or liberating transcendence from the world of suffering. The most secular of moderns could yet worship the artistic imagination.
>
> (p. 373)

This final point is one of the features that set the flowering of the Romantic imagination apart from its precursor in the Renaissance. Whereas at the end of the medieval period, experiencing the divine creative spark in man meant participating in and expressing the Christian mythology and cosmos, for the Romantics this spiritual creativity could take any form whatever. This entailed a radical empowerment of the individual to participate in creating the world, but it also threatened a loss of ground. In this way, Romanticism contributed both to a newly ascendant individualism, as well as the coming existential dilemma that would soon be expressed by Nietzsche.

Imagination and reason at the abyss

It should be reiterated that Romanticism as a whole was not necessarily a movement against reason, so much as against the excesses of reason: the mechanistic, rigid world where reason had become a tyrant. Gray (2011) writes that balancing or integrating reason and imagination was an important project for many Romantic thinkers. Shelley (1965/1840) wrote that while reason contemplated the relations between thoughts, imagination takes those thoughts and "colors them with its own light, and composing from them, as from elements, other thoughts, each containing within itself the principle of its own integrity" (p. 25). A similar integration was expressed more poetically in Wordsworth's famous declaration that imagination is "clearest insight, amplitude of mind/ And Reason in her most exalted mood" (Wordsworth, 1926/1850, p. 483). Rather than being opposed to reason, or a servant of reason, Wordsworth asserts that imagination is in fact the height of reason, an elevated consciousness that apprehends more clearly the complexities of the world. Balancing the excess of reason also entailed a higher valuation of feeling and emotion. Egan writes that the Romantic imagination was inherently "tied into our emotions, evoking responses to what was not present as though it was present" (n.d., p. 9). In this way, sympathy and passion were naturally bound up in the individual's creative response to existence. Imagination became a matter of feeling the world deeply rather than standing above it with distant analysis and logic. "Imagination and feeling now joined sense and reason to render a deeper understanding of the world" (Tarnas, 1991, p. 369). Ideally, the Romantic worldview was meant to be a corrective, a means to a more balanced and enriched human experienced. But as is often the case with counterbalancing cultural forces, in some regards it went too far.

There is of course a dark side to anything in excess, and while Romanticism may tell a tale of human empowerment and limitless possibility, it also recalls the myth of Icarus. "Coleridge seems to be implying enthusiastically that Adam and Eve were right to eat the forbidden fruit and Prometheus was right to steal the fire, and that it is our job to exercise the creative powers we have been given" (Egan, n.d., p. 9). These are the very myths, of course, that have for millennia warned humans that too much creativity might mean trouble. One clear manifestation of the shadow-side of this dynamic is the persistent linkage of overactive imagination to madness in modern thought:

> The common Romantic and Post-Romantic association of unbridled imagination with various forms of insanity represents one of the peculiar flash-points between the order of reason and the disorder of creative vision, and the modern history of imagination displays a marked tendency to waffle between these positive and negative evaluations.
>
> (Gray, 2011, p. 6)

Imagination was a means to freedom but it could also be a road to ruin. In its exalted state it might reveal the deepest of truths, but it could also bring confusion, projection, and delusion. These lines were not always clear, and they held real danger. Needless to say, though their influence was powerful, the Romantics did not win the battle of ideas going into the twentieth century. Nor can it be said that the Romantic imagination has ever fully left us. C. M. Bowra (1950) argues that although many ultimately disagree with the philosophical premises and conclusions of Romantic thinkers, we still naturally tend to regard them as a source of inspiration, for their work is at heart a creative effort toward a better world. The Romantic poet still commends our respect, because "he believes that in exercising his imagination he creates life and adds to the sum of living experience … an active agent in a world that exists by a perpetual process of creation" (p. 292). These historical figures remind of us of our own creativity, our potential to remake ourselves and remake the world, whether that potential is fully realized or not.

Kearney (1988) argues that where the Romantic imagination reached its point of excess and met with the vicissitudes of history, existentialism was born. Friedrich Nietzsche (1844–1900) is generally classified as an early existentialist, but many also regard him as the last of the Romantics. Tarnas in particular writes about Nietzsche's philosophy as a powerful expression of the Romantic ethos. Nietzsche rejected positivism and asserted instead a "radical perspectivism: there exists a plurality of perspectives through which the world can be interpreted and there is no authoritative independent criterion according to which one system can be determined to be more valid than the others" (Tarnas, 1991, p. 37). For Nietzsche, the only way out of this chaos was a creative act of will, a process of self-overcoming in which man would "imagine himself into being" (p. 37). But whereas Tarnas frames this as a positive, creative act, Kearney's analysis of Nietzsche takes a darker tact: "the truth is no longer between truth and fiction, but between two kinds of fiction: fiction that masquerades as truth, and fiction that knows itself to be fiction" (1988, p. 215). For Nietzsche there is nothing tangible beyond what we create. The Idealists and early Romantics were inclined to view this as a co-creation with a divine power, but Nietzsche saw it as process of making meaning out of a fragmented world. In contrast to the Divine Mind of Neoplatonism, Nietzsche draws our attention to the abyss, to the depths of darkness, nothingness, and chaos in human experience. To the extent that imagination reveals this shadow-side of life and overcomes it through a creative act of will, it is indeed offering up a deeper truth in the Romantic spirit. But where imagination is used to deny the darker side of human experience—to cover up irrationality and chaos with fictions that claim to be privileged literal truths rather than created fictions—Nietzsche condemns it as folly, and walks the road of existentialism instead.

The road to disenchantment: imagination in the twentieth century

Arriving at the end of the Romantic period, imagination would soon find a new and perhaps surprising home in the emerging field of depth psychology. Sigmund Freud (1856–1939) would publish *The interpretation of dreams* just 10 years after Nietzsche succumbed to madness. Chapter 5 will pick up the story of imagination in depth psychology as it developed through Freud, Jung, and the depth psychologists who came after them, and lay out some psychological frameworks for the discussion of neuroscience to follow. Nevertheless, the road of depth psychology was admittedly the road less traveled in the twentieth century. German Berrios puts this somewhat extremely: "By the late nineteenth century imagination had begun its decline, and by the first half of the twentieth century it had become extinct as a psychological function, only to survive in the field of aesthetics" (2010, p. xix). Overstated by Berrios or not, this tangible decline deserves some attention as a matter of context. Thus, the remainder of this chapter will offer a brief sketch of the fate of imagination in the mainstream intellectual discourses of the twentieth century.

From imagination to the imaginary

Richard Tarnas' intellectual history lauds the Romantics not only for their creativity and passion, but also for their challenge to rigid cultural doctrines and their advocacy for both a more integrated human existence and a broader and more inclusive view of the cosmos. However, "these radically broadening conceptions of reality ... could not be easily integrated with the more positivist side of the modern mind" (1991, p. 374). The Romantic vision was ultimately overtaken by the rising tide of positivist philosophy and reductionistic science that would characterize the twentieth century. That the Romantics were prone to decry pretensions to objective certainty while passionately expounding the mystical and transcendental aspects of human experience naturally put them at odds with the ascending scientific worldview. Tarnas frames this as a "general schism between scientific rationalism on the one hand and the multifaceted humanistic culture on the other" (p. 375). Science would eventually become the authority of external or "outer" matters regarding the nature of the material cosmos, while Romanticism would plant its flag in the inner life or "soul" of humanity, especially as expressed through literature and the arts.

Historian Lorraine Daston (2005) writes of a subsequent "loathing" toward imagination that emerged in the sciences in modernity: the world-creating individualism of the Romantics seemed anathema to the blossoming sciences, which measured success by removing subjectivity and replicating objective results across communities, languages, and cultures.

Daston makes a compelling argument that as scientific progress accelerated, it also began to rapidly replace its own established theories (the early
"paradigm shifts" described by Kuhn). "No theory was safe from this
breakneck progress, not even Newtonian celestial mechanics … hence the
fervor of proponents of mechanical objectivity in fending off all possible
adulterations and distortions of facts by judgment or, especially,
imagination" (p. 29). Amid the rapidly changing fields of science and a
rapidly transforming modern world, imagination was all the more
threatening to the purity and stability of the scientific endeavor.

Kearney (1988) does not share Tarnas' rosy view of the Romantics as
early pioneers of holistic culture. In his brief treatment of Romanticism, he
describes an inflated imagination that, after becoming a world-creating
cosmic power, had nowhere left to go except for a dramatic fall from
grace:

> Given the extravagant claims for man's creative power, it was
> inevitable that disillusionment would set in sooner or later. The
> romantic imagination could not possibly deliver on its promises.…
> Henceforth, it seemed, the creative imagination could only survive as a
> recluse. It could continue to form *images*, but it could no longer hope
> to transform *reality*.
>
> (p. 185)

The only way to preserve imagination, Kearney argues, was to create a
firm partition between "reality" and "unreality." Thus we see emerge, in
fresh distinction to *imagination*, a new concept of the *imaginary*. The
creative powers of humanity could make worlds, but only as illusions, self-
contained with no bearing on external reality, at best expressed as
humanistic art, at worst escapism, delusion, or madness. "With nature
becoming increasingly dominated by the mechanistic principles of the
positive sciences, and society riven apart by industrial strife … imagination
felt more and more compelled to recoil into a magical world of its own
making" (p. 186). The imaginary realm was unreal except perhaps as
matter of culture—but irrelevant to the objective material world now being
described and dominated by science. In popular understanding, imaginary
worlds were derided as the intangible playthings of children, or illusionary
escapes for adults who cannot handle adulthood in the grim "reality" of a
disenchanted world.

Philosophically this conception arguably had its greatest articulation in
the work of Jean-Paul Sartre (1905–1980), whose early work *The
imaginary* takes as a basic premise "the object as imaged is an irreality"
(2004/1940, p. 125), and devotes much thought to relationship between
real and unreal. Sartre maintained that the generation of mental images
was absolutely essential to human consciousness, but also emphasized the

existential dilemma of relating these internal images to an external reality. Imagination was the ultimate means to freedom in human experience, but to engage this freedom fully necessitated an alienating break from the reality of others: "Hell is other people!" [*L'enfer, c'est les autres!*] as his play *No Exit* famously declares. Examining the context of Sartre's larger body of work, Kearney concludes: "The existential imagination found itself incorrigibly bound to a life of pathological negation ... the negating consciousness cannot be free and at the same time sustain ethical relationships with other human subjects" (1988, p. 247). This somewhat dismal dilemma can be taken as an extreme articulation of the post-Romantic split in the Western psyche, where the objective scientific world, by its nature "soulless," could not be reconciled with the inner "soulful" world of humanity. Tarnas (1991) identifies this split as the root of the modern contest between the sciences and humanities. As the twentieth century dawned, this "inner division was experienced as the sensitive human psyche situated in a world alien to human meaning. Modern man was a divided animal, inexplicably self-aware in an indifferent universe" (p. 378). From here, the discourse on imagination was largely confined to the arts and aesthetics on one hand, and to dramatically reduced accounts of cognitive functioning on the other (i.e., the "propositional imagination" discussed in Chapter 1). The life-world was stripped of soul; the disenchantment of the world was complete.

Deconstructing imagination

If this were not enough, imagination would face a new foe come the late twentieth century. Kearney's entire intellectual history is presented within a framework of the demise of imagination, not from positivism or scientism, but from the discourses of post-modern thought. Indeed, his title, *The wake of imagination*, has the double meaning of a funeral wake to parallel the notion of awakening. Noting the "deconstructive" project inherent in post-modernism that dismantles cultural assumptions into "an anonymous play of language," Kearney claims that in the post-modern discourse, imagination is "subjected to suspicion or denigrated as an outdated humanist illusion spawned by the modern movements of romantic idealism and existentialism" (1988, p. 251). The criticism of humanism Kearney refers to is a reaction to the notion of a bound, self-creating subject that somehow exists apart from the larger field of meanings, interactions, and material circumstances into which they were born. Post-modernism has been critical of the notion of the "individual subject," as well as the notion of anything "original" being produced by the individual subject. "The deconstruction of the category of 'origin' is heralded by the famous *textual revolution*. The humanist concept of 'man' gives way to the anti-humanist concept of intertextual play" (p. 253). Words come to reference words in an endless circle that ultimately relativizes linguistic truth and undermines dominant cultural understandings. Insofar as "imagination" is claimed as an individual production of original meaning, it falls under the same scathing criticism. To some extent, the post-modern deconstruction of imagination is simply an extension of a larger project in undoing the pretentions of modernity. Imagination attracts particular ire to the degree it claims that an individual is capable of entirely autonomous creation, as if language, meaning, and ideas were not inextricably socially constructed and shared.

Kearney also draws attention to the flood of contemporary consumer–culture images that inundate us through various channels of mass media. With this onslaught of manufactured, profit-driven images, "the representational image soon began to overshadow reality itself. History became a pale replica of its own reproduction" (1988, p. 252). There is a fierce skepticism in post-modern thought that something "imagined" under such circumstances could be anything but the re-production, ad-nauseam, of representations of representations. Contemporary images of cowboys refer to other contemporary images of cowboys, and the historic reality from which this family of images originally sprung is presumably forgotten. At the same time, computer-generated imagery undermines the notion that image-creation is privileged human capacity. In this hall of mirrors the center is lost, the human soul is deconstructed into a textual play of referents without end, and imagination never was.

Because I have addressed reductionism and scientism elsewhere in this volume but will not have cause to speak again of post-modernity, I feel compelled to offer here a brief rejoinder to this post-modern deconstruction of imagination from the perspective of depth psychology and somatics. First, I would note that the epistemological prominence of the *unconscious* in depth psychology in itself offers a partial solution to the problem of the modern, supposedly autonomous and self-creating subject. The post-modern criticism of subjectivity focuses primarily on the rational conscious mind. As Chapter 5 will show, depth psychology has long de-centralized the rational, conscious ego against the unconscious forces of the psyche, in both personal and collective aspects. The deconstructed subject facing a cultural sea of textuality is not entirely dissimilar to the relativized ego facing the vast collective unconscious. The latter model at least allows for meaningful growth and dialog to occur between the opposing forces of conscious ego and unconscious ground of being.

Second, I would point out that the post-modern emphasis on *textuality*—the observation that all meaning can be reduced to textual references—turns on the assumption that human meaning is fundamentally and exclusively linguistic rather than imagistic. On the contrary: words are by nature referential to something beyond themselves, but images have a capacity to present a level of meaning that is self-contained in their initial presentation. An image of *a ripe red apple hanging on a tree at dawn in a tropical forest* can be apprehended imagistically as a kind of meaning in itself, prior to being translated into linguistic terms. Not only is the image comprehended in its basic self-presentation prior to language, but the human body is also capable of experiencing a somatic felt response to the image, offering another level of embodied, experiential meaning prior to elaboration in verbal language. Such an image certainly may *also* point to something beyond itself: in the case of the apple tree, perhaps a cultural or symbolic meaning, such as the Garden of Eden, or a personal association, such as a childhood love of tree-climbing or grandma's apple pie. But any such additional reference does not change the self-contained meaning presented in the original image first arising in consciousness. In imagistic consciousness, primary meaning *is* the image itself.

Furthermore, whatever thing that the initial image of the apple "points to" for a given person may well be another image that is similarly self-contained—the image of grandma holding a steaming pie, perhaps. That is to say, the basic meaning of one image may connect to the basic meaning of another image and so on, without *necessarily* ever bringing language into play. This linking of image-to-image without words is generally what is meant by "thinking in images." Of course, in the context of consumer images flooding our minds through the mainstream media, there is often little room for "thinking in images" because our minds are thoroughly preoccupied absorbing and sorting the maddening onslaught. Whereas a single evocative image invites contemplation, an endless succession of images may crowd out deeper reflection. A contemporary cartoon cowboy on the television may well only be referencing other commodified cowboy images. But somewhere along the way a particular cowboy image, artfully rendered, may yet strike the imagination of a young boy or girl, awakening a mythic instinct and perhaps even spurring historical research into the "lost" meaning of the image. The problem may not be that these media images are inherently meaningless, but rather that we are so inundated by them that we have forgotten how to slow down and pay attention, to see what inner meanings might arise. In a consumer culture, the soul of imagination may be lost—but that does not mean it cannot be reclaimed once more within the human heart.

Even in the case of the apple tree image generating an association to the Garden of Eden—an established textual myth with many layers of linguistic meaning—we need not necessarily assume an immediate pivot to language. The person experiencing this association may well next experience a subsequent internal image of a naked woman and a snake, charged with a complex and disturbing somatic–emotional experience of erotic desire and fear. Again, that somatic experience of image-and-affect is expressed as meaning in the body prior to elaboration in language, regardless of any linguistic discourse on biblical texts that might follow. Image and bodily experience become the referents that subsequent descriptive language would attempt to point to. Broader cultural forces may be at play, and may be revealed—but the initial somatic–imaginal encounter remains a meaningful referent in itself as a phenomenon of consciousness, regardless of any subsequent linguistic elaboration. This of course does not solve the problem of language itself: the challenges of communication and meaning in purely linguistic terms. But I contend that a discourse that recognizes somatic and imaginal experiences as self-contained meaningful referents offers an escape from post-modernism's more nihilistic tendencies. The challenge in this case becomes a matter of communicating direct, non-verbal human experience with imperfect, abstract language. Daunting as that may be, it is a far cry from a complete loss of truth. In this regard, imagination may yet have a role to play in healing the fractures of post-modernity.

Signs of life

Of course, the twentieth century was an incredibly complex time in which a great multitude of perspectives took hold, and any singular narrative about the fate of imagination over the last 100 years will inevitably be far too simple. As the human world continues to diversify, ideas that fall out of favor in the mainstream may still live vigorous lives on the fringe, only to surface suddenly in the unlikeliest of places. In 1871, Charles Darwin would write: "The Imagination is one of the highest prerogatives of man. By this faculty he unites former images and ideas, independently of the will, and thus creates brilliant and novel results" (2005a/1871, p. 784). Fifty years later, Albert Einstein would make his famous declaration: "Imagination is more important than knowledge. For knowledge is limited, whereas imagination embraces the entire world, stimulating progress, giving birth to evolution. It is, strictly speaking, a real factor in scientific research" (2009/1931, p. 97). Meanwhile, though imagination was largely relegated to the arts and the philosophy of aesthetics, each of those fields would continue to assert a quiet claim to a more expansive role in human life. John Dewey (1997/1934) argued that aesthetics is not only a matter of art, but a way in which the human being makes coherent meaning of their experience in the world. In the realm of social philosophy the French philosopher Cornelius Castoriadis (1987/1975) wrote extensively on the role of creative imagination in the formation of social institutions of all kinds. And Richard Kearney's wonderful history of imagination, published in 1988, concludes with a passionate call for a new ethical imagination that forever orients itself toward engagement with the "other," rather than lauding the subjective self. I offer these names as a sample of contrary thinkers who refused to conform to the prevailing spirit of the times. Though for the most part imagination was boxed and caged in the Western psyche, its promise of possibility stubbornly refused to be fully contained.

Among the more surprising developments in the early twenty-first century is a renewed interest in the topic within the field of analytic philosophy, particularly the work of philosopher Amy Kind (see Kind, 1997, 2016; Kind & Kung, 2016). In the introduction to *The Routledge handbook of philosophy of imagination*, Kind writes:

> The early years of the twenty-first century have witnessed a groundswell of philosophical interest in imagination. Much of the philosophical research sits at the intersection of philosophy of mind, aesthetics, and moral psychology, though interest in imagination extends even more broadly from ethics to epistemology, from philosophy of science to philosophy of mathematics.
>
> (2016, p. 1)

Although this renewed interest in the topic is promising, it is worth noting that the treatment of the topic within Kind's *Handbook* remains fairly conservative, at least in the context of the historical narrative I have presented here. Most of the contributors to the *Handbook* focus on linguistically parsing the logical relations between ideas, as is analytic philosophy's wont. The model of imagination common to most of its papers seems largely rooted in the Aristotelian tradition—what Coleridge would call *fancy*. This is an important contribution, but as I hope the preceding discussion has demonstrated, it does not begin to exhaust the possibilities of the topic.

I conclude with one particular point of contention, where Kind's analytic philosophy and depth psychology sharply diverge. In the opening to the *Handbook*, Kind (2016) cautiously outlines a common philosophical definition, which includes the assertion that "Imagination is intentional, i.e. imaginings have intentional content" (p. 3). This would suggest that imagination is always something that one *does*. However, depth psychology has long decentralized the conscious, rational ego as the sole creator of the contents of its own psyche. Whether Freud's crude and wild *id*, Jung's mysterious *collective unconscious*, or Hillman's poetic *memoria*, there is a longstanding essential premise in depth psychology that just because something is psychologically experienced does not mean the conscious ego actively created it. On the contrary, depth psychology is prone to recognize imagination as an activity of the psyche that operates with or without conscious intention. In this perspective, engaging with the phenomenon of imagination is not only a method for producing fictions or a tool for solving problems—it is also a means to deeper psychological engagement. And because psyche is the medium through which we apprehend and make meaning of the world, engagement with psyche means facing up to how the world itself is imagined.

It is to these possibilities that we now turn.

Chapter 5

Imaginal psychology

Call the world, if you please, "the Vale of Soul Making."

John Keats

Depth psychology is a broad field that includes myriad, sometimes divergent viewpoints. I concur with Paul Kugler that the essential premise of depth psychology is an acknowledgment of "the ultimately unknowable, the unconscious itself" (2005, p. 38). To my mind, this indicates an ontological starting point of epistemic humility—a hermeneutic awareness of incomplete pictures; unseen depths extending beyond our assumptions, cultural constructs, linguistic constraints, and unreflective experience of the "surface" of things. Critiques of depth psychology have tended to focus on deconstructing one theory of the unconscious or another (for example, Freudian psychoanalysis), whereas I understand depth psychology proper as the broader field in which all theories and models of the unconscious, and our relation to it, are at play. That there is an unconscious element to human beings has been a preoccupation in Western discourse at least since Kant philosophically addressed the "root unknown to us" in human experience. Furthermore, this root idea finds more than ample contemporary evidence in the great proliferation of "non-conscious processes" that show up in the brain scans of modern neuroscience. Depth psychology, broadly speaking, seeks to understand these unconscious aspects of humanity and how we might consciously relate to them. Freud's theories tended more toward a medical model of the conscious–unconscious relationship; Jung expanded into more eclectic philosophical and spiritual territory; and Hillman would take an arguably post-modern approach to deconstructing our basic assumptions about what "psychology" means. Through each of these different approaches runs the thread of imagination as an essential bridge to the unknown.

Tarnas (1991) views the emergence of depth psychology in the early twentieth century as an early attempt to mend the growing split between mechanistic world and romantic soul. In particular, he credits Jungian and post-Jungian thought as offering a new epistemic evaluation of the role of imagination in psychological life:

> With this awareness of the fundamental mediating role of imagination in human experience has also come an increased appreciation of the power and complexity of the unconscious, as well as new insight into the nature of archetypal pattern and meaning.
>
> (p. 405)

But while Tarnas suggests a richer depth psychology emerging from this Jungian emphasis on imagination in the human psyche, Kugler (2005) argues that a concern with mental images was present from the very beginning of the field: "Depth psychology developed out of an attempt to explain the role imaging plays in personality formation and psychopathology. Both Freud and Jung struggled to understand the functions of 'mental representations' in psychic life" (p. 3). The discourse on imagination in the Enlightenment and Romantic periods had provided fertile ground for this new psychology to take root.

Both Freud and Jung were psychiatrists trained in the medical tradition—but they were also widely read and influenced by literature and the "human sciences." Jung is often ascribed as being the less scientific, more philosophical of the two, but Freud also spoke to the poetic foundations of his work: "my books, in fact, more resembles works of imagination than treatises on pathology" (cited in Hillman 1994/1983). Downing (2006/1997) reminds us that Freud believed a background in literature and the arts would provide a better foundation for the practice of psychoanalysis than medical training (p. 105). And Tarnas writes that Freud and Jung were both "deeply influenced by the stream of German Romanticism that flowed from Goethe through Nietzsche" (p. 384). Positivistic science was on the rise in the early days of depth psychology, but had not yet dominated the academy; there was yet room for thinkers who, following the example of Goethe, sought a middle ground between rigorous scientific inquiry and a more poetic, perhaps even Romantic philosophy of life. In depth psychology, imagination would come to play an increasingly central role in understanding and engaging the human psyche as the twentieth century unfolded.

The birth of depth psychology: from Nietzsche to Freud

Sigmund Freud is generally viewed as the great initiator of depth psychology, but Walter Kaufman (1992/1985) argues that this honor should in fact be accorded to Nietzsche. In his aptly titled paper "Nietzsche as the first great (depth) psychologist" Kaufman cites Freud's declaration that:

"the degree of introspection achieved by Nietzsche had never been achieved by anyone" and that furthermore Nietzsche "had a more penetrating knowledge of himself than any other man who lived or was ever likely to live" (pp. 911–912). Coming from Freud, these are astounding words of praise—and yet on closer inspection they are not so surprising. Robinson's (1976) history of psychology also credits Nietzsche for foregrounding the degree to which the rational mind is driven by deeper primal forces. As Robinson reads Nietzsche, "we think and reason as we do in the further-ance of desires that are all too human. The discoveries of philosophy are but inventions. Not illuminations of what is in the natural world ... but the crafting of things of cultural or personal value" (p. 291). That is to say, rational systems of thought arise in response to non-rational, primordial elements in the psyche. We see here the beginnings of the psychological concept of "rationalization"—the idea that we produce rational thoughts to organize and justify deeper, irrational experiences and impulses. Kaufman sees this as one of Nietzsche's central projects: "In many different contexts he showed how the role of consciousness in our psychic life had been widely and vastly overestimated" (1992/1985, p. 913). Nietzsche's emphasis on the *will* is often misunderstood as a domineering power of the conscious mind, but Robinson interprets Nietzsche's *will* as a deeper phe-nomenon: "as with instincts, it operates beyond consciousness. It uses con-sciousness, with the latter simply being a merely superficial aspect of the mental" (1976, p. 290). As Nietzsche wrote in his final work, *Ecce homo*, "Consciousness is a Surface" (1967/1908, p. 254). As such, Freud's rever-ence for Nietzsche is no great mystery; the wily existentialist had dragged the "id" into the village square for all to see.

In Kaufman's reading, this unearthing of the unconscious was manifest throughout Nietzsche's larger project of cultural criticism. "It appears that nobody else has done nearly so much to alert us to the psychological back-ground of philosophers and religious figures" (1992/1985, p. 912). In this sense, Nietzsche can be said to have initiated an enduring feature of the depth psychology tradition: to inquire into the psychic background, assumptions, and motives of thinkers throughout the ages, asking what might be hidden behind their words, perhaps even hidden to the authors themselves. Here too, we see a firm grounding of psychology within the humanities. "Nietzsche's psychology, like Freud's has its roots primarily in imaginative literature, notably including not only Dostoevsky but also Shakespeare and Goethe" (p. 912). As the previous chapter pointed out, Nietzsche cannot entirely escape association with the Romantics, though his raw existentialism often imagined the world quite differently than that of his predecessors. Kaufman laments the fact that although Nietzsche described himself as a psychologist repeatedly and emphatically, he is rarely remembered as one by contemporary audiences. In *Beyond good and evil*, Nietzsche asserts that psychology should be "recognized as the queen of the sciences, for whose service and equipment the other sciences exist. For psychology is once more the path to the fundamental problems" (Nietzsche, 1997/1886, p. 17). This question of what psychology is, and what psychology does, was essential to his thinking. But in the twentieth century the field of psychology would become largely relegated to consulting rooms, asylums, and scientific laboratories—all places that Nietzsche did not fit.

Given these challenges, it is easier to understand why Sigmund Freud (1856–1939) would come to be more widely recognized as the founder of depth psychology. Freud's impact was immense not only in the emerging discipline of psychology, but for Western culture as a whole. Tarnas (1991) writes that Freud "radically undermined the entire Enlightenment project" by decentering the rational, reasoning ego as the dominant aspect of the human mind:

> Beyond the rational mind existed an overwhelmingly potent repository of nonrational forces which did not readily submit either to rational analysis or to conscious manipulation, and in comparison with which man's conscious ego was a frail and fragile epiphenomenon.
>
> (p. 328)

In short, Freud not only recognized a pronounced unconscious element in human behavior, he foregrounded it at the center of human psychology. The Freudian unconscious ceased to be a matter of philosophical speculation or impassioned aphorism, and instead became a personal day-to-day reality of human experience.

That said, Davis (2005) reminds us that while Freud certainly popularized the notion of the unconscious mind, the idea of an unconscious aspect of human experience was not his original creation and had in fact existed in one form or another throughout history. Robinson (1976) concurs, noting that a similar idea is evidenced as far back as Homer's Gods planting "ideas and fears" in the dreaming minds of sleepers, and henceforth surfaces repeatedly throughout history in an ongoing discourse about whether "underneath the veil of reason, our mental life actually proceeds according to the mandates of passion" (p. 313).

The specific term, *the unconscious*, was coined by Schelling in 1800 as an essential tenet of his idealist philosophy, where it was conceived as the poetic creativity of the universe, underlying human experience. Kearney (1988) directly traces Schelling's *unconscious* back to Kant's "transcendental imagination," noting that Kant originally discussed it as "the 'root unknown to us' which forms our apprehension of the objects of our world … redefined by Schelling as an 'unconscious poetry' operative in our every day natural existence" (p. 182). Thus, in this original formulation from Kant to Schelling, *the unconscious* was a synthesizing force in human experience, operating beyond (or beneath) the rational conscious mind, and implicated in imaginative process. In 1869, Eduard von Hartman would publish the widely read *Philosophy of the unconscious*, which synthesized the philosophical systems of Boehme, Schelling, and Schopenhauer, with particular regard to their articulations of *the will* (Ellenberger, 1970, p. 209). The notion of a *mythopoetic unconscious* that continually generates myth and fantasy was first suggested by Frederick Myers and elaborated by Theodore Flourney around the turn of the century (Ellenberger, 1970, p. 318). And although Nietzsche did not use the term often, he nonetheless offered this definitive statement in 1882: "For the longest time, conscious thought was considered thought itself. Only now does the truth dawn on us that by far the greatest part of our spirit's activity remains unconscious and unfelt" (1974/1882, p. 262). Thus Freud's contribution, considerable thought it was, came after a century of robust discourse on the topic.

What might be more accurately said of Freud is that he took an abstract philosophical notion of *the unconscious* and concretely applied it to the human psyche, recognizing the unconscious as a primary factor for understanding and treating psychological illness. Freud's explorations of hypnosis with his colleague and mentor Josef Breuer provided him with compelling evidence for a significant unconscious factor in psychological illness and symptom formation. Observing psychological and psychosomatic symptoms shift and change dramatically under hypnosis, Freud and Breuer concluded that "the mechanism for symptom formation was unconscious" (Robinson, 1976, p. 316). Hypnosis, of course, has its own rich history, first systematically applied to psychology by Jean-Martin Charcot (1825–1893), but dating further back as a healing method to the somnambulism of Puysegur and the "magnetism" of Mesmer (see Crabtree, 1993, Ellenberger, 1970 for a fascinating account). Freud concluded from his own observations of hypnosis that something vital in the psyche was buried or held back, and these repressed aspects of the patient were responsible for psychological dysfunction.

The Jungian imagination

Carl Gustav Jung was a brilliant, complex, and sometimes confounding thinker, not easily summarized and far too easily misunderstood. In addition to Henri Ellenberger's the *Discovery of the unconscious* (1970), Sonu Shamdasani's *Jung and the making of modern psychology* (2003) offers a wonderful genealogy of the ideas that influenced Jung's life and work. Whereas conventional wisdom long held that Jung's school of "analytic psychology" was some kind of mystical rebel offshoot of Freudian psychoanalysis, Shamdasani demonstrates decisively that Jung's ideas had a complex set of roots and trajectories all their own. Jung was, among other things, an interdisciplinary synthesizer of disciplines: "His signature concepts contained many different ideas which attempted to resolve major debates in philosophy, psychology, sociology, biology, anthropology, comparative religion, and other fields, and enable the formation of a distinct discipline of psychology" (p. 17). In this sense, Jung was following Nietzsche's injunction to recognize psychology as the "queen of the sciences"—for in Jung's understanding, psyche was at the root of every human endeavor.

In this also we get a hint of how deeply rooted Jung was in Kantian philosophy; Kant's "Copernican revolution," which asserted that human experience of the world must necessarily conform to the structure of the human mind and not vice versa, was foundational to Jung's psychology. "Critical philosophy," said Jung in reference to his intellectual forebears, is "the mother of psychology" (1958, p. 475 [para. 759]). But unlike Kant, Jung would not remain limited to strictly rational analysis and logical linguistic structures to engage the human psyche. As he wrote in 1926: "The psyche consists essentially of images ... a structure that is throughout full of meaning and purpose" (1960b/1926, p. 325 [para. 618]). Though he was a dedicated empiricist, Jung pushed back against the tide of positivism and articulated instead a psychology firmly rooted in phenomenological engagement with *meaningful images*. Nietzsche and Freud had shown humanity the irrational id underlying our reason, and now Jung would tap deeper into a primordial realm of imagery, an expression of human experience unbound by the structures of verbal language.

Many volumes have been written about the relationship between Freud and Jung and their respective psychologies. To some extent, their theoretical differences can be framed as a matter of divergent philosophies. Tarnas (1991) writes:

> While it was Freud who penetrated the veil, it was Jung who grasped the critical philosophical consequences of depth psychology's discoveries. Partly this was because Jung was more epistemologically sophisticated than Freud, having been steeped in Kant and critical philosophy from his youth ... by intellectual temperament, Jung was less bound than Freud by nineteenth-century scientism.
>
> (p. 423)

In contrast to Freud's emphasis on sexuality, Jung focused on a broader range of psychic processes that are not directly accessible to consciousness. He was more prone to question how the psyche mediates knowledge and understanding across all spheres, philosophical, academic, and personal. "Jung extends Kant's critique of pure reason to an analysis of the finitude of the human psyche, thereby shifting the epistemological 'object' of depth psychology from sexuality to psychic image" (Kugler, 2005, p. 15). Jung's divergent psychology did not exclude sexuality, but saw it as one psychic component among many, and consequently shifted focus to understanding how psychic contents, in general, express themselves through *imagery and myth*.

This new emphasis on imagination came with a new valuation of the images themselves. In contrast to Freud, who saw dream and fantasy images as "disguises" for the latent content beneath, Jung recognized that there could be meaning in the particular image in-itself. "Image and meaning are identical; and as the first takes shape, so the latter becomes clear. Actually, the pattern needs no interpretation: it portrays its own meaning" (1960a/1947, p. 204, [para. 402]). This marked a move away from the attribution of fixed conceptual meanings to psychic images, and emphasized instead a more open-ended exploration of meaning for the patient through both personal and collective (i.e., mythic) contexts. Rather than the image of a tree being automatically interpreted as a "disguised penis," the image might have different meanings for different patients, sometimes personal, sometimes archetypal—or both. In fact Jung had a rule for himself, that whenever a new dream was presented for analysis, he would always tell himself "I have no idea what this dream means" (1969a/1945, p. 283 [para. 533]), and then "collaborate" with the dreamer to uncover its meaning. Thereafter, it was for him essential to "stick as close as possible to the dream image" (1966a/1934, p. 149 [para. 320]). At the end of the day, the tree might very well be recognized as a powerful phallic symbol for a given client, but this meaning would only be arrived at after an active engagement with the particular qualities and associations of the image itself, rather than assumed from the outset.

Another important component of this shift in emphasis is that the inquiry into meaningful images became just as much a matter of psychological health as psychological illness. Davis (2005) writes that whereas Freud recognized fantasy as a psychic reality only with regards to pathology, Jung "took a much broader view of the role of fantasies in the psyche; he saw fantasies as the key to understanding normal as well as pathological behavior" (p. 83). Thus, psychic images and narratives not only expressed what was wrong, but were also involved in all meaningful psychological activity—including healthy development and personal growth. Over the course of his life and work, Jung came to recognize that while psychology must be studied scientifically, the language of image, poetry, and myth were a better fit for expressing meaningful psychological experience. "Jung, in his old age, turned not to science to describe his life in all its richness and depth but to myth, because it reflected for him the workings of psyche more accurately than science" (p. 97). Rather than viewing myth as merely an archaic fiction or falsehood, myth in this context is recognized as a meaningful pattern in collective human experience—"The Hero's Journey" as elucidated by Joseph Campbell (1968) being just one popular example. In the Jungian model, the human psyche is largely structured around mythic patterns and their expression in imagistic and narrative form.

From philosophy to psychology

Sonu Shamdasani (2003) has extensively researched Jung's philosophical underpinnings and how they contributed to the formulation of his psychology. His understanding of the unconscious was at least as influenced by the philosophical writings of Carus and Hartmann as by Freud, if not more so (p. 164). His roots extend back not only to Kant's "transcendental imagination" operating behind the scenes, but also to Schelling and the Romantics. While Jung was careful to distance himself from the metaphysical claims of Romanticism, he acknowledged their contribution to a psychology that emphasizes experiential engagement with the unconscious (p. 167). To the question of which philosopher had influenced him the most, Jung once proclaimed: "Kant is my philosopher!" (cited in Shamdasani, 2003, p. 168). This is important for understanding Jung's theory of archetypes (see below), and equally essential to understanding his essential stance of epistemic humility. On this matter, Tarnas (1991) writes: "With his philosophical grounding in the Kantian critical tradition rather than in Freud's more conventional rationalist materialism, Jung was compelled to admit that his psychology could have no necessary metaphysical implications" (p. 386). Jung thus carved out a middle-ground, an ontologically valid psychic space where Romanticism, speculative philosophy, religion, art, and culture all had inherent meaning regardless of their status in the material world. This is sometimes misinterpreted as a stance of either materialist atheism or a kind of Romantic–Idealist theism—but in fact it is neither. Rather Jung envisioned a neutral middle ground where things can have psychological or "inner" meaning completely regardless of their material or metaphysical status.

Recall Kant's key distinction between noumena and phenomena—the "thing in itself" can never be known as such, but comes to us as phenomenon through the a priori categories of the human mind. Thus, our experience is restricted to what those a priori categories allow. Jung is following the same philosophy, albeit with afresh emphasis on imagination:

> psychic existence is the only category of existence to which we have immediate knowledge, since nothing can be known unless it first appears as a psychic image. Only psychic existence is immediately verifiable. To the extent that the world does not assume the form of a psychic image, it is virtually non-existent.
>
> (1958, pp. 480–481 [para. 769])

This basic skepticism about our capacity to know what exists "outside" of human experience is equally undermining to positivistic science as it is to metaphysics, or in Tarnas' pithy summation, "Kant's insight is a sword that cuts two ways" (1991, p. 421). All we can ultimately know is the psyche, which mediates all other experience, and which itself is partially unconscious by nature.

Tarnas asserts that in contrast to Freud, Jung was "epistemologically more exacting, and repeatedly affirmed throughout much of his life the fundamental epistemological limits of his own theories (though he also reminded conventional scientists that their epistemological situation was no different)" (1991, p. 386). Jung was nevertheless committed to psychology as a science, even if his early twentieth-century definition of "science" is hard to grasp by our contemporary standards. Some of the "science" confusion stems from Jung's insistence that the psyche has an "objective" aspect, even with regards to individual personal experience. In Jung's view, "The psyche itself ... has an objective, autonomous existence" (Watkins, 1984/1976, p. 50). Jung meant by this that the contents of the psyche have an independent ontological value—the affectively charged images, narratives, and characters that arise to meet the conscious mind are not active creations of the conscious ego, but rather have an objective reality relative to the conscious mind experiencing them. Just as a material tree presents itself as an object to my senses, an image of "the tree of life" spontaneously arising in my consciousness has an objective existence as a psychic object presenting itself to my conscious mind. As such, Jung insisted these psychic contents were a kind of empirical, natural phenomenon, available to methodical, hence "scientific" study. This idea is completely lost when we assume that imagination only functions as an intentional, conscious process.

Jung designated this inner realm of image and story as *psychic reality*, ontologically real, but fundamentally different from the measurable material world. "It is a psychic fact that this fantasy is happening and it is as real as you—as a psychic entity—are real" (Jung, 1970/1955, p. 529 [para. 753]). By thus engaging with these images as psychologically real, meaning is restored to what might otherwise be dismissed as merely imaginary. Tarnas (1991) summarizes:

> Jung's granting the status of empirical phenomena to psychological reality was a major step past Kant, for he thereby gave substance to "internal" experience as Kant had to "external" experience: all human experience, not just sense impressions, had to be included for a genuinely comprehensive empiricism.
>
> (p. 386)

Jung's "scientific" psychology was thus envisioned as a kind of robust phenomenology, articulated long before the modern movement toward qualitative and mixed methods approaches to research would be recognized and codified by the academy. In this regard, I believe he was far ahead of his time.

Image as bridge to the unknown

While reality beyond the psyche might be unknowable, the contents of the psyche could be engaged and become known. To engage with the unconscious in Jungian psychology is to engage with the inner unknown for the ultimate purpose of integrating it into the conscious personality. Through this process of reconciling and integrating the unconscious, adults would experience *individuation*—movement toward greater psychological wholeness. Jung's experience, both with his own psyche and that of his patients, led him to believe that the generation of meaningful images and fantasies was a natural and ongoing activity of the unconscious. "This autonomous activity of the psyche, which can be explained neither as reflex to sensory stimuli nor as the executive organ of eternal ideas, is, like every vital process, a continually creative act" (Jung, 1971/1921, p. 52 [para. 78]). Again, we see this fantasy creation process framed as a natural phenomenon, the natural activity of a vital, living being. This generation of images requires no external stimulation or metaphysical causation, but is internally generated as a matter of course. *Generating these images is what the unconscious psyche does.* These fantasies arise of their own accord, in dreams or daydreams, and they can either be engaged and integrated or ignored and repressed. Jung goes on to say: "Fantasy therefor seems to me to be the clearest expression of the specific activity of the psyche.... Fantasy it was and ever is which fashions the bridge between the irreconcilable claims of subject and object, introversion and extraversion" (p. 52). Like Aristotle, Jung locates imagination as an intermediary between inner and outer worlds. More importantly, imagination here becomes the bridge between the conscious and the unconscious; it becomes the vessel of self-knowledge and psychological integration.

The images of the psyche may at times represent actual external objects or persons, but they may be even more important when they do not. When an image has no external referent, this may "actually increase its importance for psychic life, since it then has a greater psychological value, representing inner reality which far outweighs the importance of external reality" (Jung, 1971/1921, p. 442 [para. 744]). Following this thread of Jungian thought, Mary Watkins explains that such an internally generated image in a dream of fantasy may appear because "it represents an unrecognized or undervalued part or attitude of the person dreaming or imagining" (1984/1976, p. 44). This "unrecognized or undervalued part" might resemble the repressed sexual desires of Freud, Nietzsche's will to power—or a multitude of other contents that have become isolated from conscious awareness, be it the "inner child," "inner artist," "inner surfer-dude," or perhaps something more troubling—the violent side, the narcissist who is never satiated, the bully, the weakling, the reject, the outcast. One of the basic notions of Jungian psychology is that we are better off for becoming conscious of these aspects of ourselves and integrating them, rather than allowing them to manifest as unconscious patterns of behavior.

As we traverse deeper into the unconscious psyche, there is no shortage of images to discover. Jung (1954d/1946) writes:

> Consciousness, no matter how extensive it may be, must always remain the smaller circle within the greater circle of the unconscious, an island surrounded by the sea; and, like the sea itself, the unconscious yields an endless and self-replenishing abundance of living creatures, a wealth beyond fathoming.
>
> (p. 178)

The use of words like "abundance" and "wealth" suggest a treasure trove within for those who would go seeking. Here we come to another possibility—that the unconscious is not only a gateway to integrating the disowned pieces of personality, but to something much richer. As Paul Kugler (2005) puts it: "Perhaps the most important function psychic images perform is to aid the individual in transcending conscious knowledge. Psychic images provide a bridge to the sublime, pointing toward something unknown, beyond subjectivity" (p. 20). Following Myers and Flourney before him, Jung conceived the unconscious as a mythopoetic entity, a source of endless creativity. Here in this mythopoetic realm of creative abundance, one may begin to find intimations of the spiritual as well.

The bridging function of the imagination is perhaps most apparent in Jung's unique use of the term *symbol*. Jung contrasted symbols with signs, the latter being a representation of something known (a red light is a sign for "stop," the gender image on the bathroom is a sign for "male" or "female"). Symbols, on the other hand, are those images that go beyond the surface meaning of a word, image, object or picture. Whenever something becomes a symbol, it has complex meanings. Unicorn symbolism, for example, has throughout history carried complex connotations of the untamable wild, purity and innocence, masculine power—and in the Middle ages was even strongly associated with Jesus Christ. (Schwartz & Sherman, 2008). Jung characterized symbols as "living things that are pregnant with meaning and cannot be expressed in any other way" (Davis, 2005, p. 96). In Jungian psychology, symbols are a special class of images arising from the unconscious as an attempt to reconcile inner conflicts by pointing to something beyond conscious awareness. Jung writes that the meaning of the symbol "resides in the fact that it attempts to elucidate, by a more or less apt analogy, something that is still entirely unknown or still in the process of formulation" (1966b/1916, p. 291 [para. 492]). Thus, a symbolic image in a dream is not trying to disguise something, but rather trying to bring to awareness a new truth that is not readily grasped by the current configuration of the conscious personality. As such, Jung asserts that the proper mode of investigation into the meaning of a symbol is not semiotic but hermeneutic, looking for additional layers of meaning rather than reducing the image to a single defined value. "This procedure widens and enriches the initial symbol, and the final outcome is an infinitely complex and variegated picture" (p. 291). By focusing on complexification of meaning rather than reductive definition, engagement with the symbol becomes a process of expanding conscious awareness: the image literally accrues conscious meaning.

Archetypes: collective primordial images

The *archetypes* and the *collective unconscious* are two of Jung's most enduring signature concepts. They have courted much elaboration, much criticism, and much misunderstanding—in part because Jung himself seemed to struggle with various formulations of the concept throughout his lifetime. Briefly here I would like to touch upon these ideas both as an extension of Kantian philosophy and as a larger framework for understanding how imagination operates within the Jungian model.

Shamdasani (2003) tells us that Jung's "comparative study of mythologies led to the thesis that what underlay them were certain universal invariant forms ... which he called primordial images in 1911, dominants in 1917, and archetypes in 1919" (p. 302). Across times and cultures certain common themes emerge, patterns of human experience that appeared over and over again. This adequately expresses my own preferred definition of archetypes, whatever else they might or might not be: archetypes are primal patterns of human experience. In 1911 when Jung first began putting forth theories on the topic, he used the term *primordial image*. Shamdasani notes that Jung first adopted the term from Jacob Burckhardt's reference to Goethe's *Faust* as a "genuine and legitimate myth ... a great primordial image" (p. 298). But in fact, the German term for primordial image [*Urbild*] appears in the writings of both Schelling (p. 172) and Carus (p. 175), each of whom influenced Jung in turn. Furthermore, *Urbild* is used several times by Kant himself, where it is usually translated into English as archetype (p. 236). And in fact, Jung explained his concept of primordial images in Kantian terms, stating that although he refutes the idea of inherited ideas, "there are, however, innate possibilities of ideas, a priori conditions for fantasy-production, which are somewhat similar to the Kantian categories" (1964/1918, p. 10 [para. 14]). Just as Kant had put forward a priori categories that ordered human experience (time, causality, etc. ...), Jung was positing additional a priori modes of human experience as expressed in primordial, mythic imagery. As a priori conditions for fantasy production, they were the implicit organizing principles for imagination. "What Jung was proposing was a vast extension of the range of categories" (Shamdasani, 2003, p. 236); an extension that included the full spectrum of human experience. "What Kant demonstrates in respect of logical thinking is true of the whole range of the psyche" (Jung, 1971/1921, p. 304 [para. 512]). Thus the creative, the emotional, the irrational, the spiritual all fell into a priori categories of mythic structure. These were the "conditions for fantasy-production," the basic templates from which meaning was made.

Jung was careful to distinguish between the specific images that expressed archetypes, and the archetypes themselves, which as a priori categories were unknowable via direct experience. "The archetypal representations (images and ideas) mediated to us by the unconscious should not be confused with the archetype as such" (1960a/1947, p. 213 [para. 417]). Thus a specific image or myth (for example, Kali, Lucifer, Prometheus, Superman) is never to be taken as an archetype, but rather as an archetypal image mediated by culture. Such images have several layers of meaning: personal, cultural, and archetypal.

A corollary to the concept of archetypal patterns of human experience is that the unconscious is not merely personal, but at root has a collective layer as well. Jung writes: "The primordial images are the most ancient and the most universal thoughts of humanity. They are as much feelings as thoughts; because of that one can call them *original feeling-thoughts*" (cited in Shamdasani 2003, p. 309). As one moves beyond the complexes and rejected aspects of self in the personal unconscious to encounter these primordial and universal patterns of human experience, the personal nature gives way to a collective identity of what it means to be a human. Jung explains: "the collective unconscious is the sediment of all experience of the world of all time, and is also an image of the world, and has been forming for aeons" (p. 309). When one encounters an archetypal image, one is confronted with an essential element of humanity—a core aspect of human meaning. For this reason, such archetypal encounters, in dreams or in life, can be powerful, emotional, terrifying, or numinous experiences. Even in the encounter with the archetypal image of a primal instinct (say, lust or violence), there can be an almost religious quality that comes from directly encountering a core human truth in its raw, primal state. "The archetype as an image of instinct is a spiritual goal toward which the whole nature of man strives" (1960a/1947, p. 212, [para. 415]). What would have remained blind, potentially destructive instinct if left to the unconscious takes on a spiritual quality when expressed through imagination and integrated into the light of consciousness.

In term of practice, the realization of a collective layer of the unconscious populated by a priori archetypal forms necessitated a new treatment technique that Jung termed *amplification*. As fantasy images and narratives arose in the course of treatment, Jung recognized that certain aspects of these images may be rooted on the collective level. Thus, in addition the Freudian technique of finding personal associations to the image, Jung suggested a process of amplification, whereby the image was further understood by placing it within the context of comparative mythology. Shamdasani writes: "the establishment of analogies with mythological material ... enabled a comprehension of the non-personal images, and hence fostered the prospective development of the individual" (2003, p. 302). By comparing a dream to a sequence of similar myths from around the world, the images again began to generate additional levels of collective meaning for what otherwise might simply seem bizarre or incomprehensible. The patient was invited to discover additional meaning in a dialogical process with both the image itself and its mythic precedents. Watkins points out that this technique is particularly useful in the hermeneutics of understanding symbols: "the symbol can never be grasped in terms of what we already know. The very nature of it is to take us beyond" (1984/1976, p. 44). Through this process, the patient was working not only to resolve personal issues, but also to become more fully integrated into the collective experience of humanity. "The goal of analysis was to overcome individual alienation through revealing this unity" (Shamdasani, 2003, p. 302). I am not the first man moved to tears by the *Hunt of the Unicorn* tapestries that now hang in the New York Cloisters, and I will not be the last.

Active imagination

With imagination taking such a prominent role in both Jung's psychological theory and practice, it was necessary to develop a method or intentionally engaging imagination to access the deeper psyche. In his *The visions seminars*, Jung spoke about a particular kind of deep-looking into an image that impregnates it [*betrachten*] with meaning:

> If it is pregnant, it is alive, it produces, it multiplies. That is the case with any phantasy image. One concentrates on it, then finds difficulty in keeping it quiet; it gets restless it shifts; something is added to it or it multiplies itself; one fills it with the living power and it becomes pregnant.
>
> (1976/1932, p. 260)

Jung is describing here a basic form of *active imagination*—a deliberate process by which an individual enters into engagement with fantasy images and narratives. Unlike dreaming, in which the ego is usually not lucidly encountering the arising images, active imagination allows for more agency of engagement. The individual practicing this method does not seek to control the images as one might in a creative process, but enters instead into a concentrated, dialogical process with them. In her book *Waking dreams*, Mary Watkins (1984/1976) writes that active imagination is more effective than conventional dream interpretation, because it offers "a more active means of approaching the experience of mutual penetration of the unconscious and conscious worlds" (p. 47). By taking an active role in entering into the fantasies arising out of the unconscious, the conscious and unconscious aspects of the psyche are put into direct dialog and may begin to move toward greater integration.

Jungian analyst Joan Chodorow describes active imagination as having has two stages: "first, letting the unconscious come up; and second, coming to terms with the unconscious" and notes that this necessitates a temporary "suspension of our rational critical faculties in order to give free reign to fantasy" (1997, p. 10). Chodorow emphasized that some of the material that arises may be difficult to assimilate, and that the process of integration through active imagination may go on for many years. In addition to Chodorow, several other Jungians have offered a systematized approach to active imagination for the purposes of inner work (see in particular Robert Johnson's *Inner work* (1986) for a practical guide to practicing the method).

By most accounts, Jung developed the method of active imagination during a period of isolation and crisis following his traumatic break with Freud in 1913. In the account given in *Memories, dreams, reflections* (1989/1961) Jung recounts this process as a harrowing "confrontation with the unconscious" in which he deliberately plunged into this own unconscious mind. This was the process that would eventually produce the famous *Red book*, and provide him with the raw materials from which to forge his unique psychology. Jung's confrontation has variously been described as a "psychotic break" (Davis, 2005) and a "shamanic descent" (Smith, 2007), but for Jung it would eventually form the experiential basis for the method of active imagination. As the characterizations of Davis and Smith attest, this is not a process for the faint of heart, and may carry real danger for those who undertake it without adequate preparation. Chodorow (1997) warns that there is a danger of becoming "overwhelmed by powerful affects, impulses, and images" and it should only be undertaken by psychologically mature persons who have the ego strength to encounter such primal materials without become lost in them (p. 12). Jung (1969b/1957) further warned of the lesser danger that without sufficiently active engagement from the conscious ego, the practitioner might become "stuck in an all-enveloping phantasmagoria" (p. 68)—that is, escaping into aesthetic fantasy rather using the process for personal growth and integration in the wider spheres of their life. Once these dangers were surmounted, active imagination provided a powerful means for the patient to begin a direct engagement with the images of the unconscious psyche. "It is a way of attaining liberation by one's own efforts and of finding courage to be oneself" (p. 91 [para. 193]). Ultimately the patient was empowered to have their own inner dialog, rather than remaining completely dependent on the analyst.

Fantasy became for Jung the most important activity of the psyche, and among the most effective way to work with psychological dynamics:

> It is in creative fantasies that we find the unifying function we seek. All functions that are active in the psyche converge in fantasy.... Fantasy has its own irreducible value, for it is a psychic function that has roots in the conscious and unconscious alike, in the individual as much as the collective.
>
> (1966b/1916, p. 290 [para. 490])

It is no surprise that so much of modern dance therapy and creative arts therapy have their roots in Jungian psychology. These methods recognize spontaneous creative expression of the deep self as having a natural healing value, a means toward integration of the wounded and repressed aspects of our being. Despite the scientism of his day, Jung became an advocate for liberating the creative and playful energies of humanity as a natural and essential birthright:

> All the works of man have their origin in the creative imagination. What right, then, have we to disparage fantasy? ... The creative activity of imagination frees man from the bondage to the "nothing but" and raises him to the status of one who plays. As Schiller says, man is completely human only when he is at play.
>
> (1954a/1946, pp. 45–46 [para. 98])

The move into the unconscious through engaging the imagination is ultimately a move into an expanded sense of self, a realm where healing and transformation become possible. "My aim is to bring about a psychic state in which my patient begins to experiment with this own nature—a state of fluidity, change, and growth where nothing is eternally fixed and hopelessly petrified" (p. 46). The rigidity of fixed ideas defining who and what one was were being invited to speak, to move, to become animate, transformational images once more. Imagination, far from being the realm of the unreal, had become for Jung an essential tool for the practice of psychology.

James Hillman: advocate for the imaginal

James Hillman would be the first to clarify that his school of archetypal psychology emerged through the dialog of many thinkers and does not belong to him. In *Archetypal psychology: A brief account* (1983), Hillman identifies the immediate "fathers" of the movement as Henry Corbin and Carl Jung, but also identifies many of his own contemporaries, including Rafael Lopez-Pedraza, Patricia Berry, Paul Kugler, Murray Stein, Edgar Casey, Mary Watkins, Thomas Moore, and many others, as well as group of pioneering mythologists including Ernst Cassirer, Joseph Campbell, Karl Kerényi (pp. 2–3). Bringing greater historical context to bear, Hillman locates Jung as the "immediate ancestor in a long line that stretches back through Freud, Dilthey, Coleridge, Schelling, Vico, Ficino, Plotinus, and Plato to Heraclitus" (1976, p. xvii). Hillman was particularly influenced by Renaissance thought, with its irruption of polytheistic pagan imagination and emphasis on soul. His biographer, Dick Russell (2013), recounts Hillman's midlife encounter with the art and literature of the Renaissance as profoundly formative in shaping a psychology apart from Jungian orthodoxy (pp. 630–632).

Whereas Jung's emphasis on wholeness and integration was in keeping with the ethos of modernity, Hillman saw the psyche as a more fragmented, chaotic affair, putting him more in line with the multiple-truths of post-modern thought. Davis (2005) characterizes Hillman as "a truly postmodern Jungian analyst.... After deconstructing much of existing psychological theory, he constructs something entirely new and different, which paradoxically is also very old"; in turning via the Renaissance to Ancient Greece, Hillman invokes "polytheism with a refreshing in-your-face challenge both to monotheism and scientific materialism" (p. 5). Freud and Jung had both acknowledged the psychic reality of fantasy, and had both eventually turned to mythopoetic language to express it. But Hillman took Jung's notion that "image is psyche" to its logical conclusion, insisting on a psychology that was born out of imagination, that was expressed and understood primarily *as* a mythopoetic discourse, rather than a system of abstract rational concepts. I agree with Davis that "It is this sort of approach to what most psychologists and psychiatrists think of as a science that makes Hillman one of the most unsettling, frustrating, and seductive thinkers in modern psychology" (p. 6). In my experience, what Hillman proposes is such a radically different way of seeing and being in the world that he is both initially hard to grasp, and profoundly compelling once understood. Even at the many points where I disagree with his conclusions, I often remain enchanted by the premises from which his thoughts and fantasies flow. I happily confess that Hillman's passionate advocacy for the imagination was a powerful influence on my own interest in the subject.

Freud and Jung had labored to fit their psychologies into the frameworks of natural and medical science, but Hillman rejected and even criticized this as profound misunderstanding of the psyche.

> Hillman has frequently deplored efforts to apply the medical model to
> psychological disorders.... From his perspective, the medical model has

captured and corrupted psychology and diverted it from its true aim: the psyche and the imagination, creators of fantasy images.

(Davis, 2005, p. 28)

Hillman further extends this criticism to academic psychologists, behaviorists, and the mainstream "personal growth market" that has grown up in modern times—each of which have alienated psyche from its imaginative core (for a full account of these myriad arguments, see *Re-visioning psychology*, 1976). It is not that Hillman saw no value in those fields and pursuits, but rather sensed a dangerous and damaging lack of balance in removing the psyche so completely from its imaginal ground. Instead, Hillman wanted to find a place for the imagining psyche in all of it, and in this we find the beginnings of a truly imaginal psychology.

Henry Corbin and the Mundus imaginalis

It is telling that Hillman places the work of Corbin beside that of Jung as a principle "fathering" agent of archetypal psychology. Henry Corbin (1903–1978) was a French philosopher, theologian, and professor of Islamic Studies, perhaps best known for his scholarship and interpretation of twelfth-century Zoroastrian and Islamic mysticism. Corbin wrote extensively about imagination in this tradition; it was he who recognized the word *imaginary* was too entangled with ideas of "unreality" in the Western cannon, and instead coined the term *imaginal* to designate an experience of imagination that was ontologically real despite its non-material nature. However, this designation went far beyond carving out a new abstract philosophical category. For Corbin, this was part of the articulation of a larger view of the cosmos:

> The world of the image, the *mundus imaginalis*: a world that is as ontologically real as the world of the senses and the world of the intellect. This world requires its own faculty of perception, namely imaginative power, a faculty with a cognitive function, a *noetic* value which is as real as that of sense perception or intellectual intuition.
>
> (1972, p. 7)

To be clear, Corbin was not a psychologist, and his work contains a manifest theological element—a theology grounded in the imagination. For Corbin, the reality of the imaginal "is more irrefutable and more coherent than the empirical world, where reality is perceived by the senses" (p. 15). This is a radically different ontological starting point from the reductive materialism of, say, Richard Dawkins, for whom the real can only be given by the senses. In Corbin's view, the senses offer an imperfect and unreliable view compared to the direct experience of the imaginal, which is immediately given in phenomenological experience (this point will be taken up from a scientific perspective in the next chapter). Imagination here becomes a primary faculty of perception, a way of seeing into imaginal reality, distinct from sensate perception of the material world or abstract thinking by the intellect.

James Hillman begins his essay *The thought of the heart* (1992) by lavishing Corbin with praise. Because of Corbin's work, Hillman writes,

> the basis of our work has already been done. We do not have to establish the primary principle: that the thought of the heart is the thought of images, that the heart is the seat of imagination, that imagination is the authentic voice of the heart, so that if we speak from the heart, we must speak imaginatively.
>
> (p. 4)

Hillman is speaking poetically, and it is only by reading him poetically that we understand what he means. Corbin's imaginal cosmology was a primary inspiration and container for the development an archetypal psychology that honors the imagining heart.

That said, it should not be assumed that Hillman's psychology is thus identical to its roots. Cheetham (2015) writes that while Corbin was initially enthusiastic about the "rebirth of the Gods" in Hillman's work, he came to express reservations about the co-opting of the term *imaginal* shortly before his death. The discord stems from the fact that Corbin maintained a reverence for the mystical cultural systems from which he had derived his ideas—for him the imaginal realm was a transcendental path, "the realm of the angels and of all the phenomena of religious experience" (p. 24). Hillman, by contrast, used *imaginal* to refer to all manner of psychic experience, inclusive of the religious dimension, but also including the darkest and most fragmented experiences of the soul. Cheetham writes that "Hillman's imagination is intensely this-worldly, and profoundly concrete … he shared Corbin's hatred of idolatry and fundamentalism, but his imagination does not move vertically, as Corbin's always does" (p. 27). In fact, Hillman was often critical of transcendent spirituality (2005/1975) and hostile toward monotheism in general for imposing a fantasy of unity and wholeness on what he saw as the fragmented and chaotic experience of being human (Hillman, 1976).

Cheetham believes Corbin "was clearly alarmed by Hillman's adaptation of his work … it would, he thought, be a mistake with fatal consequence to confuse the imaginal realm … with the chaotic jumble that is the normal state of the human psyche" (2015, p. 26). But then, Corbin was a philosopher, a theologian, and a mystic, and Hillman was by his own admission a "renegade psychologist," a man who both deeply honored his intellectual forbears while vigorously deconstructing them. For

Hillman's part, he was very clear on Corbin's contribution, stating that the *Mundus imaginalis* "offers an ontological mode of locating the archetypes of psyche, as the fundamental structures of the imagination or as fundamentally imaginative phenomena that are transcendent to the world of sense in their *value* if not their appearance" (1983, p. 3). Even more importantly, Hillman writes, is "the double move of Corbin: (a) that the fundamental nature of the archetype is accessible to imagination first and first presents itself as image, so that (b) the entire procedure of archetypal psychology as a method is imaginative" (p. 4). In Corbin, Hillman found an imaginal ontology that turned on the personification of living images beyond the mind of the individual. It was the basis for a psychology that proceeded entirely through imaginal engagements. Furthermore, Cheetham argues, "what may be Hillman's central insight derives directly from Corbin. It is his account of the difference between the literal and the imaginal," a distinction modeled on Corbin's differentiation between idol and icon, the rigid idea versus the living image (2015, p. 28). Indeed, as we shall see, Hillman's constant insistence that *nothing he writes should be taken literally*—while writing so very much about so many topics and with so much passion—is one of the most wonderful and confounding things about him.

The deliteralization of the psyche

I discuss Hillman's view of literalism before exploring any of his other ideas in hopes to provide a bulwark against common misunderstandings. In short, Hillman reminds his readers over and over again that he is not to be taken literally, and that psychology and a great many other fields besides collapse when taken as literal truths. "Remember: the enemy is the literal, and the literal is not the concrete flesh but negligence of the vision that concrete flesh is a magnificent citadel of metaphors" (1976, p. 174). Hillman was a great lover of the particular, the concrete image that overflows with a plurality of meanings rooted in its particularity. The literal, on the other hand, is a reductionistic abstraction: "Literalism prevents mystery by narrowing the multiple ambiguity of meanings into one definition. Literalism is the natural concomitant of monotheistic consciousness— whether in theology or in science—which demands singleness of meaning" (p. 149). An obvious example is the believer who reads Genesis literally, who takes the richness of the myth to mean nothing but a literal Adam and a literal Eve (literally created out of Adam's literal rib) and living in a literal Garden of Eden. Instead of recognizing the world as an abundance of metaphors, it becomes de-souled, reduced and fixed into a one-dimensional narrative. Hillman goes far beyond the criticism of religion, and sees literalism at work in all spheres of human experience, wherever the metaphoric and poetic dimensions of experience have been reduced or seemingly eliminated altogether:

Psychology itself is a part of this steady withdrawal of soul into the narrow confines of the human skin. The last stage of this process is shrinking soul to its single and narrowest space, the ego ... the one personification whose function is to take itself as literally real.... Literalism is an ego viewpoint.

(p. 48)

Even the lauded sense of self, the ego viewpoint, is in part a metaphor, a fiction created by the psyche. The challenge here is to get past the association of "fiction" as "false" or "unreal" and understand that what Hillman is suggesting is that the non-literal, metaphorical, imaginal, fictitious—are in fact the basis of psyche and psychic truth.

Hillman believed that psychology was not simply a matter of isolated individuals experiencing mental illness, but that the whole culture had become ill from denying the imaginal basis of human experience. The world had been de-souled, fixed into rigid literalisms. "What is needed is a re-visioning, a fundamental shift of perspective out of that soulless predicament we call modern consciousness" (1976, p. 3). With imagination strictly confined to the arts, Western civilization had lost touch with its own depth of soul. "When imagination is not evoked, there is a deep-seated lack of confidence to imagine fantasies in regard to one's problems and to be free of the ego's literalizations, it's sense of being trapped in 'reality'" (p. 49). Thus, the therapeutic element of archetypal psychology was rooted in rehabilitating the client's imagination, their capacity to engage meaningfully with imaginal experience. In *Healing fiction*, Hillman writes:

Now if the progression from sanity toward mental illness is distinguished by degrees of literalism, then the therapeutic road from psychosis back to sanity is one of going back through the same hermeneutic passage—deliteralizing. To be sane, we must recognize beliefs as fictions, and see through our hypothesis as fantasies.

(1994/1983, p. 111)

Thus, the process of imaginal engagement was not restricted to a cordoned off practice of active imagination, in which one takes an inward journey. Hillman is suggesting something much more radical—an imaginal engagement with the wider world, that begins with deliteralizing our rigid beliefs.

One of Hillman's principle methods for accomplishing this goal was a process he termed *psychologizing*. "Through psychologizing I change the idea of any literal action at all—political, scientific, personal—into a metaphorical enactment" (1976, p. 127). All beliefs, actions, and events have a psychological, metaphorical dimension, so that by psychologizing, we "see through" the literalized surface meanings of our conscious assumptions, and engage with an array of imaginal meanings that underlie them. We can see Apollo ruling behind the positivism of science, or feel the ecstasy of Dionysos presiding over a desert festival, or trace Hermes, Guide of Souls, winding his way through a complex piece of writing. I can see the image of my mother lurking behind my perception of Hillary Clinton, and behind them both a pantheon of goddesses, presenting a complex interplay of shadow and light. "Thus soul finds psyche everywhere, recognizes itself in all things, all things providing psychological reflection" (p. 154). Our conscious experience takes place in a field of meanings, many of them unconscious and unquestioned. The point is not to reveal a singular hidden truth (i.e., "the tree *is* a phallus," "Hillary Clinton *is* Athena"), but rather to actively engage in the reflective imaginal process in which those meanings can emerge. Sometimes we may land on an especially powerful hidden truth that recasts our view of a situation, but just as likely we encounter a multitude of meanings and conflicting agendas operating behind the scenes. When this occurs, we go deeper, we differentiate, we develop greater intimacy with the contents of the imaginal psyche. In a sense, we are still following Jung, making the unconscious conscious as a means to growth. Hillman uniquely emphasized the circularity of the process, rather than becoming fixated on a "final" fantasy of wholeness.

For many rationalists, this radical departure from literal truth may sound like nihilism. I see it rather as a rebalancing from one kind of truth to another. Hillman provocatively states. "As truths are the fictions of the rational, fictions are the truths of the imaginal" (1976, p. 153). For Hillman there is abundant truth—it is the truth of metaphor, the truth of image and the multiplicity of meanings that image carries. It is, if anything, too much truth, not too little. But what of our hard-fought rational truths, the fruits of two millennia of logic, mathematics, and science? It is not part of Hillman's agenda to dwell on these things—the better part of Western civilization is doing that already—but fortunately he remembers to make room for them as well:

> I should hasten to qualify that psychologizing does not mean only psychologizing, or that statements may not have content, merit, and import in the area of their literal expression. Philosophical and scientific assertions are, of course, not only psychological statements. To reduce such assertions wholly to psychology commits the psychologistic fallacy, or "psychologism." This point is important.
>
> (1976, p. 133)

Whereas *psychologizing* invites expansion by "seeing through" surface structures to find deeper psychological meanings, *psychologism* is reductive—it reduces all meaning solely to the psychological dimension.

Thus, philosophy and science retain ample room for legitimate literal meanings; Hillman is simply not content to stop there.

Imagination of the soul

In the introduction to *Re-visioning psychology* (1976), Hillman posits "both a poetic basis of mind and a psychology that starts neither in the physiology of the brain, the structure of language, the organization of society, nor the analysis of behavior, but in the process of imagination" (p. xvii). In keeping with this starting point, he places the word *soul* at the center of his discourse, and advances his own formulation of Jungian individuation, which he terms *soul-making*. For the casual reader prone to take mythopoetic language literally, it is easy to misinterpret "soul" as reference to Christian or new age belief systems, but this is not how Hillman intends it. Rather, he goes back to Greece, to the original meaning of *psyche* [ψυχή] in psychology, and to Greek Philosophy's long discourse on soul. More importantly, the choice of "soul" over "psyche" is a deliberate move toward poetic language and metaphor. "The soul is a deliberately ambiguous concept resisting all definition in the same manner as do all ultimate symbols which provide the root metaphors for the systems of human thought" (1964, p. 46). With its romantic and metaphysical connotations, soul engages a more imaginative process than the more scientific "psyche" or cognitive "mind."

Elsewhere Hillman is quite specific about what he means by soul and how it relates to both meaning and imagination:

> By soul I mean, first of all, a perspective rather than a substance, a viewpoint towards things rather than a thing itself.... It is as if consciousness rests upon a self-sustaining and imagining substrate ... the unknown component that makes meaning possible, turns events into experiences, is communicated in love, and has religious concern.
>
> (1976, p. xvi)

In addition to this basic understanding, Hillman views soul as essential to the process of "deepening of events into experiences," and the "imaginative possibility of our nature ... which recognizes all realities as primarily symbolic or metaphorical" (p. xvi). In my reading, soul is the imaginal aspect of our being that engages with the imaginal aspect of the world. Hillman felt this perspective had largely been lost in modernity, and it was the specific task of psychology (*psyche–logos*) to make space for its return. He laments the loss of the "middle position" between materiality and divinity in the Western tradition with which soul was historically associated. Bound to both physicality and to the abstractions of intellect and spirit, soul nevertheless maintained its own distinctive space. "By having its own realm, psyche has its own logic—psychology—which is neither a science of physical things nor a metaphysics of spiritual things" (1976, p. 68). It is rather for Hillman a primal engagement with imaginal meaning and meaning making.

In this discourse, individuation becomes "soul-making," a term Hillman adopts from the Romantic poet, John Keats: "Call the world, if you please, the 'Vale of Soul-Making.' Then you will find out the use of this world" (cited in Hillman, 1972, p. 120). To make soul is to engage the world on the soul level, to become intimate with images and meanings that encompass and drive human experience. It is an ongoing, self-reflective process: "Essential to soul-making is psychology-making, shaping concepts and images that express the needs of the soul as they emerge in each of us" (Hillman, 1976, p. xviii), and one that is available to us in every moment: "making soul means putting events through an imaginal process" (p. 189). Here the distinction between event and experience becomes important, where event is the collection of facts about what occurs, and experience is the complex meaning to be found in them. Davis (2005) summarizes:

> The essence of soul-making is in the total immersion in some aspect of life at the imaginative level until it is transformed from a simple history of an event into an experience with profound and deep significance for the one doing the imagining.
>
> (p. 177)

The chaos of circumstance is worked over in the imagination, discovering and synthesizing deeper meanings, transforming the data into an experience that becomes a part of who we are. This is the process of soul-making, or ensoulment.

Clearly, the concepts of soul and imagination are completely bound up in Hillman's psychology. "To live psychologically means to imagine things; to be in touch with soul means to live in sensuous connection to fantasy. To be in soul is the experience the fantasy of all realities and the basic reality of fantasy" (1976, p. 23). Like Jung, Hillman describes the organization of the imaginal psyche in terms of archetypes, which by their nature "throw us into an imaginative style of discourse ... let us then imagine archetypes as the deepest patterns of psychic functioning" (p. xix). And perhaps even more so than Jung, he looks to myth as an expression of the basic structures of psyche. "Myth lies vividly in our symptoms and fantasies and in our conceptual systems ... a fundamental tenet of archetypal psychology [is] the interchangeability of mythology and psychology. Mythology is a psychology of antiquity. Psychology is mythology of modernity" (Hillman, 1979b, p. 23). As with Nietzsche, the rational concepts of our linear minds are suspect of always covering something more primal. But where Nietzsche saw will to power, Hillman sees an underlying structure of mythic fiction—archetypal story. Thus, the mythology of a people speaks to the structure of their psychology, and our contemporary scientific psychology is a kind of modern myth we tell about ourselves.

Even after studying Hillman for years, I still have to remind myself, when confronted with an idea such as "psychology is mythology," that he doesn't mean it *literally*. And in fact, the deep-seated compulsion to translate all of this into neat, rational, conceptual relationships is precisely what Hillman is trying to get away from. "The imaginal does not explain; myths are not explanations … they are stories, as our fantasies are, which project us into participation with the phenomena they tell us about so that the need for explanation falls away" (1972, p. 202). That last part is vitally important and easily missed—rather than a literal explanation, story invites participation—a direct experience of the imaginal truth being expressed through fiction. The Hero's Journey described by Joseph Campbell is but one popular instance—in the end, we understand it because we have all experienced some aspect of it at some point in our lives. But there are countless others, once we tear away the scrim and engage the imaginal. Hillman reminds us that to do so is the most natural thing in the world. Imagination is both our birthright and our last resort. "The autonomy of fantasy is the soul's last refuge of dignity, its guarantor against all oppressions; it alone we can take with us into the barracks behind the barbed wire" (1976, p. 39). As long as we can imagine, some part of us will always be free.

It is not that we cannot find rational concepts to correlate with imaginal meaning we find; rather Hillman is pushing back against a long history of the imaginal being crushed entirely by reducing it to an abstraction of itself. Even Freud, the great pioneer, built a psychology around finding hidden meanings behind the image rather than honoring the multivalent meanings of the image itself. "The difference between Freud and Jung is the difference between allegory and metaphor … Metaphors are not subject to interpretative translation without breaking up their particular unity" (Hillman, 1994/1983, p. 35). In allegory, an image is a simple stand-in for a concept ("death" or "marriage" or "prosperity," etc.), while metaphors are unique analogies that do not have simple translations (it would be hard to literally translate the phrase "his heart was like a thousand suns" without losing something).

> We sin against the imagination whenever we ask an image for its meaning, requiring that images be translated into concepts. The coiled snake in the corner cannot be translated in my fear, my sexuality, or my mother-complex without killing the snake … rather than vivifying the imagination by connecting our conceptual intellects with the images of dreams and fantasies, they exchange the image for a commentary on it.
>
> (Hillman, 1976, p. 39)

The rational mind may balk—if we are not to interpret these images into rational concepts, then what are we supposed to do with them? Hasn't the whole point been to demonstrate that the imagination is a source of meaning?

Indeed, it has—but an image can shower us with meanings while still remaining itself an image. We can find meaning in flesh-and-blood human relationships without transforming our friends and partners into abstract concepts. It is no different with images—we seek knowledge through relationship with them, rather than the cold logical eye of objective observation. Hence the injunction to "stick to the image" (coined by Rafael Lopez-Pedraza), to engage the image as it appears and allow its autonomy, to follow it where it wills, not where we will it, acknowledging the complex source from which it springs (Hillman, 1983, p. 9). As we learn to honor the imaginal, to remain present with it in all its manifestation, we come to know ourselves. "This return the middle realm of fiction, of myth carries one into conversational familiarity with the cosmos one *inhabits*. Healing thus means return, and psychic consciousness means Conversation, and a 'healed consciousness' lives fictionally" (Hillman, 1994/1983, p. 80). But this process goes beyond a process of healing, for in the process of healing we have come into contact with the imaginal ground of our being. Hillman speaks of an *imaginal love*, a palpable sense of being loved by the images, "a love based wholly on relationship with images and through images ... when we love, we want to explore, to discriminate more and more widely, to extend the intricacy that extends the intimacy" (1979b, p. 197). It is an intimacy with the self, but also more than that—an intimacy with the cosmos as they have touched us most deeply.

A personified cosmos

Another essential move in Hillman's psychology is to engage the imagination by deliberately personifying its myriad manifestations. That is, as much as possible, to deliberately see and interact with the images as persons. Through personification we seek a means of a) "revifying our relations to the world around us," b) "meeting our individual fragmentation, our many rooms and many voices," and c) "furthering the imagination to show all its bright forms. Our desire is to save the phenomena of the imaginal psyche" (1976, p. 3). The focus shifts here from *what* we imagine—a tree or a centaur, say—to *how* we engage the images that meet us. Through personifying we actively deepen the imaginal experience by engaging the tree or centaur not as "just an image" but as a kind of person, a being with its own autonomy and agency, cable of interaction. For as long as we wall ourselves against the possibility of engaging the image of the centaur as a person, we have diminished our interaction with it before it has even begun. By choosing to view the centaur as person, we are giving it an opportunity to complexify and deepen—to surprise us with actions and attitudes and insights which our conscious ego would never have guess at. It is a truism among creative writers (and I count myself among them), that a work of fiction truly begins to take off when the characters take on a life of their own, saying and doing things that are sometimes in defiance of the author's initial intentions. I contend that Hillman is right—that this sort of engagement with imaginal persons is available to all of us, if we approach them with an open mind and a willingness to listen.

By allowing images to become persons, we allow them to take on greater particularity and detail, and thus greater significance:

> When an image is realized—fully imagined as a living being other than myself—then it becomes a psychopompos, a guide with a soul having its own inherent limitation and necessity. It is this image and no other, so that the conceptual questions of moral pluralism fade in front of the actual engagement with the image. The supposed creative pandemo-nium of the teeming imagination is limited to its phenomenal appear-ance in a particular image, that specific one that has come to me pregnant with significance and intention.
>
> (Hillman, 1994/1983, p. 62)

Hillman implies that the seeming chaos of the multitude of the psyche is an anxiety born from not engaging the images in their particularity, assuming a vague maelstrom of phantasms. But in keeping with the dictum to "stick to the image" this supposed pandemonium gives way to the particular, a specific encounter with a specific image that we may yet come to know more intimately. "When the complex is fully personified, I can perceive its specific qualities and yield to it the specific request it requires. In Lou Salome's sense, I am now able to love it" (1976, p. 34). To use a personal example: My past struggles with emotional eating can be easily abstracted into a conceptual neurotic disorder which then sticks to me like a rigid fact that seeks a solution outside of itself. Hillman instead suggests giving emo-tional eating a face, a voice, a personhood that can both speak and listen. I can see the wounded child trying to soothe his pain and loneliness with food, I can have compassion for him, and together, he and I may find a better way.

But again, for Hillman, engaging the imaginal is not merely a matter of "going within"—it is a way of engaging more fully in the life-world. "Personifying is a way of being in the world and experiencing the world as a psychological field" (1976, p. 13). What are the fields of meaning in which we find ourselves as we travel through our days, and how might we allow them to speak to us? The imaginal fictions that emerge in the process of de-literalizing can take on a face and a voice, if only we will allow it. "The world and the Gods are dead and alive according to the condition of our souls" (1976, p. 16). The car that breaks down on the way to the job interview, the beautiful persimmon tree in the back yard, the old shirt that you never liked but can't seem to throw away: if these were persons, what would they say? Freed from the strangeness of interpreting such personhood literally, the act of personifying enlivens the image and engenders a creative process of unfolding of meanings. The world becomes richer:

> Personifying not only aids discrimination, it also offers another avenue of loving, of imagining things in a personal form so that we can find access to them with our hearts ... personifying emotionalizes, shifts the discussion from nominalism to imagination, from head to heart.... Loving is a way of knowing, and for loving to know, it must personify. Personifying is thus a way of knowing, especially knowing what is invisible, hidden within the heart.
>
> (Hillman, 1976, pp. 14–15)

By giving soul back to the world, we are able to know and love the world that much more deeply. If we can suspend our conceptual judgments about a literalized Neoplatonic metaphysics, and instead allow ourselves to actively imagine what it would mean to live in the *Anima Mundi*—we may quickly discover the *Anima Mundi* all around us.

Conclusion

James Hillman concludes his seminal *Re-visioning psychology* by stating outright that this book must not be taken as a systematic theory. He insists that his ideas are but vessels for an ongoing process of soul-making, a process far more valuable than the ideas themselves:

> In this sense, all that is written in the foregoing pages is confessed to with passionate conviction, to be defended as articles of faith, and at the same time disavowed, broken, and left behind. By holding onto nothing, nothing holds back the movement of soul-making from its ongoing process.... And when the last image vanishes, all icons gone, the soul begins again to populate the stilled realms with figures and fantasies born of the imaginative heart.
>
> (1976, p. 229)

For all the moments where I disagree with Hillman, where I find him confounding or arrogant or hyper-critical, I cannot but admire a man with enough courage of conviction to conclude his own masterwork by offering it as a sacrifice back to the imaginal fire. It is not what has been imagined, but the ongoing soul-making of imagination that matters.

What better place to end, but in a place that recognizes no end, that celebrates the circularity of an ever-deepening process of soul-making? We have come to a place of wonder —an imaginal realm of beauty and awe and terror, an ontological landscape breathing with possibility. I ask myself: why not just stay here? Why go back down, into the depths of matter and the literalisms of science, to see how imagination lives in the laboratory? And yet that is the task at hand.

Proteus takes another face.

Part III

The neuroscience of imagination

With the phenomenon of imagination fully and richly invoked through the preceding chapters on history, philosophy, and psychology, we turn now to the realm of science to explore the neurobiological correlates of imagination. What does contemporary neuroscience have to say about the phenomenon we have been exploring thus far? Taking this turn, it must not be underestimated what a radical shift this presents in the nature of our understanding. The preceding chapters proceeded through fundamentally humanistic ground, digging into the progress of images and ideas that have aggregated around the Western concept of imagination. It has always been the task of the humanities to work with the complex wholes of human experience to help us understand what it means to be human. By turning these same ideas over to neuroscience, and seeking to understand them in biological terms, we might expect a massive and perhaps somewhat violent reduction.

As a natural science, neuroscience needs simple, clearly defined concepts that can be quantitatively measured in a laboratory setting. Phenomena that are too complex will have trouble fitting through the door and so we might expect most neurobiological data on the human imagination to be grounded in relatively simple mechanisms and understandings. Any larger synthesis of the neurobiology of imagination will be a largely theoretical process of re-assembling highly reduced streams of data after the fact. To date, such a grand synthesis on the topic of imagination has not taken place, at least not in a way that addresses the phenomenon in the broader sense of its humanistic meaning.

With this in mind, the following section inquires into the neurobiological correlates of imagination by examining its component parts. Chapter 6 on sense and image focuses on the phenomenon of mental imagery and how it correlates with brain processes. Of particular interest here is the relationship between sense perception and the mental construction of images when sense perception is absent. Chapter 7 shifts the exploration toward the neuroscience of narrative and story, where images unfold and interact over time. This brings us into a discussion of the neurobiological correlates of memory and how they relate to the process of imagining the future. Of particular interest here is a discussion of the default mode network of the brain, in which memory, prospection, and fantasy are intimately entangled. Chapter 8 looks into the creative generation of new images and stories both by proposing a spectrum between conscious creativity and the unconscious generation of dreams.

Chapter 6

Sense and image

This chapter takes up the basic question: how does neuroscience understand what is happening in the brain when we experience mental images? That is, when we close our eyes and perceive sights, sounds, smells, and touch without external stimulus, what is happening neurobiologically? The point of departure for this discussion will be visual images, both for the sake of brevity and because the visual cortex has been so thoroughly investigated by neuroscience. But mental images come in all forms—we can visualize a dragon, smell its sulfurous breath, feel the rough texture of its scaly skin, and hear its guttural voice. We might further imagine, via visceral sensation in our own bodies, the somatic–emotional state of the dragon: the dragon is very angry! We might even experience all of these sensory dimensions at once, engaging with the dragon in a multisensory imaginal space. The brain processes that correlate with the phenomenal experience of such rich "inner" imagery will be the focus in this chapter, before continuing on to a discussion of narrative and story in the next.

Recall from Chapter 3 the ancient debate between Plato and Aristotle over the nature of appearances. For Plato, information received by the senses was but a shadow of the ultimate reality, whereas for Aristotle, the impressions of the senses were the means to truth. In scientific materialism (and other forms of scientism), Aristotle's claims are taken to the extreme: only that which is given by the senses and measured by the senses is real. So what does neuroscience actually have to say about the senses? How do they relate to perception and to imagination? As it turns out, a discussion of the neuroscience of mental images is impossible without a discussion of the senses and sensation for two reasons. First, the mental image itself, as outlined above, has very much in common with a sense impression, except for the fact that it is not given by external sensory stimulus. When we imagine an apple, we are experiencing something very much like the sensory impression of an apple, only without actually receiving that information through the eyes. The second reason a discussion of the neurobiology of mental images requires a discussion of the senses is that many of the brain systems that process sense data are the very same systems that process mental images.

Sensation, perception, imagination

Sensation occurs when specialized sense-receptor cells in the body receive stimulation from the environment: patterns of photons hitting the retina, sound vibrations entering the ear, chemicals coming into contact with the nose and tongue, temperature, vibration, and the texture of external objects pressed against the receptors of the skin. This classic model of five senses can be expanded to include awareness of the internal state of the body, with specializing receptors sending information to the brain regarding the position and stretch of muscles (proprioception), and the variety of visceral–somatic sensations through which we experience our internal states (see Damasio, 1999). This ongoing flood of sensation flows as information through networks of nerve cells and eventually reaches the brain, which has the daunting task of sorting this raw data out. The outcome of all this information processing is *perception*: the world as we perceive it to be. In Presti's (2016) summation: "sensory perception may be divided into two basic components: (1) the collection of information from the environment ... (2) the analysis and interpretation of this information by the nervous system, contributing to the experience of mental states of perceptual awareness" (p. 125). Note that this is not an unmediated "mirror" scenario where perception is understood to be a perfect reflection of the outside world. The "analysis and interpretation" of the incoming sensory information suggests a process of *constructing* an experience out of the available sense data, an idea that will be further explored throughout this chapter.

The question of how sensory information flowing into and being processed by the brain could somehow give rise to a conscious experience is a vexing philosophical question. A computer, for example, also processes vast amounts of information, but most of us do not assume our laptops and smartphones to be having conscious experiences of the information they process. Recently, Chalmers (2002) has popularized the notion that there is a "hard problem" and an "easy problem" with regard to consciousness and the brain. The "hard problem" was just stated above: how any amount of information processing, no matter how complex, would ever give rise to a conscious experience. What is the factor that makes data processing a first-person phenomenon rather the simply unconscious data processing such as we see in computers? Though many neuroscientists and philosophers feel there must be a material, biological cause for consciousness in the brain, there is as yet neither concrete evidence nor sufficient arguments for this position. Skeptics with regard to the "hard question" doubt if traditional objective science will ever be able to answer the question adequately. The "easy problem" on the other hand, is a simpler matter of tracking how information processing in the brain matches up or correlates with conscious experience. Another way of putting this is that the easy problem looks at how the brain constructs the various *contents* of consciousness, rather than the phenomenon of consciousness itself. Here too, the visual system is a great point of departure. We now know a great deal about how visual information is received and processed in the nervous system, and how that information converges with other information streams in the brain to influence perception and behavior.

The following discussion of sensation, perception, and imagination (and indeed, the rest of the chapters in this section) will focus on the "easy problem" of how the contents of consciousness correlate with specific kinds of brain activity. The following discussion of mental imagery begins with a review of visual perception, tracking how visual information is received and processed by the nervous system before converging into multisensory perception. This will be followed by an account of how this process changes when we do it with our eyes closed, and perceive images without sensory input.

The visual system

The following account of the visual system is a general summation of established neuroscientific knowledge, drawn from Goldstein (2001), LeDoux (2002), and Presti (2016). There is of course a vast amount of physiological minutia involved in these and all brain processes, but for the sake of focus and clarity in navigating the complex topic of imagination, I have chosen to keep my perspective physiologically broad rather than deep.

The eyes are sense organs specifically adapted to detecting electromagnetic energy in the environment in the form of light. The "visible spectrum" detected by our eyes is actually quite narrow in the full range of the electromagnetic energies that exist in our universe. Many birds and insects, for example, have eyes that detect ultraviolet light, and some snakes have special sensory organs sensitive to the infrared range; and even these animals, so far as we know, cannot see the wider electromagnetic spectrum spanning gamma rays to radio waves. Similarly, our tri-chromatic visual experience of three primary colors, enabled by specific sense receptors for those colors, presumably offers us a less visually nuanced experience than that of some birds that have tetra-chromatic visual systems. Thus, however good our vision is, it is not comprehensive in its detection of electromagnetic wavelengths, and only provides us a specific and limited visual perspective as human beings. This holds true for all of our senses; they are each imperfect windows into a more complex reality.

The retinas of our eyes contain specialized sense-receptor cells with unique sensitivity to this narrow band of electromagnetic energy entering the eyeball. When stimulated by energy of a certain wavelength, each of these receptors sends a signal to the brain. A variety of specialized receptors are activated in response to specific colors (cones) and brightness (rods), which in tandem trigger electrical signals transmitted to the brain via the optic nerve. In each eye, about a hundred million light-receptor cells are reduced to about a million axons' (nerve fibers) worth of information. Of these, about ten percent go to a structured named the superior colliculus, which is involved in unconscious "first response" reactions to environmental stimulus (i.e., unconsciously shifting your gaze to get a better look when you see a shadow in the corner of your eye). The other 90 percent of the optic nerve's axons terminate in the thalamus, which among other things acts as a sensory relay station between the body and the higher sensory processing of the cerebral cortex. In the lateral geniculate nuclei of the thalamus, the optic nerves synapse. At the synaptic juncture, the electrical signals being sent from the eyes are converted into chemical messengers (neurotransmitters), and passed on to new set of neurons, which in response send a new series of electrical signals to the visual cortex.

This stream of electrical impulses is received in the primary visual area (V1) of the occipital lobe, where the general contours of the incoming visual data are mapped out in a topographical way. That is, the pattern of activation of neurons in the primary visual area actually looks like a rough projection of aspects of the visual field itself: objects closer together in the visual field of the retina activate neurons that are closer together in the primary visual area. If an area of this part of the cortex is damaged, the corresponding location in the visual field will have a blind spot. Accordingly, LeDoux (2002) refers to this area as a "projection cortex" because the incoming visual data is actually projected onto it as patterns of nerve activation. Kosslyn, Thompson, and Ganis (2006) refer to this area of topographical mapping as the "visual buffer." The initial stage of visual processing appears to be primarily concerned with discrimination of edges and contours, and at this stage is not yet a complete visual experience.

From here, the incoming sense data is farmed out to more than 30 adjacent visual areas to process various specific aspects of the visual field. Visual area 4 (V4) for example, has cells that activate in response to specific color stimulations, and thus processes color in the visual field, whereas V5 appears to process the movement and speed of visual phenomena. Although these additional visual areas have specific processing tasks, they are all also highly interconnected, sending information to each other in both directions (Presti, 2016). In this way, the brain takes what are essentially a series of electrical impulses from the eyes and uses them to generate the complex perceptual experience that we call vision: mental images representing the external world.

As the mental imagery begins to take shape, information is sent out of the visual cortex in two divergent streams, often referred to as the "what" and "where" streams. The "what" stream, also called the "ventral" stream, runs from the occipital lobe into the temporal lobe, where it appears to be responsible for object identification: "what am I looking at?" The "where" stream, also known as the "dorsal stream," is involved in placing objects or aspects of objects in relation to each other in space. Here in the "where" stream of the parietal cortex, vision is integrated into multisensory processing of the environment. The question of how all this information could come together into a unified experience is known as the "binding problem," and it is not entirely unrelated to the question of consciousness. What is clear is that multiple sensory modalities converge and integrate in the posterior parietal lobe, generating maps of space, or spatial images.

Multisensory processing

The study of perception historically proceeded by reducing the senses into discrete channels of modal-specific information processing: visual, auditory, olfactory, etc. During the early days of neuroscience, this approach was quite successful in identifying dedicated circuits involved in each of these sensory modalities. However, proceeding this way may have unwittingly also created a false impression among brain scientists and philosophers that the senses are entirely discrete channels that only converge in the final stages of perception. Recent research into multisensory processing in the brain has turned this assumption on its head.

In fact, multisensory processing does not only occur as a final integration of sense modalities after they have been processed separately—multisensory processing appears to occur at several levels throughout the sensory–perceptual process. The lower level cortical areas, which first receive sense data at the beginning of cortical processing, also receive cross-model connections from each other (Falchier, Cappe, Barone, & Schroeder, 2012), as if raw visual data is being cross-referenced with raw auditory and sensorimotor data even before shapes, color, and motion are fully processed. Some degree of multisensory processing also occurs at the pre-cortical level, most famously the brainstem's superior colliculus, responsible for non-conscious, quick response to warning signals of potential dangers (Mchaffie et al., 2012). Even more surprising is that the thalamus itself (which is the central relay station between raw incoming sense data and the dedicated sense-processing areas of the cortex), also shows some degree of multisensory activity (Hackett, 2012). Taken together, it appears that incoming information from the senses exhibits multisensory connectivity on the full spectrum from non-conscious primitive apprehension to fully conscious immersive world-representation. In reviewing the recent explosion of research on this topic, Meredith (2012) concludes, "multisensory convergence is so ubiquitous that is seems remarkable that unisensory percepts are present at all" (p. 5). This somewhat astounding conclusion challenges both established neuroscience doctrine and much common sense about the phenomenology of perception.

To explain this, Stein (2012) argues that robust multisensory processing in the brain has an adaptive function: because each individual sense modality is prone to error, multisensory processing allows for a system of neurological checks and balances about the environment at large. The incoming data from one modality can be checked against another so as to create a more accurate map of what is really happening in the environment (p. xiii). Perhaps because neuroscience has proceeded largely by reductionistic methods, it has historically been inclined to assume the brain also operates reductionistically: in this case, one discrete sense at a time. As we are all then culturally trained to define and understand the senses as separate, this cultural framework likely influences our phenomenological perception as well—in other words, a cultural indoctrination into unisensory processing shapes our experience of the world.

If generating mental images involves the recruitment of sensory-processing areas of the brain, as will be evidenced below, then the question of unisensory or multisensory perception also becomes a question of imagination. If the cultural operating system demands that we only imagine in one sense modality at a time, it will make for a less dynamic imaginal phenomena. Likewise, reductive studies that only look at one small aspect of an imagined sensory image exclude the possibility that such an image might occur in a rich multisensory context. Indeed, I would hypothesize that those individuals throughout history who have written with such depth and beauty about the imaginal realms are those for whom imaginal processes recruited as much of the brain's multisensory apparatus as possible.

Most discussion of multisensory processing to date has been concerned with those higher areas of the cortex associated with the final levels of integration of sensory information. In particular, the posterior parietal lobe is recognized as the region of the brain that integrates multi-modal sensory inputs into spatial maps of the environment. Kosslyn et al. (2006) write: "the brain also uses depictive representations to specify information about the location of the objects in space. These representations are primarily in the posterior parietal lobes" (p. 18). These multisensory spatial maps are referred to by Kosslyn and others as *spatial images*, as distinguished from simpler *object images* that exist as a representation of a single sensory modality.

In studying spatial processing in both blind and sighted people Noordzij and Postma (2012) conclude that both groups are capable of forming spatial images as mental representations of the physical world, and that these representations contain specific information about both relative and metric distances between objects. For the blind, these spatial images are woven together from auditory and haptic sensory modalities, constructing a spatial environment through a combination of sound, touch, and motor imagery. In general, "these spatial images are presumed to have supramo-dal qualities in the sense that they rely on modality-specific brain areas [e.g. touch, vision, etc. ...] ... and also on supramodal areas, which are acti-vated independent of the original input channel" (p. 164). Whereas sighted individuals often rely heavily on the visual modality for constructing spatial images, these images are fundamentally multisensory affairs that can be constructed entirely without visual data when necessary. This model also makes room for supramodal information: abstract or propositional language-based components at work in organizing the imagery into a spatial whole.

Joseph LeDoux (2002) notes that both the multisensory processing areas of the posterior parietal lobes and the "what" temporal stream of object recognition each connect richly with the prefrontal cortex (PFC). The PFC is thought to be the seat of executive action and decision making, so this connectivity with sensory integration areas suggest that this is the final representation of the external world being presented for executive analysis and action. According to this model, the PFC receives detailed information about the what and where of the environment, and can respond (at the most basic level, initiate movement) accordingly.

But here again we find a two-way street: information does not only flow from sensory-processing areas to the executive prefrontal cortex—it also flows back in the other direction. LeDoux interprets this reversed flow: "executive control signals that help keep attention focused on the object that is represented in the workspace" (p. 183). If I understand LeDoux correctly, this directed attention in the workspace of mental sense-images would be a function distinct from the motor controls that, say, train the eye on a particular object in the visual field. This is not about shifting focus to something else in the outside world, but shifting focus within to perceive selected aspects of sensory experience in more detail. Certainly, the motor control of the eyes and internal directed attention at inner sense-images would often work in tandem. But the greater implication of this two-way communication between sensation and attention suggests that perception of sensory material as internal imagery in itself involves a top-down, willful mediation. If so, this would be yet another way our perception of the world cannot be taken as a perfect mirror of what lies outside of our nervous systems; what we perceive as reality in any given moment is heavily mediated by selective attention.

Is perception imagery?

My decision to speak of sensory perceptions as "imagery" is not entirely uncontroversial. LeDoux uses the word *representation* rather than *image* in his discussion of perception, and different neuroscientists and philo-sophers have different opinions on the matter. Rodolfo Llinas (2001) uses an image-based model of perception explicitly: "the images in our head are only a representation of the world.... The brain is a set of coordinate systems that measure or recognize abstract geometries that do not exist in the external world" (p. 109). On the other hand, Bennet and Hacker (2003) reject outright the notion that perceptions are constructed by the brain, and describe perception instead as a simple relationship between an object and perceiver. "Perception is not in our heads at all" any more than the supposition that "Jack running faster than Jill takes place in Jack" (p. 128). This includes the argument that the qualities of an object, for example its color, are not experiential properties but instead actually inhere in the object itself. Not surprisingly, Bennet and Hacker also reject the notion that imagination should be understood primarily in terms of mental images, adhering to a propositional model whereby any mental images are ancillary.

Presti (2016) describes this position—that our perceptions are a perfect fit for reality—as *naïve realism*. Naïve realism is an epistemic stance that assumes "what we perceive is identical to what actually exists in the world" (p. 127). There is considerable evidence against this position. For example, the fact that not all humans can see three colors, and that some animals apparently see more colors than humans, complicates the question of color being inherent in the object itself. How can the color red be "in" the apple if the colorblind man can't see red? Solms offers an even more common example in the "blind spot" that all humans share where the optic nerve enters the retina: were our visual perception a perfect mirror, we would expect a hole in our visual field, but our brain instead conveniently fills in the blank with a "best guess" for what's there (Solms & Turnbull, 2002, p. 156). Even more convincing are cases of damage to specific areas of the cortex resulting in radically different perceptual experiences: damage to V4 results in a loss of motion perception, so that visual reality becomes a succession of still images; damage to the fusiform gyrus in the temporal lobe disrupts the ability to recognize faces. Add to this the level of filtering and processing outlined above: a relatively small spectrum of visible light stimulation is reduced to a pattern of electrical impulses which synapse chemically before entering the elaborately interconnected regions of the visual cortex, where it is further mediated by selective attention and memory—a multi-step process of filtration, translation, and interpretation that ostensibly takes place before perception of any object or environment becomes conscious!

In the case of "Jack running faster than Jill" taking place inside of Jack, recall the discussion of first, second, and third-person perspectives from Chapter 2. From the third-person "objective" perspective, of course this event is not happening inside of Jack, but rather takes place in the environment that Jack and Jill share. Yet it is not a contradiction to assert that at the same time "Jack running faster than Jill" is also indeed taking place inside of Jack as a conscious perceptual experience—and inside of Jill as well. So too, we may recognize and measure some third-person objective properties of an apple that account for why it is usually interpreted as red instead of blue (i.e., the properties of the object that cause it to reflect a certain wavelength of light). But the "redness" itself is a first-person experiential phenomenon, and furthermore a phenomenon that is not available to all human visual systems.

The notion that perception is constructed based on the ongoing interpretation of available sense data does not deny the external world, it only acknowledges that our experience of that world is partial, imperfect, and mediated. Recall Alfred Korzybski's famous maxim: "A map is not the territory it represents, but, if correct, has a similar structure to the territory which accounts for its usefulness" (2010/1948, p. 24). Korzybski was speaking about the limits of language, but the idea can also be applied to human perception: the brain generates maps of reality based on incoming sense data. Those perceptual maps that we experience from moment to moment are not extra-sensory reality in-itself, but if the maps are correct, they will share enough structural similarity to key aspects of that external reality so as to be *useful*. Our sensory perceptions are models constructed for navigating and experiencing the environment, and certainly sometimes having a good map is a matter of life or death. Nevertheless, the map is a reduction of reality, a "best guess" representation made up of images; the reality of the environment in-itself will always be more than we can perceive.

In any case, the issue remains a topic of debate in both neuroscience and philosophy. The relationship between sensation, perception, and imagination is not a foregone conclusion and may be contested for generations to come. The question of how sensation and imagination might become blended in human experience will be discussed further below. But before exploring how imagination might intersect and even become integrated with the perception of external reality, it is important to first look at what happens in the brain when we experience mental images without any direct sensory input whatever.

Mental images

Stephen M. Kosslyn has been researching mental imagery in the brain for four decades, and much of the literature on the neuroscience of mental images is at least partially derivative from his work. Generally speaking, Kosslyn and his colleagues have offered a model whereby perception in the brain is largely a process of constructing sensory images, and that in turn constructing purely mental images without sense data makes use of the same basic brain systems. The chief opponent of Kosslyn's model is Zenon Pylyshyn, who argues for a propositional approach to imagery: that the brain stores and processes descriptions, rather than mental images per se. This somewhat esoteric debate is really more a question of the "format" of visual information in the brain (i.e., descriptive or depictive); Pylyshyn acknowledges the experience of mental images but asserts that they are not "real" because the brain does not process information via pictures. Because Kosslyn's model affirms a central role for mental imagery in the brain, I will draw primarily on his research.

In *The case for mental imagery*, Kosslyn et al. (2006), put forth a model for mental imagery in the brain that begins with the visual system. Recall that incoming sense data from the optic nerve is projected topographically onto V1, here called the "visual buffer." As the visual cortex constructs the image, information travels along the temporal "what" pathway and dorsal "where" pathway (here called "object-properties processing" and "spatial-properties processing," respectively). From here, "outputs from both of these subsystems feed into associative memories. These outputs allow associative memory to specify links among representations, creating a propositional description of an object or scene" (p. 139). If the incoming visual information matches a stored representation, it then gains access to all the information associated with that representation, thus generating layers of associative meaning for the perception. Strictly speaking their model here refers to basic identifying information (tree, large, Cyprus, beautiful, old), but given the highly interconnect nature of the cortex, it seems fair to hypothesize that associations may go beyond basic semantic meanings. Thus we might imagine that the image of the giant Cyprus tree stumbled upon while hiking deep in the canyon associates to the ancient Oak in your Grandmother's backyard, invoking family, comfort, wisdom, mystery, decay, and perhaps a sense of menace, all at once. There may be multiple associations in addition to Grandma's Oak as well. Kosslyn and colleagues further postulate that if the incoming object cannot be identified in memory, then the "best matching representation in long-term associative memory is treated as a hypothesis about the viewed object" (2006, p. 139). If we don't know what a thing is, the brain makes an educated guess and we perceive that guess as reality until further information comes into play. Thus the process of forming perceptual mental images is inherently engaged with an ongoing and imperfect process of memory-based meaning making.

In this model the formation of purely mental images, sans sensory input, is simply a matter of reversing the flow of information through the system. To generate a non-sensory mental image, abstracted, propositional information stored in memory is used to "generate mental images in topographically organized areas" (Kosslyn et al., 2006, p. 142). In other words, abstract data from memory is projected onto the visual buffer (V1) where the raw data is processed into visual imagery as if it were sense data. The process of generating these mental images is essentially the same as in sensory perception, except that the raw data is now coming internally from memory rather than externally from the optic nerve. In each case, the visual cortex is interpreting the data to generate imagery as a content of consciousness. This is a somewhat astounding turn: that many of the same brain systems are used for both external sense perception and internally generated mental images. Imagination and perception are not thus entirely distinct, but rather function across a spectrum of shared systems.

Once the mental image has been called up from memory and unpacked into the visual buffer, it can then be scanned via focused attention in the same manner as a perceptual image. "Imaged patterns are recognized by matching the input to store visual memories in the object-properties-processing subsystem, just as is done during perception" (Kosslyn et al., 2006, p. 144). After a mental image has been generated from memory, this visual information can then flow back into the object identification pathway to explore (and thus generate) further details. For example, imagining your pet cat sitting on a log, and then "zooming in" on the image to examine the cat's face specifically. This process is essential to examining and defining any spatial aspects to the image, including the distances between component parts of an image. We engage this function every time we try to estimate spatial relations, for example, imagining what pieces of furniture will fit in our living rooms.

The model also includes a limited discussion of "transforming" the image, although this is strictly constrained by simple experimental design, and as such is entirely limited to "rotating" mental images in the mind as if they were physical objects. Interestingly, subjects who imagine rotating or manipulating the objects themselves showed activity in the motor cortex of the brain, while those imagining the object rotating or being manipulated by an external force did not (Kosslyn et al., 2006, p. 146). Here too, to imagine moving the body is to activate the part of the brain that correlates with movement.

In an earlier paper published in *Neuroscience*, Kosslyn and colleagues (2001) review the wider scientific literature on mental imagery, and conclude that that there is ample evidence to support the argument that in general mental images are generated in the same systems of the brain that process sense perception. "Mental imagery draws on much of the same neural machinery as perception in the same modality, and can engage mechanisms used in memory, emotion, and motor control" (p. 635). While these systems are not identical, there is ample evidence to demonstrate significant overlap between perception and imaging not only in the visual system, but in the auditory and motor systems as well. The areas of the brain that activate during mental imagery are generally the corresponding areas that would activate in sensory perception for similar types of objects. Thus, we imagine sound with the same part of the brain that we hear it, and imagine touch and movement with the same areas that would light up during the experience of actual physical activity. In another example, O'Craven and Kanwisher (2000) found that imagining faces activates the fusiform face area (FFA), and imagining places activates the parahippo- campal place area (PPA), in similar ways to what has been found in sensory perception of those respective objects. Likewise, the PPA is not activated when imagining faces, and the FFA is not activated when imagining places. Taken in tandem, it would not be unreasonable to conclude that the per- ceptual systems and imaging systems of the brain are largely shared.

In a recent comprehensive review, Zimmer (2012) affirms the conclu- sion that mental images are generated in modal-specific sensory-processing areas, but also notes that activation of the primary sensory level is not always strictly necessary: "on the contrary, visual images of objects can be generated at different levels of abstraction (resolution), and they are pro- vided by different neural structures, depending on the content" (p. 68). This certainly helps to account for the fact that some individuals experi- ence vivid and immersive imagery while others (perhaps those more linguistically-minded) experience more vague and abstract representations. The difference seems to be the degree to which the brain recruits its own perceptual circuitry to create a rich, inner-sensory experience.

Mental images and meaning

Having identified some of the basic mechanisms of image-generation in the brain, the next task is to investigate the various ways in which that mental imagery might be considered meaningful. As outlined in Chapter 1, this book is primarily an investigation into the generation of meaningful images, where meaning is qualified as existing on spectrum of greater or lesser dynamism and depth. The simplest form of meaning for a given image may be its semantic label: the word or words used to describe it. But in the human experience, meaning can go far beyond this to include the personal, the emotional, and the symbolic.

The evolutionary case for meaningful mental images

Where in the evolutionary line did imagery first become useful? Neuro- scientist Rodolfo Llinas (2001) argues that even prior to vertebrate evo- lution, the first appearance of multi-cellular animals capable of motility (self-directed motion through the environment) necessitated a system for predicting the outcome of those movements. These predictions of how and where to move required the first simple neural networks for processing sense data. The capacity for movement, Llinas argues, is what initially dis- tinguished early animals, with primitive nervous systems, from plants, which do not actively move around their environments and do not have nervous systems. His famous example is the "sea squirt" *Ascidiacea*, which in its larval stage swims freely and has a simple 300-neuron nervous system, as well as the basic sensory capacity to detect light. But once *Ascidiacea* reaches adult form—a motionless blob filtering seawater attached to a rock—it actually digests the majority of its own nervous system, which is now superfluous to its needs. Movement through an environment, plus limited sense data from primitive receptors, required informational sensory processing that could order and form "an internal reckoning—a transient sensorimotor image—of what might be outside" (p. 18). Thus, the basis of even the most rudimentary perception was a kind of image-making, where images were used as tools for predicting and navigating the external world. The primordial function of imagery, in this model, was to allow organisms to make basic predictions for the outcomes of their actions.

Presti (2016) offers a similar evolutionary perspective, arguing that as nervous systems became more complex, they were able to create more complex representations of the environment:

> Sophisticated sentience goes along with nervous systems that conduct sufficiently sophisticated analysis of sensory information. These sensory analyses are used to construct mental models—of the environment, of other individuals, of oneself—that have adaptive utility, by enriching understanding of and ability to navigate through the world.
>
> (p. 259)

Evolution is thus not only a process of physical adaptation to the environment, but also of increasingly complex nervous systems to generate broader, more comprehensive, and more nuanced internal images as representational tools for successfully navigating that environment. By this standard, the more evolved species is not marked by primarily physical prowess, but by the utility of its image-generating capacities.

Coming to our immediate ancestors, Goodwyn (2012) also takes an evolutionary approach with regards to imagery and meaning. Given the basic evolutionary premise that the brain evolved to maximize fitness, it seems unlikely that noisy, meaningless images would be a winning evolutionary game. With homo sapiens especially, evolutionary success became wrapped up in social success, so that the kind of mental imagery favored by evolution would thus maximize social navigation. One clear example of an innate brain capacity for meaningful imagery is the ability to recognize faces and read emotional facial expressions—a capacity shared across cultures, even among the blind. Goodwyn suggests a kind of innate imagery at work in "the ability of the brain to recognize and/or reliably and spontaneously organize facial data into these expressions and link it to specific affects perceptually" (p. 142). Like a Kantian category or a Jungian archetype, the in-born capacity of the fusiform facial area to read faces and facial expressions is an evolutionary adaptation, an innate disposition to engage with specific kinds of sensory images. Goodwyn expands this argument to suggest the human capacity for producing meaningful symbolic imagery to navigate complex and ambiguous realities is also a winning evolutionary strategy. The emergence of new symbols in individuals and cultures might well be adaptive responses to complex social issues "more often than they would be random and meaningless, since brains that waste valuable resources (such as conscious processing) generating meaningless imagery would likely be selected out over evolutionary time" (p. 166). Our brain's capacity for symbolic imagery, then, can be understood as an adaptive tool for engaging the complexities of a rapidly evolving human society.

Taken in tandem, from ancient sea squirt larva all the way up to modern humans, the capacity to generate images that map the world, and to encode those images with varying levels of meaning, is a process essential to surviving and thriving on planet Earth. At the most basic level, this "meaning" might be a simple binary: approach/retreat, move left/right or up/down, eat/ignore etc. But as we move up the evolutionary ladder to more complex nervous systems, the meanings of mental imagery can take on emotional, semantic, symbolic, and even spiritual dimensions.

Image and emotion

Affective neuroscientist Jaak Panksepp (1998) has mapped out a basic emotional brain system ostensibly shared by all mammals, from mice and men to bats and elephants. It was Darwin (2005b/1872) who first suggested an evolutionary continuity of emotion from animals to humans, but Panksepp has proposed a model of specific brain circuits that correlate neurophysiological states and behaviors: fear, rage, lust, care, play, seeking, and panic/grief. In this model, emotions are understood as physiological and behavioral responses to environmental and social stimulus. Fear and rage, for example, are complex physiological processes whereby the body of an organism is primed for certain kinds of behavior, in this case, running or attacking. This would suggest that emotional evaluation—the felt sense of what is happening in response to social and environmental circumstances—is one of the earliest forms of meaning making. If this is true, we would expect the expression of emotional meaning through images to be deeply engrained in the structure of our brains.

Indeed, this account is not unlike Antonio Damasio's (1999) theory of self-awareness. According to Damasio, "the feeling of what happens" that makes up our "core consciousness" is the result of visceral–emotional data traveling from body to brain, and linking to representational images of the present circumstances.

> The images of knowing, assisted by memory and reasoning, form the basis for simple nonverbal inferences which strengthen the process of

core consciousness. These inferences reveal, for instance, the close linkage between the regulation of life and the processing of images which is implicit in the sense of individual perspective.

(p. 183)

Damasio distinguishes this "core self" from the "autobiographical self"—our personal stories about who we are. This is not to diminish the importance of autobiographical self with its more semantic and narrative-based meanings (see below), but rather to acknowledge that prior to these elaborations there is a more primal consciousness that is embodied, emotional, and imagistic.

Thus we would expect ample evidence that mental imagery and emotion are fundamentally linked in the brain, and this is indeed the case. Kosslyn and colleagues (2001) review the literature on mental imagery and conclude that "imagery of emotional events activates the autonomic nervous system and the amygdala ... visualizing an object has much the same effects on the body as actually seeing the object" (p. 641). Since then the evidence has only mounted. In a recent study of Alexithymia (e.g., chronic lack of emotional awareness), Peasley-Miklus and Panayiutou (2016) robustly confirmed earlier findings that emotionally arousing mental imagery causes a measurable increase in heart rate and skin conductivity. Suess and Rahman (2015) found that imagining faces with various emotional expressions involved similar brain activation patterns to visually being shown faces with such expressions. Likewise, Shafir, Stephan, Atkinson, Scott, and Zubieta (2013) found that simply imagining movements (i.e., motor images) generically associated with various emotional states produced an increase of affect, suggesting that such motor images can be used as a tool for emotional regulation. Whereas in a study of clinically dysregulated behaviors (i.e., self-harming), Cloos, Weßlau, Steil, and Höfling (2016) found that these behaviors correlated with both maladaptive emotional regulation and reports of intense, distressing imagery. On a more positive note, Arnaud (2013) found that mental imagery was more effective than verbal processing in producing both positive and negative emotional states, and thus argues for the use of mental imagery as a clinical therapeutic tool.

Thus, there is a strong case for a deep connection between affect and imagery in the brain. Emotional states are likely to be expressed as (or at the very least, to influence) mental images, and consciously working with mental images has a reciprocal capacity to influence emotional states. On a primal level, images have a capacity to carry emotional meaning even before language comes into play.

Imagery, meaning, and memory

Meaning expressed through language and logic is generally referred to as semantic meaning. When we remember linguistic and logical content in relation to an image or idea (i.e., "mice are mammals") we are engaging semantic memory. This is distinct from episodic or autobiographical memory, in which we remember events and episodes in relation to our lives (see Chapter 7). Semantic memory, by contrast, identifies images and their related linguistic labels. This turns out to be a process deeply related to basic perception, for as soon as we perceive a familiar face we have likely engaged semantic memory: "that is my friend Joy standing in the grocery store line." Without semantic memory, we would not be able to linguistically identify joy, nor would we be able to linguistically identify "standing," grocery," or "line." Another way of thinking about semantic memory is that it stores objective facts about the world, rather than personal experiences. It is arguable that some facts might be encoded imagistically—for example, that objects fall when dropped can be remembered as a general principle through images of objects dropping, without necessarily involving language. But that interesting possibility aside, "semantic memory" is generally understood as retained information and knowledge about the world.

Sematic memory is what gets accessed in the "what" (or ventral) stream of information processing that links incoming sense data with concrete identities and thus recognizing them as objects. This relationship appears to work both ways, with visual processing areas of the cortex lighting up in response to recognizable nouns, so that the word triggers the associated visual image (Federmeier, Segal, Lombrozo, & Kutas, 2000; Pulvermuller, Lutzenberger, & Preiss, 1999). Solms and Turnbull (2002) argue that not only does semantic memory serve as a linguistic reference for perceptual experience, but it also has the capacity to shape it. Early development in children involves experience and learning literally shaping the brain's perceptual apparatus, so that "deeply encoded and abstract knowledge derived from these early learning experiences comes to govern the perceptual processes. We therefor see what we expect to see" (p. 155). Development into adulthood involves building neural associations and circuits that filter and interpret incoming sense data accurately, and these circuits can be shaped both by experience and cultural education. This means the model of reality we settle on early in life can profoundly influence our perceptions in adulthood. "We adults *project* our expectations (the products of our previous experience) onto the world all the time, and in this way we largely *construct* rather than perceive (in the simple sense) the world around us" (Solms & Turnbull, 2002, p. 155). Indeed, Solms believes that one of the principle aims of psychotherapy is to help individuals update their internal models of reality, so that they can experience the present rather than remain trapped in the painful past, constantly re-experiencing old limitations and wounds.

Solms is reviving a very old and very persistent philosophical idea: that we see the world not as it is, but as we are. This was hinted at by Plato, philosophically expounded in detail by Kant, and given psychological life in the writings of Freud and Jung. If imagination is made up of meaningful images arising in consciousness, and the brain constructs its imperfect representations and models of reality using meaningful images, it is only a short step to conclude that our reality is always at least partially imagined. And indeed, this is what Kant alluded to by suggesting imagination held the key role in synthesizing human perception into a coherent experience. Phenomenologist David Abram (1996) takes this a step further, asserting that imagination is in fact an extension of the senses:

> Imagination is not a separate mental faculty (as we so often assume) but is rather the way the senses themselves have of throwing themselves beyond what is immediately given, in order to make tentative contact with the other sides of things that we do not sense directly, with the hidden or invisible aspect of the sensible.
>
> (p. 58)

This blending of sense and image becomes a pragmatic tool for navigating the world. Imagination is here understood not merely as something unreal within us, but as a faculty for deeply engaging the world.

From an evolutionary perspective, we would expect some serious constraints on this process: imagining a predator as a literal mate or a cloud as a literal bridge over a precipice would quickly prove a genetic dead-end. But recalling Yuval Harari's (2016) provocative thesis that most human experience relies on shared fictional realities, the possibilities expand considerably. Imaginal maps and models would still be constrained by their survival value, but in the human world where so much of survival is mediated by social considerations, the primary constraints on the imagination of reality become culturally mediated. Beyond survival, what types of imaginings are culturally tolerated, celebrated, or taboo? This fascinating question has important implications for how we understand neuroscience itself, but that discussion will be taken up later in Part IV.

Suffice to say for now that insofar as we reject naïve realism as essentially unrealistic, we must consider the degree to which perception itself is a quasi-imaginal process largely shaped by memory. Presti (2016) offers a similar valuation of the role of memory in human perception and meaning, although his approach is a bit more holistic:

> All past experience plays an essential role in determining present and future patterns of activation generated by incoming sensory signals ...

This provides a substrate for knowledge and meaning; meaning is constructed from the multitudes of linked associations that have been acquired through the entirety of one's past experiences. Meaning is a whole-body experience, and its foundation is memory.

(p. 230)

Meaning is here understood as emerging from the richness of associations attached to a given image or idea. These associations may link to other images, words, emotions, stories, past experiences, or imagined goals. In a grand sense, memory becomes the repository of all of these connections, and in this way memory would also serve as a grand reservoir for imaginative activity. Jung's idea of "impregnating" [*betrachten*] an image with focused attention might be understood like this: to stay focused on the image long enough that it becomes animated by its own rich network of associations. The point is not to find a singular semantic meaning, but to allow the associative dynamics of multiple meanings to experientially interact with each other.

From virtual reality to *Anima Mundi*

Based on the foregoing discussion, I will conclude this chapter by sketching a model for understanding the relationship between perception and imagination in the brain that ties back into Hillman's concept of the *Anima Mundi*. This model begins with the premise that naïve realism is untenable, and that our perceptual experiences are the result of incoming sense data that has been heavily filtered, pared-down, and interpreted prior to emerging into conscious awareness. Bracketing the unresolved hard problem of consciousness, it nonetheless appears that the nervous system is doing its best job to generate, or simulate, an accurate representation of the physical world for the conscious mind to experience and navigate. In evolutionary terms, survival depends on the accuracy of this simulation—but the simulation nevertheless remains a pared-down and approximated representation of "external" reality. The brain and nervous system are doing their best to interpret the raw data in such a way as to keep us alive and thriving, but the process is still vulnerable to both error and omission.

Rodolfo Llinas (2001) has come to similar conclusions about the relationship of the brain to the external physical world. In his words, the nervous system is best understood as a reality emulator. "In other words, brain activity is a metaphor for everything else. Comforting or disturbing, the fact is that we are basically dreaming machines the construct virtual models of the real world" (p. 94). This might be called the "virtual reality" model of the brain, a phrase that draws on the fantasy that some day computers will be able to simulate and immerse us in virtual realms, similar to or even indistinguishable from physical reality. In this model, the brain is the virtual reality machine, simulating (or in Llinas' words, emulating) the external world to the best of its ability. J. Allen Hobson, who spent a life-time researching the neurobiology of dreams, began to use similar language late in his career: "the brain prepares itself for perception of the outside world by first creating an internal model. I call that model a virtual reality program for the brain and propose that it arises epigenetically in utero long before the outside world is beheld in infancy" (Hobson, 2015, p. 220). We are already living in a simulation, albeit one being generated by our own brains as a best guess for what is really "out there."

This inevitable filtering, reducing, and interpreting external reality as given by the senses happens at several levels, beginning with the process of sensation itself. Ethington (2011) refers to the translation of raw data from the eyes through the optic nerve as a "bottleneck" noting that

> here and farther downstream, vast amounts of unconscious interpreta-tion are carried on prior to conscious awareness of visual objects. Stuffing the information from 125 million reception cells into 1 million ganglion cells requires compression, multiplex operations, but in any case the information has already been greatly transformed by the time it reaches the visual cortex.
>
> (p. 137)

We also know from the aforementioned example of the blind spot and other perceptual anomalies related to brain regions that the perceptual apparatus of the nervous system is inclined to "fill in" the gaps with best guesses, which may or may not be accurate. The final layer of complication comes when the brain draws on its own memory systems to complete the interpretive process. This means that perception itself can be influenced by personal and social factors. As Solms and Turnbull (2002) put it "Much of what we take to be perception is in fact memory" (p. 154) in the sense that "we all automatically reconstruct the reality we perceive from models we have stored in our memories" (p. 155). Thus, our experiential perception of the simulation is in part an expression of psyche, forged in a crucible of past experience, cultural constraints, and deeply held beliefs.

I hope the relationship of this virtual reality model to the phenomena of imagination is obvious: as Kant intimated 200 years ago, it is imagination itself at work in constructing the simulation that we experience as real. This is in any case how Kant employed the term *imagination*—as a great synthesizer of experience. Even if we ultimately prefer a more expansive definition for the term, this model still provides us at least a plausible origin for imagination from an evolutionary perspective. As nervous systems became more complex, they were capable of more complex simu-lations, and also prone to greater errors. The capacity to construct and revise these reality simulations by fusing memory and sense data would be the foundation for future imaginative activity. To put it another way, the survival of life on earth has depended on the capacity of organisms to accurately imagine what lies outside of their nervous systems, and from this bedrock of reality simulation eventually arose a capacity to simulate things that were not physically there.

This does not, however, mean that the imagination of non-physical objects must always equate to the unreal. Survival depends on accurate maps, but that means the map-making capacities of the organism would be tuned primarily to survival issues, not the broader reality per se. Thus, we would expect successful species to have excellent accuracy in identifying food, mates, predators and other physical dangers, hiding places, and eventually tools, but there would be no evolutionary imperative to develop accurate maps of any aspects of reality that did not have immediate bearing on survival. All kinds of phenomena may exist around us, things strange, fantastical and perhaps quite literally beyond our imaginations. These phenomena would not only be objectively immeasurable, but the extent of their very existence would also be immeasurable. The more complex a nervous system, the greater necessity for some kind of process of system for grasping the ineffable, apprehending and attempting to comprehend that which does not fit into neurologically established categories of existence.

This model opens up new frameworks for understanding spirituality and religion from a neurobiological perspective. Benvenuti and Davenport (2011) understand spiritual practice as a neurotechnology for integrating the fragmented experience of the individual into both a larger cultural context and the cosmology that gives that culture its meaning. Newberg and Waldman, researchers of the neuroscience of religious and spiritual experience, suggest that spiritual experiences may help us to further "bridge the chasm between these inner and outer realities, which would then bring us closer to what actually exists in the world" (2009, p. 7). One fascinating aspect of their research is the finding that as areas of the parietal lobe that process spatial mapping and relations between objects become less active, subjects report a feeling of "oneness" with reality often expressed in spiritual terms (p. 17). In the case of explicit religiosity, they suggest that under normal circumstances the parietal lobe would attempt to locate "you" and "God" as objects in a spatial relationship, but in neurological studies of intense meditation and prayer, the subject instead experiences "a sense of unity with the object of contemplation and your spiritual beliefs" (p. 43). The simulation of space falls away, and the nervous system experiences itself as part of something outside the simulation altogether.

Of course a full ontological evaluation of such claims, as well their metaphysical implications, is well beyond the scope of the present discourse. The point is rather to emphasize the ways in which imagination lies at the boundary of the known and the unknown, and the degree to which is it employed in the process of knowing. We can remain skeptical or agnostic on the matter of metaphysics and still recognize imagination as a borderland between our conscious knowledge and the unknown expanses within and beyond our own nervous systems. Such a model would certainly be in accord with Jung's use of imagination as a primary tool for healing via engagement with the unconscious elements of psyche.

The question of the neurobiological correlates of imagination in this model is less a matter of isolating a specific "imagination area" in the brain, and more a matter of seeing a great variety of brain areas/functions being employed in the imaginative project. If perception of the process of simulating the real world based on incoming sense data, creative imagination is the process of using those same systems to simulate objects and experiences that do not directly correlate with external, physical reality. The simulator is still running, but it is now generating content from within, rather than striving for fealty to sensation. Sensory and multisensory images, spatial environments, and somatic–emotional experience may all play a part in this internally generated experience. Furthermore, the imaginative experiences may be more or less vivid, more or less immersive, as Zimmer (2012) demonstrates by identifying how varied levels of abstraction in images correlates with different brain regions becoming active.

This raises this question of what sorts of root processes might be occurring in the brain that guide this simulation process. If imagination occurs when the brain recruits its perceptual systems to experience non-physical realities, what higher systems are at work to guide and facilitate these processes? What is the biological process by which an individual brain decides to experience the deafening roar of an enraged dragon, and initiates the process to make the experience happen? Given my basic hypothesis that the more vivid and immersive the imaginal experience, the more complex and global processes that accompany it, it may be that parsing out the answer to this question may be beyond the scope of current neuroscience. That said, part of the answer may be found in an exploration of the neurobiology of creativity: the deeper process by which novel images, ideas, and stories are produced to begin with. This will be the topic of Chapter 8.

In the meantime, I will end this chapter by briefly addressing the potential of this model of imagination as framework for neurobiological understanding the *Anima Mundi*. I offer this not because I think it necessary or desirable to reduce the *Anima Mundi* to a materialist account, but rather to offer an inroad for experiencing the phenomenon to those individuals who approach it from a more entrenched scientific perspective.

Reviewing the premises laid out so far: that perception is a simulation, an imagined best-approximation of the world outside the nervous system, and that this simulation is malleable and open to influence at the levels of sensation, personal memory, and cultural framework. Our perception of the world "out there" is thus an expression of neurological, psychological, and cultural bias. As Kosslyn et al. (2001) put it: "If imagery can alter activation of the early visual cortex, this indicates that some of our beliefs and expectations can (at least under some circumstances), modulate what we actually see during perception" (p. 640). In a similar vein, Newburg and Waldman (2009) conducted a study on long-term meditators and found asymmetric thalamic activity (i.e., different levels on the left and right side) when their subjects were not meditating—whereas in the population at large, activity in the thalamus is symmetrical. The thalamus, again, is the first major hub for processing all incoming sense data, and is thus fundamental to sorting data into perceptual experience of reality. In humans, the thalamus also receives inputs from the frontal lobes, suggesting that executive function has some influence on perception even at its earliest stages. From this, Newburg and Waldman argue that this is one of the functions by which the ideas we contemplate become real to us, and thus fundamentally alter our perception of the world. "If you exercise an idea over and over, your brain will begin to respond as though the idea is a real object in the world … reality will appear different from one's normal perception of the world" (p. 55).

Along similar lines, Crandall, Cruikshank, and Connors (2015) point out that the axons descending from the cortex to the thalamus outnumber ascending axons from thalamus to cortex by ten to one. The conversation between the initial sensory hub and higher cortical functions is not only dynamic, it is also quite lopsided, suggesting the cortex mediates sense-impressions extensively. From this we can conclude that the systems of meaning by which our brains are psychologically and culturally organized find expression in our basic perception of the world. This meaning-mediated perception appears to us as a play of images often taken completely literally.

Hillman's invitation is to "see through" this literalism, to become curious about the images making up our perception, and the meanings encoded in those images. In short, Hillman invites us to stop taking our own perceptions of the world as unquestioned literal truth, and to consider that everything is at least in part an imaginative landscape. The basic premise of the *Anima Mundi* is that the world itself is alive and animate. When we imagine this to be so, when we vivify the imaginal dimension of our perception, we allow the universe to express meaning back to us as a vital world of living images. This is not only a matter of seeing aspects of ourselves and our culture projected out into the world, but also recognizing the degree to which the world we experience is inextricably bound in the life process (i.e., the nervous system) through which it comes to us. Rather than take our perceptions of the external world as a crystalized, literal truth, the invitation is to let the world actively come alive as a living expression of shared being. The nervous systems (Hillman would use the term *soul*) in which we find ourselves are themselves fluid environments of active imagination. And perhaps, out there in the borderlands where imagination and perception meet, we may discover things we did not think possible. We may never know with any certainty what lies outside our nervous systems, but this is all the more reason to understand all the ways in which world of human experience is at heart an imaginal realm.

Chapter 7

Time and story

Our working definition of imagination has been: *the generation of meaningful images and narratives arising in consciousness*. The previous chapter explored the neurobiological correlates of meaningful imagery. This chapter will now shift to look at meaningful narratives and how they might be understood from a neurobiological perspective. We will begin with a brief exploration of the evolution of story in the brain and its important social functions in cultural identity and group cohesion. This is followed by a discussion of the psychosocial role of narrative for the individual, both developmentally in the child as well as later in adult life. The question of how narrative shows up in our lives inevitably leads to a discussion of episodic memory, a process in which we re-experience not only facts but immersive stories about our past. Finally, we will consider how all of these pieces fit together with imaginative processes in recent research into the default mode network of the brain. This chapter will focus primarily on how narrative is processed by the brain, with the specific question of creating new stories and narratives being taken up in Chapter 8 on creativity.

The narrative dimension

I use the terms *narrative* and *story* somewhat interchangeably to indicate an unfolding sequence of meaningful events or relationships. When we say a picture is worth a thousand words, we mean that a complex image offers many opportunities for drawing out verbal stories to explain and perhaps elaborate the imagistic contents. But as any graphic novelist will tell you, it is also quite possible to tell a story through a sequence of pictures alone, a technique sometimes referred to as visual narrative. The important point is that, whether verbal or not, narratives show images relating to each other in a sequence of events. Traditionally, this usually means the interaction of images over time in a linear sequence—we follow the heroes out into adventure and then back home. But even in cases of non-linear storytelling, where the events of the story do not necessarily follow a single linear progression of time, the story itself must nevertheless be presented as a sequence of events. Many films and novels are constructed to show events out of sequence, jumping back and forth to different points in the characters' lives, but they still present those scenes to the audience in a particular order. That is to say, even if the content of the story is non-linear, the form of the story is still constrained and defined by a sequence of one event being presented at a time in relation to other events. In music and visual arts, there is more opportunity for simultaneous presentation of contents, but the narrative storyteller can only speak one specific event or image after another. In this way, the concept of story is inherently bound up in the concept of time.

At its most basic, narrative is a method for defining and making explicit certain relations: the scorpion stung the man, the man got sick and almost died, but the roots of the red-vine helped the man get better. This simple story codifies a number of important relationships between scorpions, humans, sickness, mortality, plants, medicine, and healing. As Mar (2004) points out, casual relationships are a defining feature of storytelling. At the most basic level, a series of objects, subjects, and events, are ordered into basic narrative structures containing information to help both the individual organism and social group survive and thrive. From this basic cognitive sequencing of meaning whole oral traditions develop that contain entire social codes of behavior, personal stories about identity, intimacies between individuals and groups who come to co-create these personal and social identity stories, and mythic and symbolic storytelling to make meaning of events that don't have strict physical correlates in the material world. At their most complex, these stories can become whole imaginary worlds.

In the last chapter I outlined a model of the brain as a simulator of detailed spatial imagistic environments. As the contents of those environments begin to flow forward in time, narrative sequencing emerges. The idea that "time" is an organizing category of human experience was (again) first put forward explicitly by Kant. In recent decades, time perception has become its own focus of study within the neurosciences. It appears that brain has multiple internal clocks for tracking the passage of time in very short/precise intervals, for distinguishing longer periods of activity, and maintaining the larger circadian rhythm of the organism (Jacobs, Allen, Nguyen, & Fortin, 2013; Reas, 2013). David Eagleman, a specialist in the neuroscience of time perception, writes that just as the brain constructs a representation of the environment, it also "builds a representation of time. When we examine the problem closely, we find that 'time' is not a unitary phenomenon" (Eagleman, 2009, p. 2). He goes on to detail a number of experiments that reveal the brain making best guesses about how temporal events line up, and fills in the gaps accordingly to create the perception of seamless experience. The visual system, for example, appears to experience a 1/10th second delay between stimulus and perception, but will synch the timing of various sensory inputs as simultaneous as long as they co-occur within small enough windows. Eagleman proposes the subjective phenomena of "time slowing down" during a traumatic event is due a heightened influx of sensory information in relation to the crisis—the perceptual system becomes saturated with vital sense data and the flow-forward of events is slowed in a kind of bottleneck.

But narrative construction proper is about more than just time perception: it involves the construction of a specific sequence of images, events, and relationships. In theory, we can be fully "in the present moment" without actively constructing a narrative about that experience. But if we then turn to a friend and say "you know, I was totally in the present moment just now," we have defaulted back to our storytelling nature, constructing a narrative relating self to an experience of deep presence.

The evolution of story

Recall Yuval Harari's (2016) provocative assertion that the primary thing to set homo sapiens apart from other intelligent species is our acquired capacity to create fictions. Whether or not we agree that fiction is the singular defining feature of recent human evolution, it has certainly played a pivotal role. Egan (n.d.), Abram (2006), Cron (2012), Mehl-Madrona (2015), and many others have argued persuasively that vivid and emotionally compelling storytelling among early hunter–gatherer tribes was not only a means of entertainment, but also a key to survival. Compelling narratives encoded important survival information and tribal wisdom, transmitted social customs, and helped groups socially bond over collective identities as expressed through their stories. From an evolutionary perspective, then, the human groups with the finest capacity for storytelling would have a clear survival advantage; humans evolved to be both excellent storytellers and excellent receivers of stories told.

Neuroscientist Louis Cozolino (2016) thoroughly agrees with this perspective: "As social groups grew larger and language became more complex, more cortical space was required to process a greater amount of social information. This expanded topography was a contributing factor to the emergence of abstract thinking and imagination" (p. 25). In fact, Cozolino believes that the massive growth in the homo sapiens' cerebral cortex is largely for the purpose of meeting this need: encoding and storing complex narratives to share among the social group and pass on to the next generation. Narratives came to serve an integrative function both in the brain of the individual and across the brains of the members of the group. A group's stories tied the one back to the many in collective identity and parameters for behavior. Again this theory suggests our brains not only excel at story, but are in a real sense made for story. Cozolino further notes empirical studies demonstrating that information presented in a vivid and emotionally compelling narrative is generally better remembered than information presented as a list of facts. He argues that storytelling/listening is an ancient social process "containing all the elements to stimulate neuroplasticity and learning" (p. 240). This would imply that even today human beings are biologically wired for story, that on a primal level, we both learn about the world and experience the world primarily through stories or narratives. The recent field of "narrative therapy" takes this as a basic premise: that our selves and our worlds are largely constructed through narrative, though we may often mistake our stories for literal objective facts. Here too Cozolino agrees: "Stories are, in fact, so ubiquitous in human experience that we hardly notice their existence" (p. 236).

That storytelling provides cohesion and shared meaning within groups of humans is not only a cultural and behavioral observation, but has neurobiological evidence as well. Hasson (2008) devised an experiment that involved showing subjects cinematic clips in narrative and non-narrative format under functional magnetic resonance imaging (fMRI). The narrative clips resulted in more overall brain activity in individuals, and greater harmony of brain activity patterns between individuals, thus suggesting elements of collective or shared experience. Paul Zak, one of the pioneers in researching the role of neurotransmitter oxytocin in the formation of trusting bonds between mammals in a social group (including humans), has investigated the relationship between oxytocin and emotionally charged storytelling. Generally, oxytocin levels rise as a correlate for pro-social, trust-building interaction with humans, including intimate, comfortable hugs. Zak (2015) describes new sets of experiments indicating that oxytocin also rises in response to compelling dramatic stories in which the subject experiences empathy for the character. In a related series of controlled experiments, subjects who received a nasal infusion of oxytocin before watching videos about a social problem were 56 percent more likely to contribute money to that cause. Taken together, these results indicate that powerful storytelling can elicit a pro-social bonding effect, creating a sense of connection and community through the sharing of stories.

Hasson, Ghazanfar, Galantucci, Garrod, and Keysers (2012) conducted a fascinating study on brain-coupling that involved a portion on telling and listening to stories. Brain-to-brain coupling is here defined as the activation of one brain by another; just as one part of an individual's brain might activate another part of that same individual's brain, brain-to-brain coupling looks at how we might activate each other's brains in a similar fashion. In the storytelling portion of their study, they found that the brain activation pattern of the storyteller and the brain activation of the subject listening to the story were significantly similar. In effect, the storyteller was transferring a pattern of brain activation to the listener, implying "a causal relationship by which the speaker's production-based processes induce and shape the neural responses in the listener's brain" (p. 6). Among the most notable differences in activation patter between speaker and receiver was that the receiver had a tendency to attempt to predict what the speaker was going to say next. That is to say, the listeners' preconceptions of what the story was going to be about had the capacity to introduce "noise" into the system and disrupt the synchrony of the coupling. This certainly supports Gadamer's assertion that we always approach understanding through our own preconceptions, and only slowly achieve a fusion of horizons through careful and receptive investigation.

Studies such as these give an indication of just how essential storytelling has always been to the human condition, and how it continues to shape our lives even when we are not fully conscious of it. In Cozolino's words,

> From primitive tribes to modern families, co-constructed narratives are at the core of human groups. Group participation in narrating shared experiences organized memories, embeds them within the social context, and assists in linking feelings, actions, and others to the self.
>
> (2016, p. 242)

Oftentimes when we speak about family values or national identity, we are speaking of the stories around which we have organized our social understandings. Here again we come up against the insidious notion that "fiction" should be equated with untruth, when in fact fictions about ourselves, our families, and our communities can be among the most meaningful aspects of our lives. To "die for one's country"—or to die for any cause—is an enactment of narrative meaning. Even those cynics who would say that "life is meaningless" are still arguably subscribing to a deeply experienced story of cynicism from which a particularly nihilistic sense of meaning is derived. Positive or negative, story is a tool for engaging the world that is difficult—perhaps impossible—to do without.

Theory of Mind: agency in a storied world

One of the things that can happen when images are placed in the context of a story is that they begin to resemble persons. As we watch, for example, literary characters accrue experiences, interact with others, and face obstacles, we may begin to experience them as if they are real people. And as many writers attest, a well-developed character in a novel not only begins to seem real to the reader, but can even seem to take on a life of its own for the writer, who sometimes finds the actions of the character genuinely surprising. More will be said about this element of surprise in Chapter 8—for now, I want to focus on the phenomenon of images coming to seem like persons. So pervasive is this need, we find throughout human literature that even objects and places can seem to take on shades of personhood when described and integrated into the story with great detail. The expressive landscape and moody weather-wrapped cities of Dickens; the sinister jungle in Conrad's *Heart of darkness*; the entire Indian sub-continent in E. M. Forster's *A passage to India*; the house sitting empty for years at a time in Woolf's *To the lighthouse*—in each case, the place takes on aspects of personhood, expressing itself to the human characters in a variety of ways, affecting them to the core of their beings. Nor is his merely a literary phenomenon: whether in the modern children's books like *The giving tree* or centuries of mythic tales about talking animals and nature spirits, the capacity and need for imaginal persons seems deeply ingrained in the human condition.

Cognitive science has long been fascinated with the capacity of one subjective mind to recognize another mind in someone else. The technical term for this is *Theory of Mind* (ToM): the ability to recognize thoughts, intentions, desires, and experiences in others that are different from those of oneself. Kerr (2008) reviews a conflicting set of theories in this field between ToM proper, which holds that we construct a cognitive map of the minds of others, and the competing theory of Embodied Simulation (ES), which holds our understanding of others is based on perceptual inference of their movements and actions. In the former (ToM), it is thought that the capacity to recognize other minds is acquired through healthy development between the ages of 3–4 years, and appears to heavily engage the superior temporal sulcus and temporo-parietal junction on the right side of the brain. The latter theory (ES) holds that we infer the intentions of others by using our motor-neuron system to run micro-simulations of their behavior in our own nervous systems. Kerr's conclusion, which I heartily endorse, is that this seeming divide is rooted in a nineteenth-century dualist framework, and the real challenge is to see how these two models might be integrated. She proposes that "intersubjectivity is part of a more striking, miraculous capacity for developing flexible attentionality driven sensory filter by which we see what is salient to us. Intersubjectivity arises out of this broader capacity" (p. 212). Kerr is proposing that our cognitive maps of others are informed by our embodied simulations of others, and vice versa. Our mirror neurons use incoming perceptions to create embodied simulations that help us understand what others are doing and thinking, informing the cognitive maps which in turn help us predict what is happening in their minds.

Lisa Zunshine's (2006) *Why we read fiction: Theory of Mind and the novel*, advances the argument that all modern literature exists by engaging our ToM circuitry to understand fictional characters. The brain functions that evolved to navigate complex social contexts are exercised, strengthened, and put to the test whenever we hear a story, read a novel, or watch a film.

> Literature pervasively capitalizes on and stimulates theory of mind mechanisms.... As a sustained representation of numerous, interacting minds, the novel feeds the powerful, representation-hungry complex of cognitive adaptions whose very condition of being is a constant social stimulation delivered either by direct interactions with other people or by imaginary approximation of such interactions.
>
> (p. 10)

Zunshine argues that novels exist only by virtue of our robust ToM abilities, and that they serve us by allowing us to practice and refine our ToM skills by engaging with fictional characters. Furthermore, she suggests fiction is appealing because it reassures us about our ability to understand the motivations of others in a way that real life cannot. After all, we are usually granted much more direct insight into the thoughts and feelings of fictional characters than we are to the living humans that surround us.

The fact that we are able to empathize and believe in our favorite literary characters is evidence that the brain's ToM functions are not restricted to physical persons. "On some level our evolved cognitive architecture indeed does not fully distinguish between real and fictional people" (p. 19). This is important to a general theory of imagination for two reasons. First, it helps us understand the emphasis in depth psychology in personify the meaning-charged images that come us; to engage with images as persons with their own wants and needs. To engage a "fictional" entity as a kind of person appears to be a natural function of our cognitive architecture. Second, it suggests that ToM is itself bound up in a process of producing meaningful fictions about others. We naturally produce stories to help us understand the actions and intentions of others, but we do not always know that our projected stories are correct. Our fictions about our fellow humans may be more or less accurate—but we inevitably still relate to one another through the medium of fiction. That is why communication is so important to relationship; fiction may be inevitable, but in the act of speaking and listening, we have the opportunity to co-create the stories we live in. We allow other minds to speak for themselves, and compare their statements against the fictions we have created about them.

As a final note on ToM, I want to emphasize that understanding the world as made up of other persons is a primal aspect of human experience. When we see persons in non-human entities—in animals or landscapes or spirits or something even stranger—we are referencing a deep and primal experience of reality. Literary terms such as *personification, anthropomorphism,* even *allegory* and *metaphor* can become rationally distancing devices that prevent us from becoming experientially immersed in the story. Whether *Lolita* or *Star wars, Harry Potter* or the *Giving tree,* or a tribal tale of cosmogonic creation, when we are truly taken in by storytelling, when we are fully impacted by its emotional salience, we are allowing ourselves to see fictional characters, animals, even plants and objects, as persons.

Perhaps the most important character in any given brain is the character known as "self." If we know others through a process of fiction-making, certainly we must have the greatest number of fictions for the task of expressing our own being back us. The next section will take up the question of how narrative plays out neurologically in the psychological development of the individual, both in early childhood and in adult life.

Self-stories, individual development, and healing

The notion that narrative plays a key role in psychology is one that has gained much traction in recent decades. The stories we tell ourselves about ourselves, others, and about life are increasingly recognized as an entry point to our psychological structure and pathology. Although many clinical modalities now make some use of work with narrative, "narrative therapy" proper is a specific therapeutic technique developed by Michael White, David Epston, Martin Payne, and their colleagues. As outlined by Payne (2006), the process involves listening to and affirming the clients' story, creating distance from the life problems by "externalizing" them as characters, and then enriching and complexifying the life narrative by weaving it with contrary and unique episodes, emphasizing the details around these other stories, until a new big picture emerges. A remarkably similar approach was developed independently by osteopathic physician Lewis Mehl-Madrona (2015), a form of narrative healing work developed in part out of his cultural roots with the Lakota tribe. After listening and fully affirming the story of the client, "we invite fantasy, speculation, and projections into the future. The art of working with a story is the art of creating future narratives of success and reframing past narratives to mine them for new, more versatile, and empowering meanings" (p. 6). In both of these approaches, story is the medium through which both wounding and healing occur. How can we account for the success of these methods neurobiologically?

Cozolino's (2016) research affirms that stories serve a powerful organizing role in the brain and go to the root of the psychological construction of the self. "Positive self-narratives aid in emotional security while minimizing the need for elaborate psychological defenses. The role of language and narratives in neural integration, memory formation, and self-identity make them powerful tools in the creation and maintenance of the self" (p. 24). Long before we are trained to memorize and think logically in stand-alone facts, we apprehend ourselves, our relationships, and our world in narrative form. Efrat Ginot, a psychotherapist specializing in the neuropsychology of unconscious processes, concurs about the essential nature of narrative in the brain: "Reinforced neural activations eventually coalesce into a solid pattern of fantasies and linguistic 'knowledge' about various aspects of the self" (2015, p. 115). This accounts for the power of story to create coherence across groups and within individuals. It also helps us understand the debilitating power of negative narratives taking neurological root in the brain.

Ginot (2015) focuses specifically on the relationship between negative narratives and dysregulated states in the nervous system—that is, states where affective charge becomes overwhelming and regular adaptive cognitive process is impaired. When such dysregulation is triggered, rational assessment of the situation can become compromised and destructive behavior can result, both toward self and others. Debilitating fears, crushing sadness, and blind rage are all prime examples of highly dysregulated states. According to Ginot, the negative emotional reality of this state inevitably contains a linguistic, narrative component. "During dysregulation, the automatic and familiar narratives about the self are subjectively experienced as entirely couched in objective facts. In this case, an unconscious internal reality becomes the only dimension of one's experience" (p. 97). Similar to Jung's concept of the *complex*, these emotionally charged negative narratives can prevent us from seeing the situation clearly, driving us to shadow-box with phantoms from the past and engage in other destructive behaviors. "Such self-narratives can acquire an intrusive, autonomous life; they surface unbidden and flare up as familiar thoughts, fantasies, or images and end up dominating our intrapsychic and interpersonal experience" (p. 95). While not stories themselves, these dysregulated states are bound up in a narrative story about self, others, and world. Formed during negative or traumatic past experiences, these stories become a filtering imposition on the present even when they do not accurately map present circumstances. These narratives can function in a stubborn, negative loop, imposing old traumatic stories where they are inappropriate, and thus intensifying and reinforcing dysregulated patterns of behavior despite the lack of any present threat. In this sense, individuals can become trapped within the stories that they have internalized about themselves, neurologically blocked from effectively imagining their lives in a different light.

Ginot believes that many of the deepest narratives that shape our lives operate as largely unconscious driving forces. "Self narratives can be seen as consciously felt manifestations of an unconscious system.... Among highly dissociated patients, self narratives may be the only manifestation of their hidden emotional and relational core" (p. 98). In Ginot's understanding, these narratives are primarily an elaboration of affect, an added layer of linguistic meaning to create coherence and understanding around emotional experiences. For patients who have become severely dissociated from their own painful emotional experiences, the cognitive story they tell may be the only trace of the deeper unconscious self-system at work.

The formation of these self-stories begins at a very young age, when children first start creating linguistic labels for their non-verbal experiences through intersubjective interactions with their caregivers. Because early development is an inherently interpersonal process, problems in the relationship with the caregivers can result in the construction of destructive narratives. The earliest development of self appears to begin in the more holistic–emotional right brain hemisphere, with linguistic elaborations developing more slowly as the left hemisphere subsequently comes online. If there are aspects of the young child's experience that the caregiver cannot affirm and mirror—or worse, if the child is attacked or criticized for its experiences—that child may begin to develop a distorted self-narrative which has the potential to play out throughout its adult life.

> The distorted explanations given by the child are made even more destructive by the slower-developing left hemisphere … and the [prefrontal cortex] as a whole…. Consequently, while in the minds of traumatic, painful, or shameful experiences, the child has no choice but to arrive at distorted conclusions about its own self-worth, competency, and importance to the parent and to his age group.
>
> (p. 105)

This is especially destructive for very young children whose sense of identity is still undifferentiated from its caregivers, whose emergent self-stories may involve intense fear, shame, and dissociation. "All of these processes occur on a continuum of awareness, and if reinforced over time, they become part of an unconscious map" (p. 108). Unless these narratives are uncovered and worked through consciously later in life, they may profoundly influence the individual's life choices and relationships throughout adulthood.

Fortunately, there are potential healing solutions to these self-destructive narratives, and indeed, Ginot and Cozolino are both writing with the ultimate intention of outlining the neural correlates of effective psychotherapy. In this context, therapy becomes a corrective interpersonal process of rewiring the brain through mindfully examining and rewriting the narrative. "Through the co-construction of coherent self-stories, we are able to enhance our self-reflective capacity, creativity, and maturation" (Cozolino, 2016, p. 18). This process is aided by the formal container of psychotherapeutic practice for several reasons, chief among them that individuals tend to be self-blind to the unconscious forces at work.

> Our narratives, indeed, can be seen as an emotionally "true" reflection of our negative self-systems. When they are activated, they are in essence an important manifestation of our identity. This is why they seem so "real and convincing" when we are in the midst of a dysregulated state.
>
> (Ginot, 2015, p. 107)

The most powerful self-stories can be deeply engrained in the unconscious, often formed in tandem with our earliest self-understanding as small children. As such, the experience of such narratives can feel like an irrefutable and essential truth, even if from an outside perspective the narrative seems to be entirely self-created. To logically insist to such a person that they are objectively wrong about their story is unlikely to be effective, and may even be perceived as an attack on the person's deepest identity.

Because so many of these destructive self-stories arose from failed interpersonal processes with caregivers and early peers, the interpersonal nature of "talk therapy" with a mindful and compassionate practitioner allows the cognitive rewriting of the story to be reinforced in the context of a corrective, healing relationship. Cozolino writes "the purpose of sharing our stories with others is to gain active participation in the co-construction of new narratives. Our own stories tend to becomes closed systems in need of new input" (2016, p. 25). The therapeutic process from this perspective is an empowerment of the client to edit and rewrite destructive narratives, and perhaps to even write new narratives for their lives altogether. "Positive self-narratives aid in emotional security while negative ones perpetuate low self-esteem, anxiety and pessimism. In this way, our stories become blueprints for our future" (p. 237). Although neither Cozolino nor Ginot speak to imagination specifically, I would argue that they are describing therapy as a process in which self, others, and world come to be imagined differently. This turns out to be hard work, far beyond simple exercises in creative visualization. Because the negative stories we imagine about ourselves and our world are so deeply entangled with powerful negative emotion and wired into our brains at the deepest level of identity, learning to imagine differently necessitates a deep and committed interpersonal healing process in a safe and supportive context.

But even in putting deep healing aside, Cozolino offers much evidence for the power of narrative to improve brain health in general, both personally and collectively. He asserts, for example, that storytelling serves a basic function of neural integration:

> The combination of a linear story line and visual imagery woven together with verbal and nonverbal expressions of emotion activates circuitry of both cerebral hemispheres, cortical and subcortical networks, the various regions of the frontal lobes, the hippocampus and the amygdala.... Further, shared stories contain images and ideas that stimulate imagination and link individuals to the group mind.
>
> (2016, p. 24)

This is further bolstered by a positive correlation between individuals who present coherent life-narratives while also reporting secure attachments in their relationships. In particular, Cozolino sees the integration between the linear–linguistic left hemisphere and the holistic–emotional right hemisphere as a prime benefit of telling and listening to stories. "A coherent and meaningful narrative provides the executive brain with the best template and strategy for the oversight and coordination of the functions of brain and mind across the two hemispheres" (p. 239). Individuals with clear positive narratives also tend to have higher capacity for emotional regulation and higher self-esteem, and more rewarding social lives. Furthermore the activation of prefrontal cortical areas during narrative formation, both in conversation and in the process of journaling, can help to create a healthy sense of control and down-regulates amygdala activation, effectively reducing anxiety and fear. On a neurological level, good storytelling appears to have real power to heal.

Imagining memory

In discussing the vital role that stories play in the brain, we come inevitably to the neurobiology of memory. This is not only because the individual bits of information that comprise these stories must be stored in our neural database—but also because our autobiographical memories are a kind of narrative experience about our own pasts. It may seem startling at first to think of memory as being on the same spectrum of mental phenomenon that includes imagination, but the last two decades of neuroscientific research have increasingly shown just that.

The neurobiology of memory

Neuroscience has differentiated and studied several distinct phenomena of memory that should be clarified before proceeding. LeDoux (2002) offers a history and summary of memory research in neuroscience, distinguishing between working memory, long-term memory, implicit versus explicit memory, semantic memory, and episodic or autobiographical memory. Working memory is the information that is currently "online" in the brain at the present moment and is quite limited—remembering even seven digits of a new phone number can require some concentration. Information and events that pass a threshold of significance undergo a process of consolidation into long-term memory, and can later be recalled and, as it turns out, reconsolidated with new information. A further distinction is made between explicit or declarative memory, which can be recalled consciously, and implicit memory, which involves largely unconscious processes, like how to ride a bike. The most complex form of memory is episodic or autobiographical memory, in which past events are encoded in rich, multisensory and emotionally salient experiential narratives.

Eric Kandel, who won a Nobel Prize for his work in identifying the neurobiological mechanisms of memory, describes episodic memory with reverence and poetic license: "Remembering the past is a form of mental time travel; it frees us from the constraints of time and space and allows us to move freely along completely different dimensions" (2006, p. 3). There is a rich potential for imaginal depth and breadth in such a conception of memory, the possibility for immersion in a profoundly meaningful multi-sensory inner experience. Although this sort of richly imagined memory recall may not be available to all humans to the same degree, it remains an important capacity that, like so much else involving the brain, may be strengthened through practice (see Doidge, 2007).

Unlike the relative simplicity of semantic memory, which involves retrieval of discrete bits of information, episodic memory proceeds by a much more complex process of re-constructing an entire past event. "Episodic memory involves the literal 're-experiencing' of past events—the bringing back to awareness of previous experiential episodes" (Solms & Turnbull, 2002, p. 160). For Solms, this most complex form of memory essentially consists of linking self-states to external circumstances over time. Joy at arriving at the beach house, sadness when the cat dies, sublime wonder wandering the rainforest, or the nuanced integration of all three of those emotions watching a child get married. While this may inevitably involve recalling discrete bits of semantic information, that information must be holistically and imaginally reconstituted so that the event can be re-lived as both a sensory experience and an emotional state.

Indeed, there has been for some time a consensus that episodic memory recall is not a process of representing immutable facts, but a process of re-constructing a past event in the present based on an informational blue-print. LeDoux (2002) warns that while memory usually does a pretty good job of being accurate, we should be careful not to take our own memories too literally. "It's a reconstruction of facts and experiences on the basis of how they were stored, not as they actually occurred" (p. 97). Just as the perceptual system arguably constructs a simulated map of reality out of incoming sense data, episodic memory re-constructs approximations of those moments, guided by narrative and emotional outlines. Kandel (2006) takes this formulation even further: "Recall of memory is a creative process. What the brain stores is thought to be only a core memory. Upon recall, this core memory is then elaborated upon and reconstructed with subtractions, additions, elaborations, and distortions" (p. 281). Similar to the phenomenon of mental images recruiting the areas of the brain that process incoming sense data, episodic memory also appears to activate the perceptual areas through which the event was initially experienced (LeDoux 2002; Rubin, 2006). In this way, we are imagining the past every time we remember, albeit with some very specific information to guide and shape what arises.

Our autobiographical memories, those narrative structures we use to accurately imagine past events in present time, are largely organized around emotional salience. "Often, the emotional impact determines how influential a memory becomes in terms of its effects on narratives about the self" (Ginot, 2015, p. 116). This appears to be true for storing long-term memories in general: "things that have significant personal meaning or emotional salience" are much more likely to be consolidated for long-term recall than personally meaningless or emotionally neutral data (Presti, 2016, p. 222). Part of this personally significant meaning is simply a matter of what sorts of links the new information or event has to existing networks of information in the brain; if it relates to what has already been deemed significant, it is far more likely to be integrated into those networks and thus remembered in the long term. Presti also mentions the documented use of vivid visualizations to improve memory, citing a synesthete for memorizing π to 22,514 digits by visualizing a rich terrain of shapes, colors, and textures in association with the numbers.

There is also strong evidence that just as memories need to be reconstructed in order to be experienced, they may also be neurologically "updated" so that new information comes to color the old. In the process of recall, even the most stable long-term memories appear to enter into a temporary period of instability where they can be altered and then reconsolidated (Dongaonkar, Hupbach, Gomez, & Nadel, 2013; Hupbach, Gomez, & Nadel, 2009; Wichert, Wolf, & Schwabe, 2013). For example, the memory of a first date may later be updated by the positive or negative outcome of that relationship, so that the memory has a different feel when subsequently reconstructed and experienced. Obviously many of the details would remain unchanged, but a healthy marriage might update that memory of initial meeting with more positive emotion and vivid particulars, while an abusive relationship might give the memory more foreboding qualities. Ginot (2015) explicitly ties together mental health and psychological narratives with this updatable quality of memory:

> Memories that are too robust can be maladaptive and prevent new responses to a changing environment.... In this case, we can see the future only in terms of the past. Thus, the neural mechanisms that allow recurrent updating of items in long term memory may also permit a more effective and free imagination.
>
> (p. 118)

The rigidity of the memory system is then an indicator of how deeply entrenched the unconscious system, and thus the self-narratives, have become. In rigid memory the future is always viewed through the lens of the past, even when this results in a maladaptive assessment of new circumstances and relationships. A healthier memory system would show more flexibility, allowing past and future to inform each other so that past wisdom holds influence even as new personal narratives unfold.

Rubin (2006) offers a fascinating model for episodic memory whereby multiple systems in the brain (i.e., visual, spatial, olfactory, emotional, narrative, linguistic, etc.) each process information in specific ways, and thus contributing their own specific system modality to the construction of an episodic memory. This is offered in contrast to previous cognitive models based on computers whereby the entire brain was thought to have a singular information-processing language. Particularly worthy of note is the emphasis Rubin gives to narrative as an essential system with a unique form of processing, related to but distinct from the language processing centers from the brain. Narratives can, after all, be present in fully imagistic form (a silent film or comic strip, for example), relating events, actions, and motivations of its characters over time. Furthermore, damage to left hemisphere language processing brain areas has a lesser impact on narrative processing, where by contrast damage to the right hemisphere and frontal lobes can make the contextual, tonal, and thematic nuances of stories more difficult to comprehend (p. 284).

Rubin (2006) goes on to recognize narrative as one of the primary means through which our personal episodic memories function: "Narrative establishes a major form of organization in autobiographical memory, providing temporal and goal structure. Autobiographical memories are usually recoded as narrative; they are told to another person and to oneself" (p. 295). This relates to another major branch of Rubin's work: the study of oral traditions. These traditions involve the transmission of information in narrative form across generations without the aid of written language. Rubin suggests that these oral narratives are not memorized verbatim, as with an actor in a script, but rather fall within a series of schema that match the episodic memory systems of the brain: specific organization rules for linguistic, visual, spatial, emotional, narrative aspects of the story etc. His argument is that the oral traditions as a whole offer a window into how the basic functional structures of episodic memory evolved in our brains.

Given the degree to which the phenomena of episodic memory is a process of imaginally reconstructing the past based on markers of salience, we may ask if different valuations of salience lead to different kinds of memory recall? That is to say, given that meaning and even emotional valuation are to some degree culturally mediated and will inevitably vary among individuals even within cultures, it seems fair to hypothesize that patterns of brain activation during episodic recall might be highly variable. Perhaps different individuals and groups will use their brains to remember and imagine in different ways? Kandel (2006) cites one fascinating instance of this, where a study showed a marked difference in the way women and men recall and communicate directions. In the study, women tended to use sensory and spatial markers (turn left at the blue house and look for a bridge), and showed more activation in the right prefrontal and right parietal cortices; men focused more on numbers and internalized geometry (drive 5 miles north, then 1 mile east), and showed more activation in the left hippocampus. Fascinating as these results are, it remains difficult to sort out which gender differences are actually rooted in biology, and which are more the result of cultural expectations and gender socialization. Nevertheless, that the differences exist at all suggests an intrinsic variability in the way brain systems might be recruited in imaginal process from one individual or group to the next.

Mental time travel

One stunning discovery to come out of modern neuroscientific research is that the act of imagining the future ("prospection") appears to engage many of the same brain areas as remembering the past. This has led to a discussion of memory and prospection existing along a spectrum of "mental time travel," where the brain constructs past and future scenarios based on the data at its disposal. A review by Schacter, Addis, and Buckner (2007) found ample evidence that prospection uses many of the same systems employed in episodic memory recall, including the medial prefrontal regions, posterior regions in the medial and lateral parietal cortex, the lateral temporal cortex and the medial temporal lobe. These findings suggest the same processes involved in constructing episodic memory during recall are recruited to simulate and game-out possible future scenarios. Research by Brown et al. (2014) found that individuals suffering from post-traumatic stress disorder showed diminished specificity in remembering past episodes and imagining future episodes, further supporting the notion that past and future construction operate via shared mechanisms. This pushes back against the cultural assumption that memory recalls a literal past while thinking about tomorrow is purely a flight of fancy. On the contrary, both appear to be imaginative constructs based on the best available information. Episodic memory obviously has terrific adaptive value if it can help us accurately navigate social and physical landscapes based on previous encounters. But prospection too is highly adaptive: it allows for creative problem solving, future planning, and preparation for multiple contingencies. Prospection may be more prone to literal error because it can only make educated guesses as to future outcomes, but as we have seen memory is also an approximation, albeit one that operates under more narrow constraints.

Defining imagination as the activity of prospection is one of the favored ways neuroscience has attempted to approach the topic. This is understandable insofar as it makes the phenomenon more measurable and fits nicely within a purely functional evolutionary framework of future-simulations as a powerful cognitive tool for survival. As Richardson (2011) puts it: "memory researchers have not shown much interest in the active or "magical" character that such projection often takes, adopting a largely utilitarian approach to imagination instead" (p. 669). This is not necessarily a cause for criticism, as science can speak to only that which it can measure, and thorough research into the aspect of imagination known as "prospection" has much to offer, so long as the aspect is not mistaken for the whole. Nor is this move of equating imagination and prospection ubiquitous or settled in the field. In a comprehensive review of research on future episodic thinking, Ward (2016) attempts to differentiate between imagination and prospection. She reviews evidence that individuals who are good at one tend to be good at the other, but differentiates future episodic thinking as being temporal, plausible, and personally relevant, whereas imagination is not. Of course a depth psychology perspective would object that all sorts of imaginative activities may be personally relevant regardless of their plausibility as events in physical space–time. Here again is the late nineteenth-century cultural assumption that imagination must be associated with the unreal. More useful, I think, to view imagination as an entre into experiencing a variety of meaningful phenomena, those that plausibly correlate with external space–time events, and those that do not.

Convergence: the default mode network

Following the discovery of the memory–prospection connection, the fore-front of current neuroscientific research into imagination has largely focused on the brain's default mode network (DMN), the convergent region where many of the aforementioned imaginative processes meet. Raichle et al. (2001) first developed the idea that the brain would have a natural conscious "resting state" when not engaged with task-specific executive functions, and named this state the "default mode" of the brain. Since then, further research has mapped out a specific network in the brain that constitutes this default mode. This includes interactions between the ventral medial prefrontal cortex, the posterior cingulate, inferior parietal lobule, lateral temporal cortex, dorsal medial prefrontal cortex, and the hippocampal formation, including the entorhinal cortex and parahippocampal cortex. This network of brain systems comes online when we disengage our attention from taking action in the external world and experience inner awareness, including remembering, day-dreaming, spontaneous stream-of-consciousness, speculating about the thoughts, feelings and motivations of others ("theory of mind"), and imagining the future (Buckner & Carroll, 2007). This particular constellation of inner mental activity has led to strong associations between the DMN and the phenomenon of human imagination, with neuroscientist Scott Barry Kaufman (2013) going so far as to christen the DMN "the imagination network."

Buckner and his colleagues (2008) published a comprehensive review of the DMN in 2008, concluding that in addition to activating during solitary reflective thought,

> The default network also increases activity during mental explorations referenced to oneself including remembering, considering hypothetical social interactions, and thinking about one's own future. These properties suggest that the default network functions to allow flexible mental explorations—simulations—that provide a means to prepare for upcoming, self-relevant events before they happen.
>
> (p. 30)

Buckner notes a variety of studies in which the content of the inner reverie recruits additional brain regions as needed: visual, auditory, emotional, etc. "One possibility is that the regions within the default network transiently interact with sensory, motor, and emotional systems to represent the content of the imagined event" (p. 30). This is of course keeping with the neurobiological mechanisms of mental images discussed in the previous chapter, where there same sensory, motor, and emotional areas recruited to processing real world events are active in engaging with imaginal events. Buckner reviews additional evidence that the DMN retrieves specific information from specialized brain regions and engages in a process of complex scene construction, creating mental simulations with rich imaginal content. Furthermore, the DMN shows increased activation when one imagines oneself at the center of the simulation, participating in it, rather than viewing it from a third-person perspective.

The capacity of the brain to generate such simulations has obvious benefits from an evolutionary perspective. Organizing and referencing past experience in rich detail allows for better decision making, while the capacity to imagine potential outcomes of future scenarios makes for more effective planning. The capacity to imagine the minds and motivations of others has clear adaptive value for any social animal and especially so for humans, in which our personal and professional lives are largely built around social interactions of one kind or another. Furthermore, having a general ability to imagine things differently from how they are in the present moment opens the door to detailed creative problem solving, and thus to creativity itself (the subject of the next chapter). With regards to the common understanding of imagination as an opening up of possibilities, the DMN appears to be a key neurobiological correlate of the imaginative process.

Given the data on the DMN presented thus far, we would also expect it to be involved in narrative storytelling and fiction in general, and indeed it is. Mar (2004) found story processes in the brain involve regions associated with episodic memory, causal sequencing, and ToM, and Spreng, Mar, &

Kim (2008) note a significant overlap between narrative processing areas and the DMN. ToM in particular is essential to both producing and comprehending characters in a fictional story, and in fact without believable and emotionally engaging characters, stories will likely fail to engage us. The same brain regions that allow us to understand the motives of others and navigate our social milieu are essential to the processing of story, suggesting again that narrative structure is a basic mode of social cognition. Mar and Oatley (2008) argue that one of the primary uses of fiction is to provide a map for the brain to construct immersive simulations of potential social realities and reactions. Both the reception of narrative and the creative production of narrative allow for a simulated social–emotional learning process to take place, whereby the individual is able to process emotional potentials and circumstances they might not otherwise have access to. This allows us to better prepare for potential future scenarios as well as better understand the thoughts, feelings, and motivations of others. Rather than being merely entertainment, narrative fiction has the potential to serve as a powerful education tool about self and world.

Another significant feature of the DMN discussed in Buckner et al.'s review (2008) is the potential for the DMN to "compete" for resources with other networks in the brain. Most notably, there is evidence for a pronounced competition between the DMN and the brain systems that monitor external attention and action. With limited attentional resources, consciousness becomes focus either on internal processes like reflection and fantasy (the DMN) or external processes such as real-time interactions with others and goals or tasks in the environment. Activation of the external attention and action networks correlate negatively with activation of the DMN. This would explain why those who are deep in reverie or fully absorbed in creative process may "tune out" the external world and miss details and even whole events that are happening around them. More recently, Agnati et al. (2013) have reviewed further evidence that indicate three "large-scale" networks in the brain: the DMN, the central executive network (CEN), and the salience network. The CEN supports external attention and goal-based action, and is comprised of the dorso-lateral prefrontal cortex (DLPFC) and the posterior parietal cortex. The salience network, comprised of the ventro-lateral prefrontal cortex, the anterior cingulate cortex, and the anterior insula, acts as a discrimination system, selecting which stimulus are worthy of attention, and thus serving as a kind of mediator between the DMN and CEN. Dysfunction with the salience network has been implicated in autism spectrum disorder, psychosis, and dementia (Uddin, 2016), all pathologies involving a diminished capacity to relate internal and external worlds.

Story tellers

This chapter has taken up the question of narrative as the meaningful sequencing of images, events, and relationships over the dimension of time. In discussing the neurobiological correlates of this phenomenon, we have looked at the powerful role storytelling has played in human history, and how this continues to play out in both modern society and the psychological development, wounding, and healing of the individual. Tracking this process into the unlikely but robust relationship between imagination and memory, we come at last to the DMN, where the inner world of narrative, ToM, and memory converge into what Kauffman calls "the imagination network."

While this takes us far in developing a neurobiological understanding of imagination, there is still at least one missing vital piece. We can understand what is happening in the brain when meaningful images arise, when we reminisce about the past or daydream about the days to come, and when we sit by the fire and hear a stirring story told. But where did that story come from to begin with? When a meaningful image crashes into our consciousness suddenly in powerful dream, or a whole imaginary world begins to flow from a writer's pen—from whence do these powerful imaginative forces spring? How are meaningful stories and images generated when they did not exist only moments before? The answer may prove beyond twenty-first-century neuroscience altogether, but the best place to begin such an investigation would be an exploration of the neurobiological correlates of *creativity*.

Chapter 8

Creativity and dream

I imagine that for many readers the combination of creativity and dream under a single topic heading might be somewhat perplexing. Creativity is after all associated with the process of making something, or at least the process of thinking something up; both examples of actively *doing*. Dreams, on the other hand, are a perplexing phenomenon that happen to us while we are passive and quite literally doing the least—unconscious and asleep. My basic premise with this topical conjunction is that a good part of creativity, especially that scientific and artistic creativity deemed "extraordinary," arises from the unconscious mind, rather than the conscious ego. There is certainly a vital place for the rational, deliberate, conscious aspects of creativity, and the neurobiological correlates of such processes will be discussed in detail below. But the productions of the conscious mind only go so far; even at their best, they are making something out of the materials that the unconscious obligingly provides.

Creativity

Perhaps even more so than imagination, creativity is a topic that enchants and confounds—it seems essential to the human condition, but it is not so easily boxed into neat and manageable concepts. It is also a topic of growing fascination: between 1999 and 2009 over 10,000 papers were written on the topic of creativity across a wide variety of fields (Kaufman & Beghetto, 2009).

Harvard psychologist Sherry Carson (2010) writes that the essential definition used in contemporary creativity studies is that creative ideas or products have to be both *novel or original, and adaptive or useful*. Vartanian, Bristol, and Kaufman echo this *novel and useful* framework as the standard definition for the field in their 2013 anthology on the *Neuroscience of creativity*. Thus, a parent who tells the bedtime story "Little Red Riding Hood" to her daughter every night in exactly the same way would not be exhibiting creativity, however vividly both parent and child may imagine the story unfolding. This allows for a helpful distinction between creativity and imagination as it is understood in depth psychology. A procession of images may be deeply meaningful without necessarily being judged novel, and thus imagination can convey many levels of meaning apart from whether or not those meanings are ultimately deemed to be creative per se. Indeed, the possibility of archetypal imagination as outlined in Chapter 5 calls into question the assumption that new is always better, suggesting instead that human meaning is rather constellated around a core of meaningful patterns, as exemplified in Joseph Campbell's formulation of the Hero's Journey. At the same time, allowing for profound meaning in archetypal imagery and stories does not diminish the unique allure of creativity; if anything, it makes the capacity to tell new stories all the more mysterious.

The second part of the standard definition for creativity, *usefulness*, is a bit more complicated, because what is useful or not can become a debate in itself. I accept the *usefulness* aspect of the definition as long as "usefulness" is defined broadly and holistically. A person walking alone on a mountaintop may make up a song and sing it only to himself, and find that it brings him great joy and delight; I contend that the creation of joy is in itself a great *use* for a song, even if no other person comes to hear it. This is in contrast to more socially oriented understandings of creativity, where a creative idea or product must actually have use in the larger community or culture to qualify as creative. Mihaly Csikszentmihalyi's famous 1996 study on the psychology of creativity, for example, omitted from his definition of "creative" any product or idea that did not make a concrete impact on the social domain within which it occurs. While applying such constraints is certainly understandable in designing a rigorous psychological study of highly creative individuals, I fear it leaves out all the creativity we humans can experience from day to day—arguably an important source of meaning in our lives.

Indeed, many more recent studies and theories have tried to reframe creativity as a basic human birthright. Nancy Andreasen and her colleagues (2005) differentiate between ordinary creativity, which we all use every day, and extraordinary creativity, which produces great works of art, science, and other aspects of culture. Kaufman and Gregoire's (2015) *Wired to create* argues that the human brain is inherently creative, and that some individuals simply develop this inherent capacity more than others. Some individuals are able to make extraordinary creative contributions to their field in the course of their lives, but many others can access and enjoy personal creativity without making such contributions, and arguably we all use creativity now and again for even the most basic of activities. In any case, a spectrum can be drawn between creativity that has an external, productive focus, and creativity that has more inner or personal meaning.

The chapter is especially concerned with the latter end of that spectrum: when a meaningful new idea, image, or story emerges into consciousness, where does it come from? Elizabeth Gilbert (2015) discusses the curious phenomena reported by writers across the centuries whereby whole poems or paragraphs suddenly come upon them fully formed, seemingly out of nowhere. Of course, this phenomenon is counterbalanced by the great amount of work that most creative individuals go through working through and refining their creative ideas and images in order to arrive at a final product. Kaufman and Gregoire (2015) distinguish two basic neurobiological stages of the creative process as *generation*, where ideas and images emerge into consciousness, and *selection*, in which those ideas are sorted, evaluated, and worked over consciously. Similarly, Dietrich and Haider (2017) differentiate between *spontaneous* and *deliberate* creativity, each with their own set of brain mechanisms, and argue that neuroscience must study these mechanisms independently rather than treat them as a single monolithic phenomenon.

My working definition of imagination, *the generation of meaningful images and narratives arising in consciousness*, certainly seems to conform more to the first kind of creativity that involves spontaneous generation. But an inquiry into the neurobiology of the selection process (or deliberate creativity) is also worthwhile, insofar as it may help us better understand how imagination engages with other cognitive functions to achieve results. To this end, the next section will focus on a "whole brain" account of creativity as a conscious process that forms some kind of final product. From there, we will gradually proceed deeper into the unconscious generation of raw images and ideas.

Creative production

Much of the growing field of creativity studies focuses on the external: the generation of something new that has usefulness in the world. At its most stringent, this might be restricted to great works of art or philosophy and major scientific breakthroughs. But most discourses on creativity are open to a wider range of products; arts and crafts, architecture, home design, business ventures, corporate leadership, product development, scientific progress, technological innovation, video games, cooking, gardening, city planning, event planning—these are just a few areas that may involve high levels of creativity. I would go so far to say that any field of knowledge or practice can experience creative renewal when some aspect of it is re-imagined in a way that has a meaningful impact. This kind of creative production may occasionally occur as the sudden emergence of a fully formed insight, but more often it involves a sustained and often elaborate work process. Books and works of art are often outlined, worked over, and revised in multiple iterations. Major projects, whether in business and politics or in the garden or kitchen, often involve a great deal of care and consideration, and no shortage of trial and error over time. This process of "working out" a creative product (Kaufman and Gregoire's process of *selection*; Dietrich and Haider's *deliberate* creativity) goes beyond imagination in itself. Imagination may generate meaningful images and ideas, but creative production implicates other brain functions in order to refine, develop, and complete a successful finished product. Success in this context is of course mediated by the language and knowledge of whatever field the creative project is taking place in, as well as the specific aims of the creator: a garden overrun by weeds would for many gardeners count as a failed creative project, but a garden that intentionally cultivates and showcases weeds might yet count for a great creative success for the gardener who felt called to create it.

The "classical model" of creative production, first attributed to Helmholtz (1896) and/or Wallas (1926) usually proposes four stages to the creative process: (a) preparation, (b) incubation, (c) illumination, and (d) verification (or elaboration). The creative individual first prepares for the work by learning all about the problem or topic, or in the case of an artist, immersion in both the rules and constraints of their art-form and the aesthetic raw materials of sensory and personal experience. Phase 2, incubation, introduces an unconscious process, whereby the creator stops consciously working out the problem and allows for fresh insights and images to emerge. Phase 3 is the moment of illumination, sometimes referred to as the "aha" or "eureka" moment. In phase 4 the process then returns to conscious work, carefully applying the unconsciously generated materials to the problem at hand, working them over to refine a finished product.

Over the years the classical model has received criticism, both for being too simplistic, and because not all creative processes necessarily involve an "aha" moment. That said, so long as we don't take it too literally, I would argue the classical model is a viable framework for one of the means by which creative process can unfold. If we view the four stages as a more dynamic cycle of conscious–unconscious dialog, allowing different stages to have different levels of import under different circumstances, and allowing for the creative process to revisit past stages repeatedly rather than proceed in a rigid linear fashion, a great deal of creative activity can be accounted for. We can find "aha" moments in events as simple as the selection of the right word choice, the perfect color, the right filter through which to interpret confusing scientific data. In each of these cases the mind has produced a small solution, emerging suddenly into consciousness: illumination does not always require fireworks.

But whether or to what degree we accept the classical model as viable, it fits with a growing consensus that creativity is among the most complex of brain functions and that it recruits multiple areas in the course of making a creative product. In fact, Pfenninger (2001) considers creativity to be the highest of brain functions, because it involves the integration of otherwise unrelated systems of information. Arne Dietrich in particular has been crit-ical of attempts to localize a monolithic conception of creativity into spe-cific brain regions, quipping that "we might as well try to locate the neural centers for thinking" (2007, p. 24). Shelley Carson (2010) maps out mul-tiple brain regions that must work together for creative production, stating "there is, of course, no 'creativity' center in the brain ... creative cognition is a complex mental phenomenon that involves multiple sequential acts that utilize widespread circuits in the brain" (p. 45). The brain regions she identifies as crucial to the creative process include the executive centers of the prefrontal cortex, active during planning, reasoning, and decision making; the association centers, including the angular gyrus, supramar-ginal gyrus, and Wernicke's area, which integrate disparate sensory information and relate knowledge about one concept to something else that seems unrelated; as well as brain centers involved in judgment, motivation, sense of self, and ToM. Each of these brain functions play an important role in the creation of something novel and useful.

This whole brain model is a large step forward from the late twentieth century, when a popular notion held that the right hemisphere of the brain was the creative hemisphere. This notion has its origins in the Nobel Prize-winning research of Roger Sperry and his graduate student Michael Gazza-niga, which studied "split-brain" patients whose corpus callosums had been severed, essentially isolating the two brain hemispheres from each other (Sperry, 1974). Kaufman, Kornilov, Bristol, Tan, and Grigorenko (2010) describe how following these early breakthrough studies, "There are now extensive data indicating that the right hemisphere specializes in global, parallel, holistic processes, whereas the left hemisphere specializes in sequential and analytical processes" (p. 221). From this many surmised that the right hemisphere was specialized for novelty, finding new connections where the left hemisphere was prone to taking things apart through reason and analysis. And indeed, the right hemisphere appears to be important in the generation phase of creativity. But most researchers now agree that creative production happens through the right and left hemispheres working together: "the sequential and interactive engagement of both hemispheres, an interdisciplinary engagement between two 'experts' " (p. 222). Furthermore, McGilchrist (2009) points to data that split-brain patients actually show impaired imagination and creativity, strongly suggesting that "the integrated functioning of both hemispheres is needed for such activity" (p. 198). Linear analysis and holistic synthesis are both important ingredients for successful creative production.

Just as the left and right hemispheres of the brain must cooperate for creative production, so do the front and back of the brain need to work together. The executive center of the prefrontal cortex works with information incoming from the sensory and association areas that identify facts, generate images, and make new connections. Along these lines,

Damasio (2001) sees creativity in the brain as being first of all contingent on the "strong generation of representational diversity," by which he means "the ability to generate—to bring to your conscious mind—a variety of novel combinations of entities and parts of entities as images" (p. 65). However, not all of these images will be relevant to the problem or project at hand, and most of them in fact may be discarded. This latter process of selection relies on the executive reasoning of the prefrontal cortex:

> The images are not realized as such in the pre-frontal cortices—but rather in the early sensory cortices—but they are conducted or ordered from there.... I suspect that a marvelous pre-frontal cortex generating many new items and holding them "on line" would be of little use if we did not have the ability to execute good selections based on aesthetic or scientific goals.
>
> (p. 65)

In essence, the planning, reasoning, decision making regions at the front of the brain must play an active process in shaping, editing, and elaborating the creative imagistic contents that are generated in regions that are further posterior.

Arne Dietrich and his colleagues have developed a detailed model that differentiates and relates *deliberate* and *spontaneous* creativity, with particular regard to the role of the prefrontal cortex. While the ventromedial prefrontal cortex (VMPFC) is involved with regulating emotional and social considerations, and thus involved in the many social considerations of creative output, the dorsolateral prefrontal cortex (DLPFC) engages with the sensory and association cortices and is implicated in working memory, or the workspace of ideas (Dietrich, 2004). Information and imagery that is held "online" in working memory can be consciously worked over, tinkered with, and recombined during a deliberate creative process. However, while much can be achieved through this conscious workspace, it is also limited. Dietrich and Haider (2017) argue that because this process is heavily controlled by top-down processes, it is subject to biases and expectations about how the creative problem should be solved. Deliberate creativity is thus constrained by "paradigmatic" and "common-sense" solutions that draw on a much smaller range of associative possibilities. Thus, the focused attention of deliberate creativity has the drawback of narrowing its possibilities, or as Dietrich and Haider humorously put it: "While the deliberate mode has the advantage of limiting the solution space, it has the disadvantage of limiting the solution space!" (p. 5). Moving outside of the solution space of deliberate creativity in the prefrontal cortex means opening up to spontaneous creative processes arising from deeper brain regions. Of course, once new ideas and images are generated and enter into working memory, the solution space may close and the deliberate creativity can resume.

An important point to consider here is that one of the basic constraints on the solution space of working memory are the cultural frameworks and other belief systems that organize perception of reality. Dietrich (2015) acknowledges this as one of the primary limitations of the deliberate mode:

> Being at the top of the neural pyramid, the prefrontal cortex also houses a person's cultural values and belief system. This gives the deliberate mode—initiated and supervised by the prefrontal cortex as it is—a number of critical built in predispositions as it generates new ideas.... The deliberate mode is, for all its sightedness, pretty useless when the solution violates something we think is true about the world.
>
> (pp. 150–151)

Hence the association of creativity with "thinking outside the box"— getting outside of assumptions and rigid thought structures to allow the unexpected to emerge. This notion first nicely with Thomas Kuhn's theory of paradigm shifts in science involving a dissolution and refinement of entire systems of scientific understanding. It also, incidentally, helps make the case for model agnosticism as an effective strategy for engaging complex problems.

A related late twentieth-century notion that continues to be researched and debated today is the proposition that creativity requires a "disinhibition" function that allows the brain to activate creative capacities that are otherwise usually kept on lockdown. Kaufman et al. (2010) review theories of disinhibition dating back to the mid-nineteenth century, and focusing in particular on the late twentieth-century work of Colin Martindale, which showed that creative people show lowered activity in cortical regions that inhibit "abnormal" behavior. More recently, R. Jung and Haier (2013) reviewed evidence of frontotemporal dementia and brain lesion studies to argue that "lower brain integrity within left hemisphere brain structures—particularly left anterior temporal and inferior parietal lobes—serves to 'disinhibit' other brain regions associated with increased novelty generation" (p. 243). The authors go on to cite several studies of their own to further evidence "a decidedly left-lateralized, frontosubcortical, and disinhibitory network of brain regions underlying creative cognition" (p. 244). These findings are further supported by Vishkontas and Miller (2013), who undertook a review of the effects of various neurodegenerative disorders on creativity, and concluded that "diminished language function via neurodegenerative diseases that target the left frontal or left anterior temporal lobes sometimes leads to the emergence of previously unrecognized visual or musical creativity" (p. 128). Likewise, Radel, Davranche, Fournier, and Dietrich (2015) found additional evidence that decreased inhibition improves idea generation. The disinhibition hypothesis suggests that the linear, analytical left-brain usually actively inhibits generative creative process, and that a disinhibition function is required to allow creative cognition to take precedence.

A final point of consideration with regards to whole-brain conscious creative production is to revisit the DMN. Recall that Scott Berry Kaufman has taken the bold move of christening the DMN as the *imagination network* (Kaufman, 2013). He has further asserted that the DMN is "involved in as much as half of our mental lives.... Its three main components—personal meaning making, mental simulation, and perspective taking—often work together when we are in what researchers call 'self-generated cognition'" (Kaufman & Gregoire, 2015, p. xxviii). This model emphasizes the interplay between the inwardly focused DMN and task-focused CEN, noting that creativity is at its best when these two networks are working together. Kaufman and Gregoire point out that "creative people are particularly good at exercising flexibility in activating these brain networks that in most people tend to be at odds with each other" (p. xxix). That is to say, whereas most individuals have an inner tension between the inner-focus of the DMN and the more externally focused CEN, highly creative individuals have developed a capacity to move back and forth between these networks consciously. It has been further theorized that shifting between these two networks is moderated by a third: the salience network (Agnati et al., 2013). This would imply that successful creative individuals have both a well-developed salience system, and have acquired some facility for working with it consciously.

The creative unconscious

For all the twentieth-century criticism leveled at depth psychological discourse on the unconscious mind, it now seems glaringly obvious that the majority of information processed by the brain in any given moment does not reach conscious awareness. Indeed, Deitrich's (2004) entire discussion of deliberate creativity takes as given that "the working memory buffer of the prefrontal cortex holds the content of consciousness, and that the attentional network of the prefrontal cortex is the mechanism to select and limit the content" (p. 1016). Selecting and limiting the contents of consciousness would of course not be possible were there not a great reservoir of unconscious material to draw from. And indeed, given the heavily processed and filtered streams of information discussed in Chapter 6, it seems fair to suggest that the immediate reservoir of material from which the prefrontal cortex draws is itself surrounded by a veritable ocean of additional information processing that never feeds forward. Nor am I alone in my recourse to metaphoric language: Damasio declares that "there is a subterranean underneath the conscious mind and there are many levels to that subterranean" (1999, p. 319). The question then is not a matter of whether unconscious processes play a role in creativity, but rather how they do, and to what degree.

Damasio's assessment of the unconscious mind is also helpful to the present discourse because he explicitly frames it in terms of images. "Not all the images the brain constructs are made conscious. There are simply too many images being generated and too much competition for the relatively small window of mind in which images can be made conscious" (1999, p. 319). His theory rests on the notion that images function as representation aggregates of meaningful information, a kind of "currency" for the mind. There is some risk here of falling back into the imagery debate (i.e., Kosslyn vs. Pylyshyn), as to whether unconscious images should properly be called images prior to becoming conscious. Rather than getting muddled in that distinction, we can consider instead that what are experienced consciously as "images" are meaningful aggregates of information whether they have a representational (or sensate) form outside of consciousness or not. The point being, the brain has all manner of meaning making capacities—and myriad bundles of meaning already made—to populate this reservoir (or ocean) from which the prefrontal cortex selects in the process of deliberate creativity.

As the previous section on creative production demonstrates, there is great emphasis in recent scientific research into creativity on its conscious, deliberate, and perhaps rational properties. Dietrich (2007) in particular is extremely critical of formulations of creativity that overly emphasize divergent thinking, defocused attention, or altered states of conscious. And yet I think creativity has come to be widely associated with non-linear, non-rational, and unconscious processes for a reason: it seems to me implicit in the very idea of creation that *something emerges from nothing*. Whereas we saw the problem (or painting, or novel, or garden) one way, suddenly we are able to see it differently, to experience something new. Creation entails coming-into-being. Even in highly externalized group creative processes that seem to proceed mostly by conscious trial and error—Watson and Crick's discovery of the double helix is a great example—there may be any number of small new thoughts, ideas, and perspectives emerging suddenly into consciousness along the way. While these thousand tiny insights are not the dramatic "aha" of classic illumination, they nevertheless require a capacity for staying open to ideas outside of current conscious awareness. It seems that even when proceeding deliberately by trial and error—especially in consideration of the limited capacities of working memory—that engagement with unconscious processes during a prolonged creative project is inevitable. And as many artists attest, this engagement with the unconscious, or "unknown within," is not only one of the central mysteries of creativity, but also one of its principle delights (see Cameron, 1992; Csikszentmihalyi, 1996; Gilbert, 2015).

Free association revisited

Years before the DMN became a hot ticket in the neuroscience field, Nancy Andreasen became curious about the "resting" states of brains that were not focused on a specific task. She devised a study (Andreasen et al., 1995) that compared brain activity during spoken episodic memory recall with non-directed states when no task was present. In the task-free state, she found increased activity in areas often designated as "association cortex"—parts of the frontal, temporal, and parietal cortices with "a more complicated columnar organization than other parts of the brain" that gather and link information "in potentially novel ways" (Andreasen, 2005, p. 73). In her interpretation, this provides a window into how the brain generates unconscious thoughts and thus feeds the creative process through new and exciting combinations. Pfenninger (2001) also discusses the importance of association cortex, which he describes as "a structure characterized by extensive connections with other areas of the cerebral cortex and specialized for holding 'mental images'" (p. 96). In keeping with his theory of creativity as the highest of brain functions, the association cortex integrates disparate information from otherwise non-associated regions into greater wholes. Harkening back to the disinhibition hypotheses, Andreasen (2005) sees the intercommunication of the association cortices as a process "running unchecked, not subject to any of the reality principles normally governing them" (p. 77). This also fits with Dietrich's model of reducing the top-down control of prefrontal deliberate creativity in order to open up the solution space to possibilities that lie outside of conscious paradigmatic constraints.

Deitrich is highly critical of the idea that there are specific circuits that process information creatively as opposed to non-creatively. Outside the deliberate creativity performed by working memory, "the recombination of bits and pieces of information into novel configurations must come from the very neural circuits that normally store those bits and pieces of information" (2007, p. 25). This parallels the notion that the brain systems that generate internal mental imagery are largely the same systems used to process incoming sense data. In this case, the same circuits that retrieve "correct" information in a linear fashion are the circuits that recombine that information in a novel fashion. This, Dietrich argues, is inevitable once we concede that the brain is a non-linear information processor; generating novelty is inherent to the system and can in principle arise in any brain circuit. For Dietrich, this is the core of spontaneous (as opposed to deliberate) creativity—a wide-ranging sweep of associative activity that occurs "outside the box" of paradigmatic conscious working memory. Future research, he argues, should focus less on localizing creativity and more on applying existing neuroscientific knowledge of cognitive circuits to see how a creative process engages the same circuits differently.

One noteworthy line of research in this direction is Gabora and Ranjan's (2013) work on associative neural cliques, or "neurds." They begin their paper by boldly asserting that their neural model of unconscious associative process explains the "magic of creativity"—that is, how creative insight emerges seemingly out of nowhere. This theory depends on the "distributed, content-addressable architecture of memory" (p. 22). The distributed nature of memory means that the various features of grandma's apple pie are widely distributed across different brain regions (sight, smell, taste, social contexts, emotional contexts, specific memories of grandma herself, and so on down the rabbit hole). The content-addressable nature of memory means that related ideas, images, and concepts are stored together in a neural clique of associations. The connections between these neurons across specific memories are what makes associative thought possible. This means that while a specific memory may have a specific network of neurons encoding its features, those neurons also have associative connections to similar bits of information that do not belong to the memory episode.

Using Freud's distinction between analytical and associative thought, Gabora and Ranjan assert that while linear analytical thought seeks a single source of correct information, non-linear associative thought activates the wider range of neural connections. They further point to evidence that some neurons will respond maximally to a particular microfeature (a particular vocal tone, for example) while others will have a weaker response to the same stimulus. Analytic thought ignores these weaker connections while associative thought invites them. Thus they define their concept of *neurds* as neural cliques "that would not be included in cell assembly if one were in an analytic mode of thought, but would be included if one were in the associative mode of thought" (p. 31). They go on to argue that most of the time, for most people, neurds aren't active in regular task oriented thinking. "Their time to shine comes when one has to break out of a rut" (p. 31). Thus, they assert that this activity accounts for the magic of creativity, insofar as the brain reaches into its memories to produce something that was never there to begin with.

I find both Deitrich and Gabora and Ranjan's accounts to be compelling and plausible as far as they go, but as both a lifelong scholar of creativity and a creative writer myself, I can't help but feel that they have yet to address creativity in its most awesome aspect: the generation of whole fictional worlds, living characters that surprise their authors, and emergent visions of reality, across all disciplines, that fundamentally remake the paradigms that constrain them. The accounts given thus far still seem to adhere to the model of a computer solving problems; appropriate and understandable coming from the scientific world, but still not quite touching those qualities of creativity that for so many artists make it a spiritual or even cosmic experience. Andreasen (2005) gets a bit closer by framing creativity in the brain in terms of complexity theory: "the human brain is perhaps the most superb example of a self-organizing system … it is constantly and spontaneously generating new thoughts, often without external control" (p. 63). In addressing the widely reported phenomenon of whole creative works (poems, stories, visions, and other detailed schemas) emerging ex nihilo, she speculates that during creative process "multiple regions of our highly developed human association cortex interact with one another…. The brain is working as a self-organizing system … as if the multiples association cortices are communicating back and forth" (p. 77). Rather than trying to reconcile and integrate external data with internal frameworks, as is usually the case during waking life, during a creative process the brain is reconciling and integrating the different parts of its own emergent process. The vast resources of the brain given to us by evolution for decoding and integrating reality are turned instead toward creating reality. The simulator begins to run itself.

Incubation and insight

The central stage of the much-debated classical model of creativity circles around a process of incubation and illumination. The conscious mind, having done the hard work of research and preparation, lets go, and like a mother bird incubating an egg, allows the rich warmth of the creative unconscious to do its work. Sometime later, while out for a stroll or taking a shower or becoming engrossed in some other unrelated activity, the moment of illumination suddenly occurs—an idea or image or story emerges into consciousness. In contemporary parlance, this is often described more modestly as a moment of insight: when out of the dark of unknowing, new knowledge emerges. Phenomenologically, Csikszentmihalyi's (1996) study of highly creative individuals affirmed that incubation is often experienced as a vital part of the creative process. With due respect to those advocates for deliberate forms of conscious creativity in which such incubation plays a minimal role, it is nevertheless an important phenomenon in its own right worthy of deeper investigation. As Dietrich (2015) puts it with regards to major scientific progress: "the fact that groundbreaking discoveries in science are the result of the mind idling in neutral should give us pause the next time we want to credit creative thinking solely to the higher cognitive functions of the cerebral cortex" (p. 153). It may be wounding to the ego to think that major creative breakthroughs are thus received from the unconscious rather than consciously achieved, but this certainly appears to be the case some of the time.

For all of his criticism of traditional conceptualizations of creativity in neuroscience, Dietrich offers a thorough defense of creative incubation. Even in his early work on the topic (2004) he suggests: "It is plausible that incubation is successful because it leads to the spontaneous processing mode, which in turn results in the relaxation of constraints" (p. 1019). More recently (Dietrich & Haider, 2017), he gives a more thorough account, arguing that once the "task-set" of deliberate creative process in working memory has failed, it leaves behind a goal-oriented inertia that continues unconsciously at a slower pace. "We can expect that a strongly interacting coalition of neurons does not instantly decay back to baseline. Any disintegration phase would take time, during which a new task set would be subjected to interference from the previous one" (p. 4). The general goal remains, but without the constraints of the established solution space in working memory. Dietrich and Haider further relate these ideas about the spontaneous mode of creativity and incubation to the DMN:

> The notion that the DMN is a proactive system implies that there must be a continuous search process taking place that reduces uncertainty even when no task is at hand. This constant anticipatory drive in the DMN during moments of passive contemplation brings it into close contact with the concept of task-set inertia and the specific phenomenon of incubation.
>
> (2017, p. 5)

While skeptical of the rush to proclaim the DMN as the source of creativity in the brain, they suggest that mapping the spontaneous mode of creativity onto the DMN and the deliberate mode onto the CEN may prove a fruitful hypothesis for further investigation.

The importance of daydreaming and mind-wandering, both strongly associated with the DMN, are taken up repeatedly by Kaufman and Gregoire. "Research has supported the idea that the creative incubation that occurs during daydreaming is critical to creative thought and achievement and also to insightful problem solving" (2015, p. 34). Daydreaming here is framed as a sort of liminal space where a relaxed consciousness can play with the emergent contents of the unconscious. The daydreaming itself is of course a conscious process, but one that is more receptive to the spontaneous generation of images and ideas from unconscious processes. Conscious but receptive engagement with the unconscious helps the creative process come to light.

The parallels to Jungian thought should at this point be obvious. A central theme running throughout Jungian psychology is the "mutual penetration of the conscious and unconscious" (1954b/1931, p. 152 [para. 327]). Jung is sometimes criticized for suggesting a deep wisdom or intelligence to the psyche that can at times seem mystical in nature. But Kaufman and Gregoire argue that the idea of non-conscious intelligence is amply supported by scientific research. "The brain's implicit processing system can, in fact, be very intelligent. Non-conscious processes may indeed be faster and structurally more sophisticated than our conscious thinking systems" (2015, p. 66). The existence of so-called "idiot–savants" who test low on conventional IQ scored but are nevertheless capable of extraordinary mental and artistic feats are offered as a further example of unconscious implicit intelligence can look like. Although this fails to fully explain the phenomenon of incubation over particularly long periods of inactivity, it does further emphasize the importance of being able to periodically surrender conscious control during the creative process.

Dream

For all his excellent analysis, I must admit find Dietrich's reductionistic account of creativity ultimately dissatisfying. He certainly makes the case for the benefits of reduction as a methodology—it has the benefit of narrowing a search into utmost specificity. There is clearly an immense amount to be discovered by sorting through the minutia of the particular. But how such a reduction could ever comprehensively explain an unfathomably complex phenomenon as human creativity continues to perplex me.

Perhaps because Dietrich is a scientist, he is naturally inclined to think of creativity as it occurs for most scientists: creative problem solving in scientific projects. Running throughout his writing is focus on creativity as a way of finding a distinct solution to a rational problem. Of course problem solving is one important form creativity can take—but creativity at its most vital and mysterious goes far beyond this. The whole-world and deep-character generation of writers, the unprecedented complex aesthetic creations of artists, the transformational visions of leaders of all kinds, and perhaps most importantly, the thrill of creative living when individuals experience a taste of what Nietzsche meant by life itself being a creative work of art—each of these phenomena speak of a holistic complexity that no simple set of brain mechanisms are likely to predict. For all out scientific prowess, we still do guesswork when it comes to predicting the weather—and weather has nothing on the complexity of the creative brain.

To dig deeper into what might be happening in the brain when the creative unconscious astounds us, we have recourse to a much more common area of human experience where complex imaginal wholes are generated spontaneously without direction by the executive ego. I am speaking, of course, of dreams. Every night we enter into an imaginal process that is experienced as something happening to us, a weaving of images, environments, actions, and stories that we do not control. The idea that creativity and dreaming are somehow connected is not new. Discussions of creative incubation often references creative ideas emerging through dreams. Andreasen (2005) remarks: "the unconscious creative processes that we 'run in the background' during waking hours … may also occur during sleep" (p. 67). In both cases, something other than the executive ego is engaged in a complex imaginal process, sometimes with spectacular results.

Dreams have long presented a special problem to science, in that as a subjective phenomenon they cannot be directly measured, and any brain correlates to dreaming must be matched to the imperfect verbal dream transcriptions offered by subjects after the fact. The scientific literature is rife with disclaimers about the challenge of this area of study—a challenge that of course applies equally to any scientific study of imaginal phenomena.

In searching for a scientific definition of dreaming, Dang-Vu, Schabus, Desseilles, Schwartz, and Maquet (2007) write: "dreaming is experienced every night by most humans as multisensory mental representations occurring spontaneously during sleep, often organized in a narrative manner" (p. 96). Voss and Voss (2014) provide an alternative definition: "Dreams are altered states of consciousness in which the brain constructs a virtual world of vivid images that we are unable to identify as hallucinogenic" (p. 24). Running through these two definitions are many of the ideas that have been discussed in this discourse already: spontaneous generation, multisensory imagination, virtual reality, and narrative construction. Dream scientists also often emphasize that dreamers usually can't "reality test" and realize that they are dreaming, except in the special case of lucid dreams, which will be discussed toward the end. The inability for dreamers to recognize that they are not experiencing physical reality is all the more curious in that dream content is so often characterized as bizarre, bending rules of space, time, and identity as if they did not exist.

Continuity in dreaming and waking consciousness

One of the themes that has clearly emerged in this study of the neurobiological correlates of imagination is that imaginal and creative process do not have their own dedicated brain regions so much as they use normative brain regions in specific ways. It should come as no surprise, then, that the neurobiological correlates of dreaming would overlap significantly with brain systems that are also utilized for waking, conscious processes. There are some clear unique physiological markers to dreaming that will be outlined below, including the notable absence of executive control. But it is also worth considering the ways in which the dreams that take place during sleep have continuity with waking imaginal processes, such as creative artistry or Jungian active imagination. Goodwyn (2012) reviews several studies comparing the content of dreams with the content of waking fantasy during sensory deprivation, and concludes that "under the right conditions, dream *content* and waking mental imagery *content* are indistinguishable" (p. 36). Kaufman and Gregoire (2015) also make an argument for continuity between dreaming and daydreaming, "as both involve an exploration of various aspects of who we are, including self-representations, strivings, current concerns, and autobiographical memory" (p. 36). They further point to the neurotransmitter dopamine as a common link between dreaming and daydreaming, noting that "people who are high in openness to experience report dreaming more often and having more vivid dreams than those who are less open to experience, very likely due to their higher dopamine production" (p. 87). Solms and Turnbull (2002) also discuss the role of the neurotransmitter dopamine in dreaming, including studies that correlate artificially increased dopamine levels with more frequent, intense, and bizarre dreams, and suggest that the goal-seeking function of dopamine may be the chemical engine underlying all dream activity (more on this below).

That said, there are also some pronounced and undeniable discontinuities between dreaming and waking. Hobson (2015) dedicates the final chapter of his book *Psychodynamic neurology* to examining the phenomenological aspect of these discontinuities using one of his own dreams as an example. Echoing his earlier work (2002), he emphasizes that dream content is cognitively bizarre, showing little regard for the rules of time, space, and identity that fundamentally organize our waking experience. Perhaps the single most striking discontinuity from a neurobiological perspective is the deactivation of the DLPFC during REM sleep (see Maquet et al., 1996; Muzur, Pace-Schott, & Hobson, 2002; Nofzinger, Mintun, Wiseman, Kupfer, & Moore, 1997; Pace-Schott, 2007). As mentioned above, the DLPFC is crucial to executive decision making and working memory. As such, its deactivation during REM sleep is often cited in accounting for the irrational and bizarre aspects of dream phenomenology (Hobson, 2002; Solms & Turnbull, 2002).

An interesting point of contrast to the DLPFC shutting down is that the neighboring medial prefrontal cortex (MPFC) "has been shown to be as active during REM sleep as during wakefulness ... in contrast with its significant deactivation during non-REM sleep" (Dang-Vu et al., 2007, p. 105). Dang-Vu and colleagues review literature on the MPFC indicating that it is involved in "theory of mind" (ToM) processes, and conclude that this is the source of the colorful characters we meet in our dreams and experience as having minds and intentions of their own. A further review by Pace-Schott (2007) confirms that other areas most commonly associated with ToM are active in dreaming, including "the superior temporal sulcus and temporal poles including the amygdala" (p. 140). In an echo of James Hillman's affirmation of our psychological need to personify, the dreaming brain appears to deeply value engaging with "other minds," while asleep.

Returning to the deactivation of the executive functions of the DLPFC, Dietrich (2015) has proposed and long advocated for what he calls the transient hypofrontal theory (THT). In short, THT holds that the prefrontal cortex represents the zenith of human brain evolution, and as such is responsible for the highest functions of human consciousness. Altered states of all kinds, according to this theory, are marked by a transient down-regulation of prefrontal activity. "In altered states that are marked by severe prefrontal hypofunction, such as dreaming or the various psychopharmacological heavens and hells, this modification results in extraordinarily bizarre phenomenology" (p. 156). Dietrich uses this hierarchical model to argue that these altered states of consciousness should be viewed as lower and less evolved forms of consciousness. I find this formulation problematic, not in the least because assigning the seat of rational ego function a privileged role is a culturally mediated assumption and perhaps a self-fulfilling prophecy. A full critique of this model and the scientific culture that supports it will be taken up in more detail in Chapter 10.

Physiological origins of dreams

Since its discovery in the 1950s, REM sleep has been associated with vivid dreaming (Aserinsky & Kleitman, 1953; Dement & Kleitman, 1957). REM sleep marks periods of punctuated cortical arousal in otherwise peaceful slumber, arising roughly every 90 minutes. As summarized by Presti, "during REM sleep clusters of cells in the in the pons and midbrain become active and spread neural activation to the cerebral cortex. The neural transmitter acetylcholine is central to this excitation" (Presti, 2016, p. 236). In essence the reality simulator starts running without any sensory input, with cortical activation in sensory and motor areas presumably resulting in dream experiences of sensation and movement. Part of what makes this possible is that motor output via the spinal cortex becomes inhibited during REM, preventing the body from actually moving and reacting to or acting out the dream content. The fact that this inhibition is necessary at all indicates just how close to waking "reality" these sensory-motor brain processes are.

Presti further reminds us that we all dream every night whether we remember the dreams or not, and that for most people dream recall can be improved with dedicated practice. "The networks activated during REM sleep may be novel ones, not necessarily associated with previous learning and experience, and thus prone to ready dissipation" (2016, p. 237). Dreaming might then paradoxically be understood as altered form of waking consciousness, one for which we often do not make memories, thus creating the illusion of an entire night's sleep spent unconscious. Hobson (1988) proposed a mechanism for this dream amnesia, whereby only short-term memory functions in the cholinergic environment of REM, and long-term memory is shut off without sufficient stimulation from the aminergic system. "If, and only if, aminergic signals arrive at the many neurons storing that trace memory will the perceptual and cognitive experience of the dream be transferred into intermediate memory" (p. 214). Emotional salience might do this, as when we make up from a nightmare, but an intentional practice of recalling and valuing dream content seems to help as well. I would further posit that the chronic lack of dream recall in contemporary Western civilizations may be heavily culturally mediated as well. Because recall is a skill that can develop with practice, societies more prone to honoring dreams are more likely to foster individuals wired to remember them.

However, the understanding that REM sleep is the sole physiological process that underlies the phenomenon of dreaming has recently become more controversial. In a pivotal clinical–anatomical review, Solms (1997) concluded that dreaming can and does occur even when the brain is not in the REM state. The vast majority of dreams appear to arise during REM, but they are occasionally reported at other periods of the sleep cycle as well, especially during the period just after sleep begins, and just before it ends—both moments marked by higher cortical arousal. From this Solms offers the alternative hypothesis that the physiological trigger for dreaming is brain arousal in the broader sense, REM being the most common form that this arousal can take: "a certain amount, rather than a certain type, of arousal is a necessary precondition for dreaming" (Solms & Turnbull, 2002, p. 196). Furthermore, epileptic seizures completely contained in the limbic regions of the forebrain have also been accompanied by dreams outside of REM sleep and with no prompting from the brainstem. "Dreaming, it seems, can triggered by arousal of any type, arising from any place—including the emotion-and-memory generating structures of the limbic forebrain" (p. 198). Thus, while acknowledging REM as one of the primary physiological triggers for the dream experience, several other mechanisms may trigger dreams or dream-like states, quite possibly including mechanisms that have yet to be discovered.

Solms and Turnbull have developed the alternative hypothesis that while the arousal necessary for dreaming may come most consistently from REM sleep as initiated by the brainstem, dreaming itself has physiological origins distinct from REM. Again working from extensive clinical–anatomical review, they identify two forebrain regions that are essential to dreaming: the occipito-tempero-parietal junction and the limbic white matter of the ventromesial quadrant of the frontal lobes. While damage to other parts of the brain can change the form and content of dreaming, damage to these two regions appears to cause dreaming to cease altogether. The role of the occipito-tempero-parietal junction remains controversial, as Solms' lesion data contradicts other brain-imaging studies (see Yu, 2001). But it is the limbic forebrain that is advanced by Solms and Turnbull as the most likely "primary driving force" (2002, p. 198) for dreaming in the brain. This conclusion is drawn in part from Panksepp's (1998) studies in affective neuroscience, and in particular the emotional SEEKING system associated with the limbic forebrain. This system of curiosity, appetite, and reward relies on the neurotransmitter dopamine as mentioned above. The activation of the SEEKING system, in according to this hypothesis, is what initiates the dreaming process:

> Activation of the SEEKING system during sleep is commonly, but not exclusively, triggered by the REM state. A thought process occurring during any stage of sleep can presumably also activate the SEEKING system.... If [a] memory or feeling activates the interest of the SEEKING system, this would be enough to begin the dream process. ... This is experienced as imaginative perception and cognition— which, however, differs from waking thought in that it is unconstrained by frontal inhibition.
>
> (Solms & Turnbull, 2002, p. 212)

This suggests that dreams are inherently emotional processes, and that they are essentially a meaning-seeking process carried out in the cortex without executive control. This proposition is now gaining greater acceptance after a period of some decades where the scientific community was far less accepting of the notion that dreams might be meaningful.

Dreaming and meaning

Following their 1975 discovery of the brainstem origins of REM sleep, Hobson and McCarley (1977) published a second paper that proposed a physiological model for dreaming itself. Their activation synthesis model proceeds from the assumption at the time that REM sleep and dreaming were the same thing, and thus the cholinergic arousal provided by the brainstem was activating cortical activity on a purely physiological basis. This was widely interpreted to mean that dreams were a kind of random noise generated as a byproduct of physiological REM arousal. Solms and Turnbull (2002) lament that after Hobson's presentation to the American Psychological Association in 1976, the membership voted that Freudian dream theory was scientifically untenable. The idea that meaningful dreams emerged as expressions of unconscious psychological truth was replaced with a skeptical stance that dreams were more likely an epiphenomenon of undirected cortical arousal. Hobson (2015) has since made a rather stunning disavowal of this position, insisting that he never meant "to imply that dreams were meaningless and therefor of no use to psychology.... I have claimed that dreams are very meaningful but that their meaning was not so much concealed as revealed by dream bizarreness" (p. 217). Hobson's agenda in 1976 was not so much to argue against meaningful dreams as to argue against Freudian theory in general, and indeed, any comprehensive review of his work reveals a deep anti-Freudian bias. But the fact that Hobson felt the need to defend himself so unequivocally on the issue of meaningful dreaming indicates how pervasively his earlier work was interpreted to imply meaningless dreams.

As this discourse has argued from the beginning, meaning comes in a many shapes and sizes. Solms and Turnbull (2002) and Yu (2001) argue that much of Freudian dream theory is affirmed by recent neuroscience, while Hobson (1988, 2002, 2015) has led the charge in dismissing Freud's work as unscientific. One of the principle forms of meaning that Solms and Hobson do agree on is that dreams are emotionally meaningful—that is, they express emotional activity and emotional concerns. Bulkeley and Hurd (2014) write that dreams represent a form of emotional processing far more intense than in normative consciousness: "the 'emotional brain' is more active than in waking life ... the amygdala goes into overdrive during dreaming, which is notable because this structure is known to mediate fight or flight responses" (p. xvii). Hartmann (2007) has developed a model that brings symbolism back into play by suggesting that images in dreams are primarily expressions of emotional contents. In this understanding, the image is more than its literal meaning (i.e., just a red bird)—the symbolic or metaphoric meaning of the image is its emotional charge, which the dreamer also ostensibly experiences simultaneously. Hartman argues that in this regard dreams can serve an important healing role in integrating difficult emotions by allowing them to inhabit representational forms other than their original raw affective form. The image can carry more complex connotations and nuanced layers of understanding, and thus help the dreamer develop a more integrated emotional intelligence. This model is further substantiated by Kunzendorf (2007), who reviews evidence that "lingering emotion" (p. 156) can exist without a conscious source, and that these unintegrated emotions may find symbolic expressions in the context of dreaming. In addition, Ribeiro (2004) argues that the phenomenon of recurring nightmares in trauma victims is evidence of a deep psychological dimension to dream meaning. If dream images were random or even mostly random, how could the same dream images and narratives arise repeatedly?

While the emotional theory of dream meaning is generally agreed upon and supported by substantial evidence, it would be premature to conclude that emotion is the only form of meaning that dreams carry. Harvard psychologist Deirdre Barrett argues that dreams include thinking and problem-solving processes while the brain is in a different biochemical state from waking cognition (Barrett, 2007). "Dream content touches on virtually everything waking thought does, though in different proportions" (p. 138). She reviews extensive evidence, including both first-person phenomenological reports and her own empirical studies, to demonstrate that creative problem solving in dreams is a common occurrence. Subjects in the studies were sometimes able to solve logical brain-teasers through dream content and also commonly reported dreams that addressed the problem even if no solution emerged. Furthermore, subjects were more likely to find dream solutions when highly motivated and tasked with solving problems that were more personal in nature. A fascinating report from her popular book *The committee of sleep* recounts a physician sleeping on the brain-teaser "what word starts and ends with 'he?'"—a bizarre dream scenario unfolds including twisted "hee-hee" laughter, intense chest pains, consultations with doctors and the image of a brain in the road. The dream concludes with the dreamer exclaiming "Riddles give me headaches," at which point his pain vanished (Barrett, 2001, p. 161). The dreamer awoke with the two correct solutions to the brain-teaser: "heartache" and "headache." Reviewing this evidence, it seems likely that dreaming and creative incubation are related and overlapping brain functions, and that dreaming may offer us a first-person perspective into the deep, non-linear, and imagistic processing that unconscious creativity entails.

It is interesting to note that Hobson's (2015) assertion that dreams reveal rather than conceal meaning is also the basic hypothesis advanced by Wilkinson (2006) in her study of the neurobiological correlates of Jungian psychology. In fact, a similar formulation was used by Jung himself: "[Dreams] do not deceive, they do not lie, they do not distort or disguise, but naively announce what they are and what they mean" (1954b/1931, p. 103 [para. 189]). For Jung, the content of the dream represented something in the unconscious psyche that the waking ego had yet to understand and integrate. The fact that the rational ego is prone to describe dream content as bizarre or random actually strengthens the argument that non-rational brain regions are communicating something psychologically true but as yet not comprehended or integrated by the rational mind. The neurobiological evidence discussed so far supports this assertion both in the form of otherwise inhibited emotional contents becoming conscious, and in the case of creative incubation and insight detailed above. And given the holistic and interconnected nature of the brain, it seems plausible and perhaps likely that if dreaming can express meaning on these levels, it may well be capable of expressing more complex constellations of meaning as well.

Hartmann (1998) argues that although both waking and dreaming consciousness involve the activation of associative neural networks, dreaming specifically "connects more broadly and more widely than does waking; in this sense, dreaming can be considered 'hyperconnective'" (p. 80). For Hartmann, this is intimately bound to the notion of metaphor, where microfeatures of images associate to and thus imply each other. "In the nets of our minds (and that's all we have) metaphor is real; the similarity between a personal relationship and a journey by car is just as real as the similarity between a car and a truck" (p. 106). In the hyperconnectivity of the dreaming state, much more distant connections between images and ideas can theoretically emerge in the form of metaphors. This idea of a broader associative network in dreaming states has striking similarities to Gabora and Ranjan's (2013) theory of "neurds" in creative processes. Wilkinson also emphasizes the importance of metaphor a complex meaning-maker in the brain: "Emergent metaphor stimulates the possibility of an encounter with the unconscious in a powerful way for metaphor has been found to light up more centres in the brain than any other form of human communication" (2006, p. 147). Here too is a parallel to Andreasen's (2005) theory of creativity whereby multiple association cortices communicating with each other as a basic correlate to creativity.

In this model, images, narratives, ideas, and symbols with sophisticated layers of meaning can emerge spontaneously into consciousness as the result of unconscious networks of complex meanings having conversations with other unconscious networks of complex meanings. While this type of activity might produce a certain amount of nonsense and white noise, there is good reason to believe that evolution would select for brains capable of generating more useful meanings with the greatest frequency. As Goodwyn (2012) argues, "new undirected symbols are unlikely to be random and meaningless, but related to species survival, emotional expression, and the activities of unconscious circuits in the deep layers of the brain/mind" (p. 167). Furthermore, given the narrow attentional window of working memory in comparison to the raw processing power of the whole brain, it strikes me as more than plausible that the non-conscious processing of the mind may present a richness of sophisticated meanings far beyond what the DLPFC can easily comprehend. Particularly insofar as working memory and executive function operate through linear, rational planning, the full scope of unconscious knowledge and meaning would be excluded automatically and constantly except in highly filtered and greatly reduced form. If this is true, a spontaneous complex symbol might indeed be the best way to get the executive ego's attention, however incomprehensible or bizarre the emergent symbol might at first seem.

Considered in the context of the above conversation about unconscious creativity, the case for meaningful dreams is further strengthened. The brainstem may indeed initiate levels of arousal conducive to dreaming, but the content that emerges from that arousal seems as likely to produce meaningful combinations as an incubated creative process would. In fact, dream process may involve the expression of multiple incubating creative problems and projects. The creative unconscious and the dreaming brain may have far more in common than most contemporary creativity scientists suspect.

Lucidity: the paradox of dreaming awake

I conclude this discussion of conscious and unconscious creativity by coming full circle to the fascinating and paradoxical phenomenon of lucid dreams. If dreaming represents the unconscious mind at work, lucid dreaming cycles the experience back toward consciousness as the dreamer becomes "awake" within the dream, aware that she is dreaming, and capable of exercising executive cognitive capacities usually unavailable in the dream state. "The term *lucid* is used in psychiatric sense, indicating a condition of clear insight and correct orientation to reality in opposition to the clouded insight and deluded disorientation of the delirious" (LaBerge, 2007, p. 307). In addition, lucid dreaming can also sometimes involve various levels of control over the dream story and environment, though actively exercising this control over dream contents is only one path lucid dreaming can take. Bulkeley and Hurd (2014) lament that recent growing popular interest in lucid dreaming has skewed too far in the direction of learning to control dreams, and that in so doing, something vital may be lost. In their words:

> If people treat lucid dreaming merely as a kind of personal virtual reality where ego can command the imagination to do its bidding, are they missing the deeper potentials of lucidity? After all, lucid dreaming has been honored by shamans and sages throughout history for its unparalleled access to the unknown and the ineffable, and for bringing new information to consciousness.
>
> (p. xiv)

Here again is the theme of engaging with the unknown and allowing something new to emerge into conscious awareness. While the possibility of controlling dreams is a fascinating topic in its own right, I will focus specifically on the phenomenon of waking consciousness within the dream state, without emphasizing the need to control.

Stephen LaBerge (2007) has dedicated his life to researching and scientifically validating the existence of lucid dreams. Some of his most important experiments involved training regular lucid dreamers to send signals in the form of specific eye movements and respiration patterns from within the dream state. Using electroencephalogram (EEG) to monitor brain activity, he found that many of his subjects were able to successfully send these signals while in an unambiguous REM brain state. He further found that lucid dreaming correlates with increased central nervous system activation, and hypothesized that this activation was required to activate working memory—a necessary precondition for the dreamer to remember to perform the signaling action. In keeping with other imaginative and creative phenomena discussed in this book, LaBerge also found evidence that activities performed in the dream showed similar patterns of brain activity as they are when performed in waking life. LaBerge's research was helped immeasurably by that fact that lucid dreaming is an ability that can be learned and honed with practice, using specific induction techniques

(LaBerge, 1990). Reviewing a wide range of these techniques, Stumbrys and Erlacher (2014) note that unlike most skills, lucid dreams tend to fade when not actively practiced, and that engaging in regular dream recall and journaling offers strong support for a robust lucid dreaming capacity.

Research by Ursula Voss and colleagues has further investigated the neurobiological correlates that distinguish lucid and non-lucid dreaming states (Voss, Holzmann, Tuin, & Hobson, 2009). Most notably, they discuss the reactivation of the DLPFC during lucidity, which predictably restores a degree of executive function to the dreamer. The REM state is further altered during lucidity in the increase of gamma wave activity. Among their most fascinating findings was that gamma frequency wave stimulation (around 40 hz) from an outside source could shift brain physiology during REM and introduce elements of lucidity, though not necessarily full-on lucid dreaming (Voss and Voss, 2014). From this they have advanced a model that understands lucid dreaming as a hybrid state of consciousness between REM and waking: "we consider lucid dreaming as hybrid because thinking is only partly ruled by lower level consciousness. … The dreamer has—however limited—access to higher order consciousness, enabling him to reflect on his present state" (Voss & Voss, 2014, p. 25). Here again is a reference to the Freudian model of primary and secondary process, whereby the dream represents the deep, primal, emotional psyche, and lucidity brings in a capacity for reflection and rational cognition. Whereas secondary consciousness operates in terms of self-reflection and linear time, "the most striking feature of primary consciousness is that it is restricted to the present—in other words, that 'time' has no meaning" (p. 33). Lucid dreaming, then, appears to represent a direct encounter between these two states of being: the linear rational ego and the timeless primal self.

Of course, this formulation of lucid dreaming begs comparison to the Jungian practice of active imagination (see Chapter 5). While many of the scientists cited above have compared dreaming with daydreaming, their understanding of the daydream state is most often understood as "mind-wandering"—an associative thinking state. Jung's active imagination technique contains an aspect of this associative thought, but is far more directed: active imagination contains an injunction to engage relationally with the emergent imaginal contents of the mind as a psychological reality. This practice of consciously relating to the manifest contents of imagination as a psychic reality seems to me a very short step from the lucid dreaming, where the ego experiences a vivid dream reality while conscious. To my knowledge, the neurobiological correlates of active imagination have never been specifically studied by brain scientists. When that research finally comes, it will be fascinating to draw comparisons between the brain states of practitioners of active imaginers and the brain states of practitioners of lucid dreaming.

Concluding remarks on the creative unconscious

In the course of this chapter, my hope is that what might have initially seemed to be two distinct phenomena—creativity and dreams—have been shown to have significant overlap in the structure and function of their non-conscious neurobiological correlates. While the conscious deliberations of the DLPFC are clearly essential to achieving goals across a variety of fields, the rational executive ego would be at a loss if it could not draw on the wisdom of the unconscious psyche. Creative incubation and dreams both involve non-conscious processes eventually presenting emergent meaningful contents, sometimes quite complex and sophisticated, for the conscious mind to grapple with. The Eureka moment of Archimedes is a moment of the ego receiving an answer from beyond itself. Whether we attribute the giving of such gifts to emergent neural processing or to the Gods (or both), it strikes me as an event that occasions gratitude and humility, rather than arrogance. The executive ego may have put the pieces together, but it surely did not create the pieces.

And in conjuring the phantom of the Gods once more, I would be remiss if I did not at least mention that it is not an absolute and foregone conclusion among all neuroscientists that all creativity and dream is entirely internally generated by the machinations of the biological brain. As just one counter-example, Kelly and Presti (2015) discuss the psychobiological implications of a "transmission" model, whereby consciousness and creativity are not so much generated by brain matter as organized and filtered by it. A thorough discussion of this possibility is obviously beyond the scope of this book— and I would argue that it is also clearly beyond the scope of any reductionistic and purely objective science. The question of how the objectively immeasurable aspects of consciousness should be related to the measurable projects of scientific inquiry is ultimately a philosophical question, not a scientific one. For all the wonderful scientific research that has been done, I conclude this chapter with the confident assertion that we still do not know with any certainty where creativity and dreams ultimately come from.

Part IV

The imagination of neuroscience

As argued in the first chapter, a truly comprehensive examination of imagination must not stop at a purely neurobiological account. From the perspectives of history, phenomenology, and depth psychology, the phenomenon of imagination exists prior to any scientific measurement or reduction. It is not enough to say that we can understand imagination through neuroscience; we must also ask in what ways we understand neuroscience by engaging the imagination. These final chapters take a decided step back toward the humanities, and employ the more expansive understanding of imagination that has emerged over millennia of human discourse to explore how imagination and science exist in reciprocal relationship to each other. As much as possible, this approach will also incorporate the neurobiological understandings of imagination that emerged from the previous section.

Chapter 9 on imagination in science looks into the various ways that imagination is essential to the scientific process in general. This includes the role of the creative imagination in science and how creativity relates to the process of discovery. The chapter also develops the idea of an onto-logical imagination that underscores ostensibly rigid worldviews, and discusses the circumstances and consequences of large imaginative shifts on that fundamental level. Chapter 10 turns more specifically to neuroscience, and asks the question of how the scientific data of brain studies is transformed into story and myth, both within scientific culture and in the culture at large. I use myth in a positive sense here, understanding it as a kind of psychological (as opposed to material) truth that guides scientific inquiry. In looking into neuroscience as a mythic cultural force, some time is also spent examining the danger of mistaking popular scientific myths and metaphors about the brain for proven, literal truths. Finally Chapter 11 concludes the discourse with a recapitulation of the relationship between scientific and humanistic knowledge, and considers what wisdom the archetypal shapeshifter Proteus may have to share.

Chapter 9

Imagination in science

We will approach the question of the role of imagination in neuroscience first by pulling back to a broader inquiry into the role imagination plays in scientific discovery in general. The epistemic, ontological, and methodological constituents of science in general must also be largely true for neuroscience in particular. To reiterate my position from the first chapter, I have no intention of completely reducing the scientific enterprise to imaginal phenomenology. Nor do I mean to deny the extensive non-imaginal aspects of scientific practice. Science progresses through careful observation and persistent and patient collection and analysis of data, and could not proceed otherwise. That said, I wonder if and to what degree imagination has been undervalued in mainstream science, and if a more inclusive inquiry into its uses might not prove fruitful.

The notion that imagination may be an important factor in successful science has some history as a contentious topic. Daston's (2005) historical research on the "fear and loathing of imagination" in science emphasizes a pushback against the Romantic imagination for both its cosmic scope and its ethos of individualism. These aspects of Romanticism became increasingly polarized against the ascending scientific culture of the nineteenth century. In contrast to Romantic philosophy, the strength of science was found in both its mundane replicability and its universally communicable nature; the force of gravity effected falling objects in England and France in the same mathematical terms. The results were measurable and that measurement was available to everyone, not just individuated geniuses. Furthermore, Daston argues that as the rate of new scientific discoveries replacing only slightly older ones began to accelerate, imagination seemed all the more potentially corrupting to a scientific worldview that was not as stable as was initially promised. In short, early indications against a clear and easily identified objective reality spurred a kind of doubling down: more objectivity, more certainty, less room to admit imagination might be a required component in the process.

Although negative viewpoints such as these have survived into the twentieth century, they no longer garner the same level of consensus. From

Einstein's (2009/1931) famous declaration "imagination is more important than knowledge" to the long discourses on creative imagination in the sciences by Csikszentmihalyi, Dietrich, and so many others, it seems clear that in our present zeitgeist imagination has a clear role to play in scientific progress. Even avowed skeptic and science defender Phil Plait (2009) is bold in provocatively announcing that "imagination IS science"—by which he means specifically that new discoveries are only available to the minds prepared to first imagine, and then rigorously test them. The task, then, is not to demonstrate *that* imagination plays a role in science, but rather to better understand the scope and limits of that role.

Types of imagination in science

It would be useful here to differentiate between three interrelated types of imagination in successful scientific enterprise. The first, *functional* imagination, refers to the most basic manipulation of mental images and symbols in the workspace of the mind while doing (or reviewing) scientific research. By contrast, the *creative* imagination refers to the generation of new ideas and approaches in tackling specific scientific problems. Finally, the *ontological* imagination refers to the way scientific cultures imagine the total context of complex relationships that make up the universe that they are studying. I posit these three types of imagination in a nested holarchy, whereby functional imagination occurs to some degree in almost all science, while active engagement of the ontological imagination happens only in those rare and momentous cases of paradigm shifts within a given scientific field. Let's review each one of these types of imagination in turn.

The persistent existence of a *functional* imagination in scientific inquiry should follow as a natural conclusion from the lengthy discussion of sensation and mental images in Chapter 6. If we accept the representation of ideas and objects as mental images as a key brain function, we would expect the use of mental images to play a role in the scientist's mind similar to linguistic thinking. Science is rife with objects that have to be imagined: intermediary forms in evolution, plate tectonics, biochemical reactions, subatomic particles, etc. Even when an instrument such as a microscope allows for a more detailed view of the phenomenon in question, the scientist must still be able to imagine and work over such details in the mind after the instruments have been put away. I anticipate objections that not all scientists are primarily imagistic thinkers and may rely more on linguistic constructs to do their work. This is a fair point, and I would merely point to Howard Gardner's (1983, 1999) theory of multiple intelligences in response. Different brains work in different ways, some orienting more toward the linguistic than the imagistic and vice versa—notwithstanding such biases, on the whole both images and words remain essential. And while many scientists might claim a primarily linguistic thought process, an excellent counter-example of the use of imagery in scientific thought comes from the great Albert Einstein:

> The words or the language, as they are written or spoken, do not seem to play any role in the mechanism of my thought. The psychical entities which seem to serve as elements in thought are certain signs and more or less clear images which can be "voluntarily" reproduced and combined.
>
> (1954/1945, p. 25)

If we take Einstein at his word, many of his revolutionary contributions to physics occurred through working with mental images rather than words. To a large extent, I feel the case for a functional imagination underlying most human mental activity has already been made in previous chapters, and thus will not be focused on here.

The *creative* imagination in science was addressed at several points in Chapter 8 on the neuroscience of creativity. The solutions to confounding scientific problems often involve the generation of new ideas and images to shape the research. This is where, as Gabora and Ranjan's (2013) theory of "neurds" posits, the mind reaches into memory to produce something that was not there to begin with. If scientists were not able to imagine new solutions to previously intractable problems, we would be forever stuck with what is already given and scientific progress would cease. However, it is not only in the generation of solutions to problems that the creative imagination plays a role in science. Creative imagination may also be indispensable in identifying new problems to be tested, devising effective experiments that test for the right things in the right ways, and interpreting confusing or contradictory data into innovative theories. As astronomer Phil Plait puts it "Without imagination, science is a dictionary" (2009, p. 1). In order to discover the hidden order of things, one must also be able to imagine beyond what seems obvious or apparent.

Most interesting and perhaps most controversial is the argument for an *ontological* imagination. By this I mean the total imagined worldview of what is real, and the entire web of complex relationships that exist within that worldview. Science aims to describe the external objective world in great detail, and rests on a mountain of data built on a series of premises about how the world works. As imaginative creatures, we humans will also inevitably come to imagine the world in a certain way that fits with the best data at our disposal. The data and theories from science, however provisional or incomplete, become the threads from which we weave the world. Quite often, it seems, we take these worldviews literally. Kuhn's (1996/1962) great insight was that while the worldviews emerging from scientific fields have offered great contributions to the human experience, the history of science shows a series of revolutionary paradigm shifts in which the fundamental premises that organize those worldviews are reorganized. The imaginal nature of a given scientific worldview only shows her hand in the advent of a paradigm shift. Then what was solid becomes suddenly protean; reality itself appears to change shape. This, again, is not to say that objective reality does not exist, only that in mapping that reality, we cannot escape the use of imagination in the many ways we organize and weave the data at our disposal to fill in the gaps. I use ontological imagination to refer both to the imaginal aspect of the current paradigm (whether it is being taken literally or not), as well as to those revolutionary moments of creativity when the paradigm shifts, like Proteus, to form the world anew.

Creative imagination in scientific method

Physicist and historian of science Gerald Holton (1996) asserts that the role of imagination in science is often covered up. If we want to see how scientists use their imagination, he argues, "we shall have to catch them unawares. For quite good reasons—to arrive more dispassionately at consensus—modern scientists try to keep their personal struggles out of their published research results and out of textbooks" (p. 78). He goes on to say that while logic, mathematics, and technical skill are essential to successful science, they are not ultimately enough. Imagination too must play a role. Similarly, physicist David Bohm argues that while mathematics is essential to scientific progress, math alone is insufficient:

> I think that verbal concepts, pictorial aspects, and philosophical think-ing can contribute significantly to new ideas. Einstein certainly appre-ciated mathematical beauty very keenly but he did not actually begin with the mathematics, especially in his most creative period. Instead, he started with unspecifiable feelings and a succession of images out of which more detailed concepts eventually emerged.
>
> (Bohm & Peat, 2000/1987, p. 7)

Ultimately such creative imaginings have to be born out through the formal structure of mathematics and the rigor of experimentation, but this works best as a secondary stage in the process. This formulation of creative science bears some resemblance to the maxim in creative writing that argues the initial generation of words and ideas should be allowed to flow freely to start, with analytical editing and refinement of those words coming into play later as an essential but separate process. The creative imagination thus becomes the soil from which more robust and specific theories spring forth.

Holton (1996) speaks of the process in terms of an underlying thematic imagination that is rarely discussed in scientific discourse. He points out that so much of scientific practice is about removing the subjective human element to get at the objective data, so that even the scientist's most cherished ideas must be endlessly put to the test. Following the falsifiability of Karl Popper, it is expected that scientists will do everything they can to disprove their own ideas and only commit to those few and far between that are left standing. And yet, Holton argues, the history of science is full of cases where individual scientists had great breakthroughs by doing just the opposite: holding onto their ideas even when they seemed to fail, incubating their intuitions over long stretches of time and numerous setbacks, only to find those ideas ultimately vindicated. "By studying their notes we now know that Isaac Newton, John Dalton, and Gregor Mendel, among many others, refused to accept 'data' that contradicted their thematic presuppositions, and were proven right in the end" (p. 97).

To further complicate matters, Holton (1996) is quite clear that the history of science also shows how the opposite has often been true. Obstinately clinging to cherished ideas and images can prevent a scientist from seeing clearly. Einstein's reluctance to accept probability in quantum mechanics and Galileo's failure to recognize Kepler's elliptical orbits (because of his culturally conditioned aesthetic preference for circles and symmetry!) are just two telling examples. Nevertheless, Holton argues, "at least in the nascent phase of scientific work, thematic presuppositions—which Einstein referred to as freely chosen 'categories or schemes of thought'—are necessary for most scientists, whether they are used consciously or not" (p. 119). Creative imagination is thus conceived by Holston as being both vital to good science, and also a potential danger to it. There is no black and white solution or easy methodological formula for navigating this contradiction. Rather, the effective use of imagination in science, like all difficult and complex tasks, requires practice, humility, and wisdom.

Specifically, we can locate several points in the traditional scientific method where creative imagination might come into play and prove an effective tool. In the first place, simply identifying the phenomenon to be studied may require creativity: looking into the interconnected complexity of the world and coming up with an idea about which particular part of the greater whole should be isolated, measured, and studied in order to solve a particular problem. As Weisberg puts it, "The really creative act in science is asking a good question, rather than answering it" (1993, p. 186). This leads naturally into the process of formulating a hypothesis about the phenomenon to be studied. There may be an obvious set of properties or reactions to study with regard to a given object, but sometimes a creative re-imagining is called for, particular when it comes to hypotheses that contradict common sense, cultural biases, or established scientific theories. Paul Feyerabend (2010/1975) advocates for an anarchistic approach to scientific method whereby new and contradictory ideas are encouraged:

> There are circumstances when it is advisable to introduce, elaborate, defend ad hoc hypotheses, or hypotheses which contradict well-established and generally accepted experimental results, or hypotheses whose content is smaller than the content of the existing and empirically adequate alternative, or self-inconsistent hypotheses, and so on.
>
> (p. 7)

Doing so, Feyerabend argues, is the only way to ensure that science will continue to relentlessly explore the truth rather than fall into rigid assumptions about the infallible scientific theories of the past. Again, this need not always be the case, and certainly a great deal of scientific progress can be made without constantly challenging the basic precepts of a given field. But for the most confounding problems, creative imagination may prove indispensable in generating new avenues to explore.

Likewise when it comes to the question of how the phenomenon should be studied. How should the experiment be designed? What factors should be controlled for? How best to isolate the object of study from its interconnected context so as not to skew the results? Coming up with a brilliant experiment can be a highly creative and imaginative act. This is all the more important because the method used to study the problem will partially determine the results. As Weisberg puts it, "the 'facts' that scientists collect are less objective than they appear and often their 'collection' depends on the development of very sophisticated methods, which itself can be seen as requiring creativity" (1993, p. 151). Every innovative experimental design, every novel method for collecting data, finds its existence in part through an original image forming in the mind.

Finally, creative imagination may come into play after the data has been collected and the process of interpretation begins. This is true both on the level of understanding the basic results of a given experiment, and the process of ultimately weaving a great number of results into a theory. "Once a set of facts is available, they must be interpreted through the construction of a theory that can explain them" (Weisberg, 1993, p. 152). Sometimes the data is clear and tells an easy story. But when the data is confusing or contradictory, or points toward something as yet undiscovered (or lying outside of established scientific theory altogether) there is room, and perhaps need, for imagination to synthesize the pieces into an original whole. For Bohm and Peat (2000/1987) this process is necessary and inevitable. In the classic case of Archimedes' "eureka" moment at the bath, they argue that the recognition of water rising and falling in connection to volume was itself an act of creative perception. "The observational data obtained by Archimedes in his bath ... had little value in themselves. What was significant was their meaning as perceived through the mind in an act of creative imagination" (p. 66). In that moment, we may surmise a whole new model for the relationship between fluid and volume took shape in Archimedes mind. Without that moment of creative synthesis, the rising of the water—the data in itself—would have remained meaningless noise.

When the data is pointing to an unseen conclusion outside of what is already scientifically known or understood, it takes an act of imagination to generate a new image or map of the phenomenon that accurately fits the new data. The faculty of creative imagination makes this leap into the unknown and fills the gap with a new functional image for the phenomenon in question. Whether this proceeds by a sudden burst of insight or is worked out piecemeal over time, it falls to imagination to generate images, models, and maps of the world that previously did not exist.

The art of making models

Molecular biologist Gunther Stent (2001) takes the unorthodox position of suggesting science and art have more in common than not. Both art and science "are activities that endeavor to discover and communicate truth about the world: they share the central features of searching for, and encoding into a semantic medium, the meaning of novel truths" (p. 33). The principle difference, Stent contends, is that science is concerned with the outer objective world, while art seeks discoveries in the inner, subjective world of human experience.

Stent argues that the recognition of patterns by the brain "is nothing other than the selective destruction of information" (2001, p. 36). For science to proceed at all a process of abstraction must take place as the scientist isolates the object of study from its complex context. Bohm and Peat echo this argument: "To be able to give attention to something, it is first necessary to abstract or isolate its main features from all the infinite, fluctuating complexity of its background" (2000/1987, p. 16). In Stent's analysis, the process of identifying and working with such isolated patterns is neither a true mirror to reality nor an invention of the mind. Rather, "the mind interprets reality as a set of structural transforms abstracted from the phenomenal world" (2001, p. 37). What this means in practical terms is that all scientific models are abstractions of reality that are just as much created as discovered.

> The structure of the DNA molecule was not what it was before Watson and Crick defined it, because there was and still is no such thing as the DNA molecule in the natural world. The DNA molecule is an abstraction created by century-long efforts of a succession of biochemists, all of whom selected for their attention certain ensembles of natural phenomena. The DNA double helix is as much a creation as it is a discovery.
>
> (p. 37)

Again, this is not to say that the DNA molecule is somehow unreal, rather that, properly speaking, it is an abstract model, an imagined map for a particular aspect of complex reality that is especially accurate and therefore useful. In this sense, it is an imaginal tool for engaging with objective reality—a tool so powerful it may yet fundamentally reshape life on earth. Even so, the tool itself is an abstracted model, and the model had to be created. If Watson and Crick and their colleagues had not been able to imagine the component parts of the DNA molecule and assemble them creatively, there would be nothing to test.

Delving deeper into the case of DNA, we find the essential data was there, and yet without the creation of the right mental model, no solution was forthcoming. Data in itself is not enough—interpretation is also necessary for discovery, and this opens the door for creative imagination to do its work. Weisberg (1993) discusses the role of interpretation in the discovery of DNA:

> The use of X-ray diffraction produced photos that gave scientists clues about the structure of DNA, but the information was not just sitting there waiting to be plucked by the scientists. Much interpretation was necessary before the scientists could understand the facts in those pictures.
>
> (p. 152)

The meaning of the data was not forthcoming without further creative process. Multiple models were generated by multiple scientists, some closer than others, and each model was in part a product of creative imagination. Weisberg emphasizes how the "unit-shell shape" first discovered by Rosalind Franklin was not actually applied by her, but rather by Francis Crick in the final synthesis:

> Franklin did not consider her own results, because she was not in favor of a helix for the crystal form until after Watson's January 30th visit carrying Pauling's paper. Wilkins did not think of anti-parallel chains in response to Franklin's result because he was not thinking at that time of a double helix, but of four chains.
>
> (p. 168)

In this case, Franklin and Wilkins lacked the imaginative flexibility to see what Franklin's data was pointing toward. And yet clearly a process of group creativity was at work. Even in an ostensibly competitive environment, there was an exchange of data, theories, and imagined models, each of which pushed Watson and Crick toward the discovery of the double helix.

In a very real sense, a failure of imagination can mean a failure of science. Thomas Cech, who won the Nobel Prize in Chemistry for discovering that RNA can play a catalytic role in cellular metabolism, recalls how several other labs were poised to make the same discovery and failed to do so. Because it was widely believed at the time that RNA could not have a catalytic role, these other labs failed to investigate what was before them—they could not imagine it. Cech recalls, "One Danish laboratory, in Aarhus, was neck and neck with us all the way, but they could not believe their results. They decided to quit working on the problem before the end" (2001, p. 13). In this case, the previous and less accurate model of RNA was taken so literally that it could not be questioned. As it turned out, the old conception of RNA was an imagined model that told part, but not all, of the molecule's story. By failing to allow the literal belief about RNA into a creative imaginal workspace, the possibility of further discovery was thwarted. Weisberg (1993) makes a similar point about Einstein's ultimate refusal to accept quantum mechanics:

> Einstein's rejection of quantum mechanics was not because his personal characteristics had changed in any fundamental way from the time when he did his revolutionary work. His basic belief in determinism and in strict causal laws motivated both his earlier work and his rejection of quantum mechanics.
>
> (p. 82)

For all his revolutionary imagination, Einstein ultimately could not let go of his own fundamental ideas about the universe, leading to a rupture in physics that continues to this day. The models were incompatible, and a literal belief in those models (or a belief that the models must be literal), prevented their coexistence in one of our greatest minds.

The ontological imagination

Thus far the discussion has focused on the role imagination plays in the success of discrete scientific projects whereby some phenomenon has been isolated for study. Now we turn to the bigger picture—the way we imagine the greater scientific and philosophical context in which those discrete studies take place. By ontological imagination I refer to both the imaginal threads that weave together our worldview, as well as to those extraordinary moments when the paradigm shifts, and the world itself is re-imagined.

In Chapter 7 I argued at length that the neurobiology of perception works as something akin to a reality simulator, generating images that represent a best guess at the objective world based on limited sense data, and further constrained by cultural factors that organize attention and interpretation of that sense data. These imaginal maps that we experience as reality are useful insofar as they help us interact with the world in beneficial ways. Following basic evolutionary theory, we would expect one of the primary constraints on this map-making capacity to be survival; internal representations of the world that do not accurately identify potential threats and promising mates would of course be a genetic dead-end. That said, it is quite a leap to then suggest that only phenomena that impact survival should be considered real! These survival-related phenomena may after all make up only a tiny fraction of the total phenomena of the universe occurring around us. According to strict evolutionary theory we would likely be largely incapable of perceiving non-survival phenomena accurately at all. And indeed, one of the most startling discoveries in recent decades is the pervasive existence of dark matter and dark energy in our universe, which according to NASA makes up as much as 95 percent of all matter and energy in the universe ("Dark matter, dark energy," n.d.). That is to say, the majority of the universe appears to be made out of something that we don't understand. Presti (2016) discusses a similar astounding discovery: the fact that only 3 percent of the human genome codes for functional proteins, with the remaining 97 percent coding for RNA with as yet mysterious functions. Once described as "junk DNA," Presti points out that cells spend considerable energy transcribing these sequences, meaning "they are clearly playing important roles and are certainly not junk" (p. 117). It seems we don't quite know what we are made of after all. And even this is not necessarily the limit of the unknown around us, as dark matter, dark energy, and dark DNA may well represent only a fraction of unknown phenomena in a universe bursting with unknown phenomena that we have yet to detect. There is no scientific measure for the ultimate measurability of the universe.

But let us also acknowledge that it would be another great leap to then proceed with the proclamation that the vast majority of existing phenomena are indeed unmeasurable. Or even worse, to arrogantly proclaim that we know with certainty what inhabits that great unknown that lies beyond scientific measurement. The point of not knowing is that in fact we do not know. While I certainly have my ideas, insights, fantasies, and hypotheses about the great unknown, I must also acknowledge that, from a scientific perspective, I can go no further without admitting speculation. And in the present discourse, there is no need to do so: the point is not to argue for one story about reality over another, but rather to foreground the basic existential condition that our senses and our science are limited, and that beyond a certain point, all we have left to work with are stories and imagination. And it is out there, beyond the data, where we encounter the imaginal substrate through which our encounters with the unknown take shape. I contend that, based on current neuroscience, this is not a metaphysical assertion but a neurophenomenological one, an inevitable consequence of the way our brains apprehend and make sense of existence.

A great deal of modern science has moved beyond what can be detected with the raw senses, in many cases studying phenomena that we cannot meaningfully "see" except through imagined models. John Tyndall recognized this in 1870: "the bodily eye, for example, cannot see the condensations and rarefactions of the waves of sound. We construct them in thought, and we believe as firmly in their existence as in that of the air itself" (2015/1870, p. 18). This has only become more true in the 150 years since, as Bohm and Peat remark, "as science developed, this aspect of perception through the mind grew more and more important. Indeed, very little of what could be called direct sense impression takes place in physics today" (2000/1987, p. 45). Furthermore, they argue that even the instruments used to do physics are increasingly remote from the senses, a far cry from Galileo's telescope. And yet has it not always been part of the mission of science to reach into the unknown and explain the unseen order behind it? Science is intimately bound to the world beyond our senses: when it works, it gives us a glimpse of the myriad phenomena and deep order that exist outside of our biologically given sense perception. Science brings us incredible riches in this regard. And yet it remains a human fantasy to assume these riches comprise the totality of the cosmos when in reality they are just as likely to be merely a glimpse of it.

Chapter 6 further argued, following evolutionary theory, that in addition to physical survival issues, human survival has been uniquely entangled with social considerations, including the adoption of cultural codes and belief systems. This means our imaginal maps of reality also skew toward adherence to the social norms of the cultures that contain us. Thus, a large part of the reality we experience as humans is as much a matter of collective imagination and shared fiction as it is effective interaction with the physical world. Again, to say this does not imply a denial of objective reality nor a descent into some kind of absolute relativism; rather I am suggesting that human reality is an imaginal synthesis of accurate-enough physical maps and largely fictional, co-created cultural maps.

Looking into the history of science, we see that what scientists believed about the world, and the stories they told their fellow humans about the world, have not always been entirely accurate. New theories replace old theories all the time; the recognition of this ongoing process of re-establishing scientific worldviews is given theoretical heft in Kuhn's work on scientific revolutions. Deeply held cultural myths of progress and anthropocentrism may reassure us repeatedly that whatever scientific understandings we've reached in the present moment *must* be the truth at last—but history suggests the worldviews inspired by science will continue to evolve. Looking back, at any given point in this history, scientists and those they influenced were inevitably employing the best scientific data and theories of their time to imagine the world. This means, for example, that prior to relativity and quantum theory, to have a scientific worldview meant imagining a Newtonian universe. And of course, these scientists and scholars had good reason to do so—the data and the mathematics were both convincing and elegant. But apart and above from the data and the math, there is the story: a collection of fictions about reality that take root in both scientific and mainstream cultures. In turn these fictions and beliefs shape our perceptions, complicating our capacity to do science that is objective in any absolute sense.

The move to call this experience of a given scientific worldview a case of ontological imagination proceeds from the simple fact that for each scient- ific paradigm that ordered human perception of reality there came a moment in history when the science underlying that worldview changed. Then what was taken as solid literal truth dissolved as the map was redrawn, and new possibilities for the organization and experience of reality emerged. Up until that moment, it does not seem like imagination at all: it is simply that way things are. But when a paradigm shift occurs, the ontological imagination is revealed at the heart of the worldview. She was there, all along, surrounding us and in plain view, but we could not see her. As Kant suggested in the first edition of the *Critique of pure reason* (1958/1781), imagination is the glue that holds human reality together.

Foregrounding the imaginal context

Science aims to reach beyond subjectivity, beyond human opinion and error, to measure what is "out there" in the world. To do so, it relies on theoretical concepts and standards of measurement that can be shared and confirmed among large groups of scientists. As suggested in Chapter 2, the objectivity reached for in science is rooted in the intersubjectivity of scientists using shared language and methods. And I would certainly agree that over the centuries, science has made remarkable and tangible gains in interfacing with the world "out there." Our world has been transformed radically—with even greater transformation yet to come—through the practice of science.

Yet it is still only through the shared consciousness of human scientists, with all its constraints, that this process takes place. However extraordinary our models and the technologies they produce, they emerge from a psyche that has always been in a constant process of imaginal construction. Humans have no way of knowing, at any given point in history, which of their imaginal maps of reality are truly accurate descriptors of the universe, and which are provisional best guesses or even outright misunderstandings with little bearing on physical reality. To see the imaginal aspect of scientific beliefs is not a refutation of the value of scientific data or the models that have proven so useful for both the prediction of physical events and the construction of powerful technologies. Rather, I am suggesting that in the vast expanses of possibility between discrete sets of data and useful pieces of technology, it is inevitable that human mind will weave stories and beliefs about the nature of reality. Those stories may be bolstered by data, but they are still stories.

The tricky thing about the ontological imagination is that, as the faculty that imagines the nature of reality itself, it is often not recognized as imagination at all. Bohm and Peat (2000/1987) refer to these unquestioned assumptions about reality as the *tacit infrastructure* of a scientific field. Most scientists, they argue, carry out their research based on frameworks learned in graduate school, and as such spend decades conducting scientific investigation without ever questioning or even deeply considering the underlying "tacit" frameworks of their field. Emerging data or theories that contradict those underlying frameworks can be easily perceived as a threat. "Because scientists are accustomed to using their tacit skills and knowledge in subliminal and unconscious ways, there is a tendency of the mind to hold onto them and try to go on working in old ways within new contexts" (p. 21). This is to say, part of education as a scientist is being taught how to imagine the world based on previous theories. Kuhn argued explicitly that science could not proceed otherwise: "Measurements taken without a paradigm so seldom lead to any conclusions at all" (1996/1962, p. 135). Paradigms are necessary to organize scientific endeavor, to provide the theoretical constraints necessary for robust and specific research to take place. Biologist Stephen Jay Gould (2003) agrees: "How could we ever discern a pattern, or see anything coherent, amid an infinitude of potential perceptions, unless we employed some theoretical expectation to guide our penetration of this plethora?" (p. 34). Trouble arises, according to Bohm and Peat, when the paradigm is held so rigidly that the enterprise becomes inflexible and innovation is suppressed. "To cling rigidly to familiar ideas is in essence the same as blocking the mind from engaging in creative free play" (2000/1987, p. 51). Absolute certainty diminishes the world and cripples discovery.

But there is an even greater danger in such rigidity, and that is the feedback loop of belief and perception that can turn paradigms into self-fulfilling prophecies. As Kuhn says, "Paradigms determine large areas of experience" (1996/1962, p. 129). The basic idea in this line of thought is that paradigms not only constrain research, they also constrain perception. The essential feature of an unconscious or tacit infrastructure of ideas is after all that it is not consciously considered—it organizes thought and perception from behind the scenes. Holton (1996) gives the example of astronomer Thomas Harriot and Galileo Galilei both looking at the moon through telescopes in the year 1609 and apparently seeing different things. From the time of Aristotle, the moon was thought to be a perfectly smooth sphere, an instance of the incorruptible celestial realm. And this is indeed what Thomas Harriot saw—the perfect moon that his culture had taught him to believe. Though he noted strange jagged lines, it was quite unthinkable to him that these lines might be mountains and valleys. That same year, Galileo also looked at the moon through a telescope, and came to the conclusion that in fact the face of the moon was like the face of the earth: uneven, imperfect, marked by high mountains and deep valleys. And what was it about Galileo that allowed him to transcend the cultural imagination of his time? Holton concludes that Galileo was able to see depth on the moon not only because of his Copernican sympathies, but because he had been steeped in Italian Renaissance art culture, which emphasized the play of shadow and light on three dimensional objects. Harriot, as an Englishman with far less exposure to such aesthetics, was not able to make the creative connection.

Surveying the scientific data on human perception and misperception, Kuhn argues that "something like a paradigm is prerequisite to perception itself. What a man sees depends both upon what he looks at and also upon what his previous visual-conceptual experience has taught him to see" (1996/1962, p. 113). And Bohm and Peat emphasize how these predispositions can affect multiple levels of the scientific enterprise: "theories determine not only the design of scientific instruments but also the kinds of questions that are posed in the experiments themselves" (2000/1987, p. 65). Again, none of this is necessarily a negative, and Kuhn would even argue it is necessary for the bulk of "normal" science to proceed. It does, however, clearly limit the possibilities of what science can discover by limiting the imaginations of scientists to a prescribed collective understanding. Paul Feyerabend argues that too often "a person's religion ... or his metaphysics, or his sense of humor ... must not have the slightest connection to his scientific activity. His imagination is restrained, and even his language ceases to be his own" (2010/1975, p. 3). And yet the history of science shows us that these moments of imaginal rigidity do not stand forever; eventually, a paradigm shift occurs.

Kuhn's seminal work, the *Structure of scientific revolutions* (1996/1962), offers one historical example after another of the scientific worldview being fundamentally re-imagined. As just one example, in the case of astronomy, he discusses the impact of Copernican theory on what astronomers were able to see. Following the assertion by Copernicus that the earth revolved around the sun, rather than being in the center of perfect celestial spheres, Western astronomers began to see, for the first time, new phenomena in the skies. Where before had been established celestial spheres, now the sky was filled with new planets, irregular comets, and strange dark spots on the sun. "The very ease and rapidity with which astronomers saw new things when looking at old objects with old instruments may make us wish to say that, after Copernicus, Astronomers lived in a different world" (1996/1962, p. 117). Phenomenologically speaking, this was certainly the case. The whole meaning of the sky, the cosmos, and perhaps humanity's place within it had to be fundamentally re-imagined. Paradigm shifts "cause scientists to see the world of their research-engagement differently. In so far as their only recourse to that world is through what they see and do ... after a revolution, scientists are responding to a different world" (p. 111). With this imaginative re-visioning of the cosmos more data was integrated and the maps and models were improved. But they are still imaginative maps and models, and we have no more capacity to know now than we did then just how much is still being left out of the current worldview science provides.

Ontological creativity

If the science of a given paradigm always flirts with the danger of becoming a closed-system and self-fulfilling prophecy, we should also note that the history of science shows that potential for creativity also always lies in wait. When the moment finally comes and the world reveals itself as an imaginal construct transforming into a new form, it remains to inquire what could make such a thing possible. The question is especially vexing given how closed the scientific worldview can become:

> Unless the perceived rewards are very great, the mind will not willingly explore its unconscious infrastructure of ideas but will prefer to continue in more familiar ways.... People will therefor tend not have the necessary energy and courage to call into question the whole tacit infrastructure of their field.
>
> (Bohm & Peat, 2000/1987, p. 22)

Perhaps it was pondering this problem that led Paul Feyerabend (2010/1975) to his radical and provocative anarchistic approach to scientific method. His *Beyond method* advocates for a constant tearing down of rigid ideas to make room for new possibilities. His advocacy for diversity of opinion within the scientific community is fierce:

> Unanimity of opinion may be fitting for a rigid church, for the frightened or greedy victims of some (ancient, or modern) myth, or for the weak and willing followers of some tyrant. Variety of opinion is necessary for objective knowledge. And a method that encourages variety is also the only method that is compatible with a humanitarian outlook.
>
> (p. 25)

This approach has some resonance with the solution proposed by Bohm and Peat above, which advocates for holding multiple viewpoints "in suspension," and to seek to understand contrary perspectives rather than reactively refuting them.

But how does creativity in science ever manage to transcend these deepest boundaries and re-vision ontological premises largely assumed to be irrefutable literal truths? One possibility, already hinted in Galileo's appreciation of the arts, is that broader, more complex worldviews are part of the answer. Kaufman and Gregoire (2015) discuss research indicating that creative scientists do not tend to restrict themselves to a narrow research area. Rather, "highly creative scientists tend to engage in a large number of loosely related activities, forming a broad 'network of enterprises.' They also tend to have hobbies and interests outside of the sciences" (p. 96). Thus, the interplay of multiple ideas, frameworks, and even worldviews may prove beneficial in breaking out of a rigid paradigm. Kuhn further suggests that one must have a tolerance for contradiction and confusion as new ideas are being worked out. "Like artists, creative scientists must occasionally be able to live in a world out of joint" (1996/1962, p. 79). Incidentally, this is quite similar to Jung's notion of "holding the tension of the opposites," tolerating painful contradiction long enough that a new synthesis may emerge. In part, Kuhn argues, this struggle is carried out by exercising one's imaginative capacities:

> The analytical thought experimentation that bulks so large in Galileo, Einstein, Bohr, and many others is perfectly calculated to expose the old paradigm to existing knowledge in ways that isolate the root of crisis with a clarity unattainable in the laboratory.
>
> (p. 88)

This "exposure" of rigid assumptions to imaginative possibilities resonates with Bohm and Peat's notion that metaphoric thought is essential to creative science because it compares things that tacit frameworks would not normally put together.

The question of worldviews during the Scientific Revolution is a deep and fascinating topic. One of the distinguishing features of Tarnas' (1991) *Passion of the western mind* is that in addition to following in great detail the popular narrative of rational thought and scientific progress, he makes a point of also tracking the threads of more esoteric belief systems as Western culture transformed. Copernicus, for example, was "armed with a sense of kinship with an ancient tradition, inspired by the Neoplatonists exalted conception of the Sun, and further supported by the university Scholastics' critical appraisal of Aristotelian physics" (p. 250). In the end it was mathematics that demonstrated that the earth orbited the sun, but the passion to do those mathematics grew out of a vision of reality that held the sun as divine. Kepler, in turn, considered his own revolutionary principles successful because they "affirmed both Copernicus' theory and the mathematical mysticism of the ancient Pythagorian and Platonic philosophers" (p. 257). Kepler was in fact the first to theorize that the sun exerted some invisible divine force on the planets, an *anima motrix*, though it was left to Newton to imagine gravity in mathematical detail. The strict materialist will insist these great minds were "only" imagining these metaphysical contexts, yet it is difficult see how their scientific models could have emerged without this imaginal framework organizing their thoughts and inspiring their creativity. Tarnas concludes that "without the intellectual bias created by a Neoplatonically defined aesthetic judgment, the Scientific Revolution might not have occurred, certainly not in the form it took historically" (p. 255). Galileo, as mentioned above, was deeply influenced by Renaissance aesthetics, and the symmetry and beauty of the Copernican system is part of what drew him to the cause.

This account is somewhat at odds with the rationalist narrative that scientific progress represented a clean break from religion, spirituality, and metaphysics. But humanistic biologist Stephen Jay Gould (2003) argues that the notion of a fundamental war between science and religion was entirely an invention of the late nineteenth century. "As so many scholars have documented, the standard episodes in the supposed warfare between science and religion are either greatly distorted or entirely fictional" (p. 88). Even the popular case of Galileo's supposed conflict with the church, Gould argues, is a bizarre distortion that ignores Galileo's hot-headed temper and lack of social grace in finding even a bare modicum of social compromise with his intellectual adversaries. Atheism simply was not a factor among the great scientists of the sixteenth and seventeenth centuries. On the contrary, Amos Funkenstein's (1986) *Theology and the scientific imagination* traces in great detail the links between religious belief and scientific progress in the revolutionary period. "Never before or after were science, philosophy, and theology seen as almost the same occupation" (p. 3). Christian theology, as Funkenstein documents, was an important imaginal substrate in which the conventions of modern science took root.

But while atheism may not have been a factor in the Scientific Revolution, free and diverse thought most certainly was. The Renaissance, after all, was a great cultural conjunction, when the linear progress of the West opened up to the richness of its own forgotten philosophical and pagan history. The role of esoteric and "magical" thinking during the Renaissance was detailed in Chapter 3, and it has a role to play again in the revolution of human consciousness that produced modern science. Westman (1977) discusses the thesis put forward by Frances Yates that magical thinking was essential to the birth of science, insofar as it offered an image of humanity as beings capable of engaging with and controlling the natural world. In the Tarot, this figure is revealed in the Magus or Magician, an archetypal figure that implies both sorcerer and scientist.

Arthur C. Clarke (1967) was getting at the same basic idea when he observed that any sufficiently advanced technology is indistinguishable from magic. If we can remove our current cultural certainty of hindsight—if we can avoid the temptation to project onto Kepler, Galileo, and Newton, the ontological certainty of scientific facts and principles in which we as modern Westerners were all dutifully trained—then we can *imagine* these men as magi, engaged in a daring encounter with the unknown, and in so doing forging a new relationship between humanity and the forces of the unseen world. The notion that an x-ray or a space shuttle or an antibiotic is not "magic" is a semantic determination rooted in a modern disposition to equate "magic" with unreality and delusion. Defined as such, "magic" will always be false—no matter what. But if "magic" is understood instead as a wonder-inducing practice of creating tangible effects in the physical world, then science and magic are potentially synonymous. In the physical world, the math and the data are the final arbiters of whether a technology works. But in the imaginal realm, we can (and inevitably will!) imagine the meaning of those "works" as best feeds our souls.

I will end with the enigmatic figure of Sir Isaac Newton, preeminent figure of the Scientific Revolution, who defined physics for generations to come and gave us gravity as we know it. "It was Newton's astounding achievement to synthesize Descartes mechanistic philosophy, Kepler's laws of planetary motion, and Galileo's laws of terrestrial motion in one comprehensive theory" (Tarnas, 1991, p. 269). At the same time, Tarnas will not let us forget that Newton's conception of gravity as a force acting at a distance was an idea whose primary precedents were found in Neoplatonism, Hermeticism, and alchemy. Sarah Dry (2014) documents the fate of Newton's unpublished papers—over five million words in his own hands—ranging from early drafts of the *Principia* to wide-ranging explorations of religion, alchemy, and even more esoteric topics. Dry emphasizes that Newton made careful preparations for his death that included burning certain papers that he did not wish to survive him. Yet a vast collection of confounding, decidedly non-scientific material remained. Dry concludes that Newton had an "awareness of both the limits of his contemporaries' understanding and the possibility of a more enlightened future. He left his papers unassigned but also undestroyed" (p. 9). In the centuries since, these papers have served as both a topic of embarrassment, and increasingly, a source of fascination.

The embarrassment, which is no doubt still alive in some circles today, is that the preeminent figure of the Scientific Revolution was not only profoundly religious, but also deeply invested in alchemy and other esoteric and occult systems of thought. Dry follows John Maynard Keynes' interest in Newton's papers through his ultimate dismissal of the alchemical and occult currents as a bizarre sideshow to Newton's true genius. In this, Dry believes, "Keynes revealed the limits of his own imagination" (2014, p. 159). The discomfort, it seems to me, was in assuming that Newton's alchemical work should somehow be equated with scientific work. But as a student of Jungian psychology, I am of course predisposed to interpret alchemy in psychological terms, as a psycho-spiritual system for individual growth. Mary-Louise von Franz (1997/1979), Jung's intellectual heir, conceived of alchemy as a form of active imagination. If we allow the imaginal realm its own ontological status (see Chapter 5), quite apart from the physical world to which science is concerned, there is no conflict between Newton's alchemy and his physics. On the contrary, it is quite likely that the former was a rich resource for producing the latter.

It was not until late in the twentieth century that a more open-minded interpretation of Newtonian alchemy began to emerge in intellectual circles. Betty Jo Teeter Dobbs (1975, 1991) has reviewed Newton's alchemical works in depth and concluded that they are essential to understanding his thought:

> By whatever route one approached Truth, the goal was the same. Experimental discovery and revelation; the productions of reason, speculation, or mathematics; the cryptic, coded messages of the ancients in myth, prophecy, or alchemical tract.... In Newton's conviction of the unity of Truth and its ultimate source in the divine one may find the fountainhead of all his diverse studies.
>
> (1991, p. 6)

Dobbs argues that Newton operated as though no single approach to knowledge would be sufficient in solving the epistemological problems that began in the Renaissance. Newton was just as willing to turn to the wisdom of the ancients as he was captivated by the modern breakthroughs of Galileo and Kepler. For him, the guiding principle was a divine unity of truth, but in that conviction, he held a remarkable capacity to investigate and integrate different frameworks of thought. Dry (2014) ultimately comes to a similar conclusion: "Newton's ability to move among such disparate intellectual realms may be best understood as an aspect of his faith" (p. 197). Newton's notion of the divine order was one of freedom of movement and expression; an idealized angelic order of existential liberty.

This is just one case in the rich and varied history of science. While Einstein may have entertained views of cosmic religion, Watson and Crick were able to successfully produce a model of the double helix within wholly mundane frameworks. It is quite obvious that great science has occurred both with and without holism or mysticism. Nevertheless, we must concede that even at the beginning, a more holistic and expansive ontological imagination had an important role to play. The point, as ever, is not to raise one worldview or system of thought over another, but simply to suggest that a diversity of worldviews can support and inspire the project of science. A mystical imagination, once cleanly differentiated from the rigorous work of mathematics and measurement, has much to offer, and a flexible mind may be well poised for unexpected insights.

Chapter 10

Neuroscience as story and myth

The immediate challenge of a chapter titled "neuroscience as story and myth" is the fact that in much scientific and intellectual discourse, both "fiction" and "myth" are words used to denote falsehood. "Fact or fiction" is a basic cultural idiom suggesting all propositions must be one or the other, while science often refers to "myths" as untrue beliefs about reality that must be "busted" using scientific evidence. Let me be absolutely clear: I am not using these terms in this way. I do not mean to imply that neuroscience is not in possession of objective facts, or that it is somehow fundamentally false or delusional. So ingrained is this way of thinking about fiction and myth that this point may bear repeating several more times.

As detailed in Chapter 5, depth psychology has staked out a phenomenal ground whereby the imaginal contents of the psyche have an irreducible ontological status that is distinct from that of material reality. Fiction is one way in which these imaginal contents can be organized as an expression of truth distinct from measurable facts. Quite apart from depth psychology, Chapter 7 further argued in detail that there is good neurobiological evidence to suggest that storytelling is not only ubiquitous among humans, but is in fact one of the primary means through which humans perceive and make sense of reality. If this is true, then story and science must inevitably intersect, not only in public understanding but also in the human minds of scientists themselves. A final perspective to consider with regard to fiction is Harari's (2016) basic thesis, which makes recourse to neither depth psychology nor neuroscience in asserting that most of what makes human life meaningful exists as a collection of fictions outside of the measurable material realm. As physically constrained as our lives may be, they are also lived in rich realms of co-created belief.

Less central to the discussion so far has been a more positive appraisal of myth, whereby it is understood not as a falsehood, but rather an expression of deep cultural truth. The anthropologist Mircea Eliade expounded this view in 1963: Myth "supplies models for human behavior, and, by that very fact, gives meaning and value to life" (1963, p. 2). This conception of myth applies not only to ancient or indigenous cultures, but also in theory drives human development in all ages, including our own. Harari (2016) for example, argues that the primary reason Europe ascended as a colonial superpower in the nineteenth century was not technological superiority so much as the driving myths of progress, capital, and mastery over nature. Depth psychology too has come to understand myths as archetypal patterns of human experience that structure how we relate to each other and find our place in the cosmos. In the words of Christine Downing (1981), "We need images and myths through which we might see who we are and what we might become" (p. 2). The premise here is that we are always living out these stories. We can either do so unconsciously, allowing the myths of our family and culture to run us as unexamined drives, or we can become conscious of the mythic dimension of our lives, and perhaps begin to choose which myths we want to live. Far beyond their simplistic literal interpretations, myths serve as containers for human meaning, and can be seen coursing through the development of both individuals and societies.

So why undertake an examination of the mythic and fictional dimensions of neuroscience? I can think of at least two good reasons. The first is that the data from neuroscience, once liberated from the dry sets of factual results found in laboratories and scientific journals, eventually comes to traverse the culture at large in the form of stories. These science-based stories about the brain may point to science, but mistaking them for science outright can be problematic, as they are sometimes several steps removed from the hard science from which they were sprung. The second reason is that category errors between mythic truths and scientific truths are not solely a matter of erroneous folk beliefs yet to be supplanted by scientific findings. It works the other way too: mythic thinking can shape science and determine its course, and without care the very scientists who think they have transcended such thinking can mistake mythic understandings for science. As Tallis (2011) puts it, we must strive to "distinguish between neuroscience and its shadow, neuroscientism" (p. 28). Both of these phenomena, the popular stories about neuroscience and the mythic thinking within neuroscience, as well as their various consequences, will be discussed in detail in this chapter.

The immediate objection to such a line of thought is that science strives toward objectivity, and insofar as it is successful, it must purge fiction and myth altogether. I would counter that this is itself an excellent example of a guiding myth of scientific culture. On some level the scientist must imagine that objectivity really exists, and strive toward the mythic ideal of contacting, measuring, and successfully unlocking the secrets of that objective reality. Again, to recognize the mythic dimension of this belief is not to deny it an objective dimension (such arguments were addressed fully in Chapters 2 and 6). Rather I am asserting that in addition to the objective dimension of scientific work, there is also a mythic dimension guiding the work. Fiction is part of the ontological fabric from which our human experience is woven. The great challenge for scientists and humanists alike is to discern the difference between these different aspects of the human condition.

Furthermore, I contend that acknowledging the human dimension of science ultimately gives us a more accurate picture of the universe, not less. Jan Golinksi (1998) discusses the balancing act of studying science as a human activity:

> [Constructivism] draws attention to the central notion that all scient-ific knowledge is a human creation, made with available material and cultural resources, rather than simply the revelation of a natural order that is pre-given and independent of human action. It should not be taken to imply the claim that science can be entirely reduced to the social or linguistic level, still less that it is a kind of collective delusion with no relation to material reality.
>
> (p. 6)

Golinski sees this constructivism as a methodological approach rather than set of philosophical principles. It allows us to study the cultural and sub-jective aspects of scientific knowledge production while still making room for the knowledge science produces to hold its own merit. As the metaphor of mind as mirror to reality fell away in the wake of Kant, and seems all the more dubious in the wake of the contemporary neuroscience of percep-tion, investigating the human dimension of scientific inquiry has the poten-tial to offer a richer and more nuanced understanding of scientific knowledge.

Nevertheless, the historical tension between science and fiction runs deep. Harari (2016), who is by varying degrees an outspoken champion of both types of truth, suggests that a certain amount of conflict was inherent from the outset. "The willingness to admit ignorance made modern science more dynamic, supple, and inquisitive than any previous tradition of knowledge" (p. 253), and yet this new capacity for doubt presented a new threat to the fictional dimension of human existence. The fictions binding society together, long perceived as literal truths, could now be doubted and deconstructed in science's renewed quest for truth and power. Harari identifies two traditional solutions to this ongoing problem. The first is to relegate science to its own sphere and attempt to set firm boundaries on which realms of human experience it is allowed to encroach upon. The second solution is scientism: the transformation of science into a religion, a numinous source of complete and absolute truth. Both of these solutions can still be seen in the twenty-first century. This entire formulation, however, seems to be based on a zero-sum opposition between fact and fiction. But if fact and fiction are instead seen as two different kinds of human truth, can we not imagine a world where they can not only coexist, but integrate?

Although part of the problem is certainly the many ways that fictions in the popular culture make false claims at being scientific, another culprit is the refusal among some factions of scientific culture to admit that science has its own mythic dimension. This is to say that it has its own guiding images, fictions, and myths that help it meaningfully cohere in human consciousness. Harari argues that "one of the things that has made it possible for modern social orders to hold together is the spread of an almost religious belief in technology and in the methods of scientific research" (2016, p. 254). In this narrative, the scientific enterprise was able to eat into the foundational fictions of society and leave that society standing only be replacing them with other fictions about the infallible power of science. Bohm and Peat (2000/1987) recognize a similar shadow in scientific culture. For many disillusioned with traditional religion,

> science became the repository of the idea that particular forms of knowledge could either be absolute truths or at least could approach absolute truths. Such a belief in the ultimate power of scientific knowledge evoked strong feelings of comforting security in many people, almost comparable with the feelings experienced by those who have an absolute faith in the truths of religion.
>
> (p. 24)

Like all tribal origin stories, this mythic account of science as the provider of the one absolute truth serves a deeply emotional function around identity and belonging. In cases of such a deep emotional attachment to this worldview, we should not be surprised to see an emotional response, rather than a strictly scientific one, when the worldview is questioned.

To reiterate: asserting that there is a mythic dimension to science is not to disparage scientific knowledge. What's more, a depth psychological understanding of myths allows us to view them as neither good nor bad in themselves. Rather myths are seen in the first place as psychologically inevitable and in the second place as existing on a spectrum of conscious or unconscious awareness. Thus, there is no insult implied in suggesting, for example, that most neuroscientists subscribe to a myth of materialism. Materialism, the belief that we are matter and nothing more, is a guiding myth that gives meaning to the life and work of many scientists. Trouble only arises when the myths are mistaken for verifiable facts, when materialism is mistaken for a scientific conclusion rather than a metaphysical premise, or more broadly when the truth-revealing power of science is mistaken as the sole source of truth.

The identification of materialism as perhaps the most pervasive myth of neuroscientific culture will be returned to at the end of this chapter. First let us proceed with an inquiry into the ways in which fiction plays a role in the day-to-day transmission of scientific knowledge. This inquiry will begin broadly in tracking the interplay of fictions in scientific discourse generally, and eventually focus in on the fictional dimension of neuroscience in particular.

Science and the bridge of fiction

In his wonderful book about the birth of complexity theory, M. Mitchell Waldrop (1992) recounts an interview with physicist Doyne Farmer about the nature of science:

> Science is about a great many things, says Doyne Farmer. It's about the systematic accumulation of facts and data. It's about the construction of logically consistent theories to account for those facts. It's about the discovery of new materials, new pharmaceuticals, and new technologies. But at heart, he says, science is about telling stories—stories about what the world is like, and how the world came to be as it is.
>
> (p. 318)

Ideally these stories contribute to our understanding of who we are and how we fit into the universe. Holton (1996) takes this assertion even further, stating that in addition to the production of knowledge and power, science has always also had a "metaphoric function—that is, it generates an important part of a culture's symbolic vocabulary and provides some of the metaphysical bases and philosophical orientations of our ideology" (p. 43). The discoveries, theories, technologies, and models that come out of science are a rich stream of images to be further woven into our cultural self-understandings.

My basic argument in this section is that in this process of transforming science into story we have inevitably shifted from one kind of truth (fact) to another kind (fiction). That fiction may indeed point backward toward hard data, and the degree that it does so should absolutely be a metric for assessing how scientific the story really is. But it has still become a story, and this shift has consequences on several levels. Some would argue that science should just be a clear transmission of pure data, but a variety of social and linguistic factors make this extremely difficult. Randy Olson (2015), a scientist turned filmmaker who specializes in helping scientists become better storytellers, assesses the problem as follows: "Scientists wish they could just pour out facts, untouched, for consumption. But they can't. The brain needs information packages in specific ways" (p. 38). He is referring to the growing evidence that emotionally salient narratives are easier to remember than dry lists of facts (see Chapter 7 for a review). As

Siegel (2017) summarizes, "stories are how our minds recall information best" (p. 18). Olson argues that "science is a newly arrived guest in an ancient narrative world" (2015, p. 37). Humans have been transmitting information in narrative form for tens of thousands of years, whereas science has had only a few centuries to develop its communication techniques. Long before the world of human experience was made up of subatomic particles, it was made of stories. Thus, Olson's argument goes, the data must become a story if it is going to have an impact on the culture.

This is absolutely not a claim that the data itself is imagined. The data is the data—it is immutable on its own terms. Data can be taken at face value: these scientists used this method to find this thing at this time, and these other scientists were able to replicate the results. Therein science finds its legitimate authority. It is what happens next that complicates the matter. In the effort to make the data comprehensible for others, a fiction-making process is undertaken to turn the data into an understandable story. The story is a new map of reality, and like any good map, it must be somewhat accurate to be useful. Ideally fact and fiction are perfectly synthesized so that one points clearly to the other, and vice versa. But whether this ideal *conjunctio* is reached or not, the medium of human communication has, like Proteus, changed shape, arriving now in the form of story rather than data.

It could well be argued that even within the most remote of specialized scientific enclaves, there is some degree of storytelling in the ongoing communication around objects of study, models, theories, and procedures. If it is human nature to experience the world through story, then this should be somewhat inevitable in laboratories and peer review journals as well, with stories operating in the background even when overt conversations between colleagues are more explicitly concerned with data, mathematics, and abstractions. My colleague Yvonne Lefebvre, a career molecular biologist, assures me that this is the case: that even within the lab, scientists hunt for stories in the data (personal communication, 2017). But for the present discourse let us leave this part of the argument to others. For the sake of simplicity, let as assume that within a given laboratory, the majority of what gets communicated within the group is in fact data rather than story. Even with this pure beginning, a considerable point of transformation occurs when scientists take their specialized knowledge out of the enclave. Now the scientists must try to explain what on earth they have been up to, to those who do not share the enclave's specialized language, knowledge base, and underlying mythology.

The first step of this transmission of scientific knowledge may be the scientific enclave next door. Even here, significant problems may start to arise. The terminology, methods, and conceptual framework of one scientific discipline may be quite different from even a relatively similar scientific discipline (neuropharmacology and psychoneuroimmunology, as just one example)—to say nothing of the gulf of understanding that would need to be bridged in transmitting that knowledge to a distant discipline, such as sociology or history. Holton (1996) laments the "atomization of loyalties within the intelligentsia" (p. 42), with fields of study becoming increasingly insular and self-referential, disconnected from their larger contexts. Bohm and Peat (2000/1987) foreground this problem as well: "Science today is becoming more and more specialized, so that an individual scientist may spend a lifetime working in a particular narrow field and never come into contact with the wider context of his or her subject" (p. 19). They further point out that many see this as inevitable—as overall knowledge increases, it becomes increasingly difficult for an individual to keep track of information outside of their immediate field. It is a practical issue rather than an ideological one. Nevertheless, it results in a fragmentation of worldview that is not easily overcome.

This means that the sort of shared storytelling that goes on within the laboratory about the objects of study does not automatically translate to the philosophy lecture hall on the other side of campus. Complex data is oversimplified, sophisticated counter-interpretations go unmentioned, small correlations start to look more certain, speculative models can sound like established theories—all without any deliberate malfeasance on the part of the scientists doing their best to tell their story. Tallis (2011) is especially critical of a recent influx of supposedly neuroscientific information into various fields within the humanities. "Most of the time you will be selling your product to an audience that is not in a position to judge the correctness, the validity, or even the probability of the claims you are making about the guest discipline" (p. 60). In a room full of philosophers who are not already also experts in the given scientific field, the degree of fiction in the transmission expands considerably. And this problem becomes even more pronounced when the story leaves the ivory tower altogether and makes its way into the culture at large.

Science fictions in public discourse

As I worked toward the completion of this book, I noticed a growing concern about dismissive attitudes toward science in the United States (Lloyd, 2015). As a supporter of science I find these trends deeply disturbing. In my view science is one of the most important sources of information on which any liberal democracy may form an involved consensus. What could account for this apparent devaluation in the public mind? Randy Olson (2015) is a strong advocate for the notion that science is not translating well into the larger culture because scientists in general lack a grasp of narrative structure and an appreciation of how important narrative is to communication in general. "Scientists are trained only as scientists—meaning they sprint passed the humanities to the best of their abilities while they are undergraduates" (p. 47). This, Olson argues, is a fundamental error, as it severely limits how scientists are able to effectively communicate their findings to humanity at large. "Narrative tools need to become a fundamental part of science.... Narrative needs to be taught at the start of science from the undergraduate level" (p. 69). This is not to say that scientific results need to be dramatized or inflated beyond what a given study actually says. On the contrary, Olson argues that good narrative structure would help scientists make even negative or inconclusive results of a study more engaging.

Whether and to what degree such narrative savvy would significantly improve public engagement and understanding of science remains to be seen. But in the meantime, the process of accurately transmitting scientific knowledge into a broader public discourse remains problematic. Olson summarizes that when it comes to "the communication of research findings both among scientists and to the general public—the problems are age old" (2015, p. 11). It is especially difficult, he argues, when communicating information-heavy material without a narrative structure to contain it. A prime example, is the finding by Sumner et al. (2014) that out of 462 biomedical papers and their corresponding press releases, 40 percent of the press releases contained exaggerated advice, 33 percent exaggerated causal claims, and 36 percent exaggerated inference. Sumner and her team found that this led to even higher levels of exaggeration in the printed news stories that reported on the scientific studies. To begin with, this shows that even within the communications that scientific teams are producing, exaggeration shows up with disturbing frequency for what should be a purely objective presentation of scientific data. An even more alarming trend is what happens to the science once the news media gets a hold of it—in order to make headlines, the news reporting took these fictional liberties in communicating science even further.

Feyerabend (2010/1975) is all too cognizant of these problems. He speaks of the moment when "theory is no longer an esoteric discussion topic for advanced seminars and conferences, but enters the public domain.... Unfortunately, this increase in importance is not accompanied by better understanding; the very opposite is the case" (p. 23). The more fictionalized a scientific understanding becomes, the more its genuinely contentious scientific points fall into the background. What would be debated carefully and relentlessly in a scientific journal all too easily becomes a series of truisms in the popular culture.

A concrete example of this sort of inflation in the realm of neuroscience is provided by Tallis (2011) in analyzing a news story claiming that scientists had uncovered the neurobiological basis for wisdom. In the original scientific paper that the news report was based on, the authors described an investigation into the various "subcomponents" of wisdom and the brain locations that seemed to correlate to those activities (see Jeste &

Meeks, 2009). The model presented by the authors was admittedly speculative and depended on a rather narrow (some might say hopelessly reductive) definition of "wisdom," and proceeded quite regardless of the lack of consensus about localization models in contemporary brain science. Nevertheless, Tallis describes how the mainstream public version of the story went quite a bit further. "Following a familiar pattern, the 'speculative' model was translated by journalists, with the help of a press release from the laboratory and rather optimistic interviews with the scientists, the article headlined: 'Found: The Brain's Center of Wisdom'" (2011, p. 75). What had initially been offered as a speculative model of the neurobiological correlates of consciousness had become in its public expression an absurdly certain decree about how the brain somehow magically creates wisdom. I use the term *magically* quite deliberately because in this succession of misunderstandings between scientific data and popular mythological understanding, quite a bit of magical thinking has taken place.

In this case, some scientists have taken a complex phenomenological truth, named in the Western context as *wisdom*, and attempted to analytically break it down into constituent parts in the language of contemporary cognitive brain science. This step, in itself, is an imaginative exercise, insofar as it takes a complex cultural understanding and reductively re-imagines into a series of cognitive terms that don't necessarily have anything to do with its original synthesis in the Western canon. I certainly do not object to the original authors' attempts to relate these linguistic and imaginal components to current cognitive theory, but I agree with Tallis that they are essentially speculative. The authors are, quite creatively, offering us a new way of looking at wisdom as it correlates to the small amount of brain activity that we currently know how to measure. There is no problem here with the science, as long as we recognize it as an essentially creative and speculative journey into understanding the material correlates to the phenomenon of wisdom. But there is nothing here that suggests any sort of final word on how "wisdom" shows up in the brain— much less how we should best understand wisdom in humanistic, psychological, or spiritual terms. Nevertheless, the public discourse transforms the study into a bizarrely certain declaration that neuroscientists have somehow accurately confirmed that a particular area/function of the brain has explained and accounted for *wisdom* itself! While the science may be sound, the public transmission of the science has become not only mythology, but the kind of mythology that frankly seems damaging to the project of honest scientific inquiry.

Consider the above example from the perspective of the public. If they have come to trust science blindly as an authoritative source of truth, then they have been misled into taking a largely fictional account of wisdom for a scientific one. For those who look at such news stories and rightly see them as being bizarrely reductive, absurd, and perhaps even a diminution of human nature, the legitimacy of science may begin to lose its luster. Such claims about the brain do not just offer us new information about potential qualities of the material world—they strike at the very heart of what it means to be human. Now it might be natural at this point for a typical human to choose to disbelieve the story, because we all know on a deep intuitive level that stories are only partial truths. But because this story ostensibly carries the stamp of science, we are being asked to believe that this story is somehow objectively true. We might expect from such a scenario the same deep intuitive resistance as we find in opposition to fundamentalist religion, which also demands that its adherents accept mythology as being inherently, absolutely, and literally true.

The honest scientist objects, of course, that science should be much more skeptical and no single study should be taken as truth. But those caveats were not included in the news story, and the general public does not have direct access to the laboratory. Within the limited public discourse on science, these stories must be for the most part absorbed and accepted or rejected in their fictional expressions. Ultimately belief in these fictions, as Harari implies, becomes a matter of which social group you belong to rather than a matter of what might or might not actually be a better correlate to objective truth. The data itself, along with its interpretive ambiguity, is left in the laboratory.

These skewed popular scientific understandings then become part of the mythic substrate for the larger cultural belief system, essentially a mythic belief system rather than a properly scientific one. This cultural substrate, in turn, becomes the social context in which new scientists are produced, suggesting that for many individuals their initial understandings of science, prior to graduate school (and perhaps in some cases well beyond), are expressions of mythic frameworks rather than scientific ones. From here we can see how the entire scientific enterprise could at times be carried forward on self-perpetuating mythic understandings quite apart from what has actually been verified—or is verifiable. As just one example, consider the long dogma in twentieth-century neuroscience that the human brain is more or less fully developed and unchangeable by adulthood (Begley, 2007). From this belief an entire generation was told, by the scientific establishment, that their brains could not continue to develop and change beyond adolescence. Imagine what a cultural impact such a belief could have on a population! The discovery of neuroplasticity in adults changed all this, but for many millions of lives the damage had already been done.

To make matters worse, so long as such mythic beliefs go unexamined, there remains strong potential for unconscious bias to skew future scientific studies back in support of the unexamined cultural myths. The fact that purveyors of these myths insist that they are fundamentally scientific makes the problem more acute. If Einstein is correct (and I believe that he is) that in science the formulation of the question is at least as important as finding the answer, it is a short step to see the degree to which unexamined cultural mythology can drive scientific enterprise toward mythic, rather than scientific, conclusions.

The human face of neuroscience

If science genuinely seeks the truth, scientific process must include an acknowledgment that science does not always do an impeccable job of seeking the truth. Apart from the failures of public relations and news media, there are considerable factors that may complicate both the purity of scientific process and the clarity of perspective of the scientists who undertake it. Because I too am a great believer in honest inquiry, I contend that an honest assessment of these compromising factors does not attack or impugn science itself. Rather, ultimately, such analysis of potential error strengthens the ability of science to get at a deeper and more specific kind of truth.

Science is, in part, guided by mythological frameworks. Myth helps to create the broad context for science whereby its sometimes-atomistic explorations may reveal larger truths. The myths themselves may lead us toward a variety of outcomes, both successful and not. The point is not to attack or laud one myth over the other, but rather to become conscious of how they operate in our lives and in our laboratories.

Myths of scientific purity and power

Let us begin with the mythos that is most apparent and prevalent. Especially beneficial as a motivating force is the guiding myth that scientific method can and does reveal deep truths about the nature of reality. Logic and evidence may demonstrate some literal truth to this assertion, but in calling it a myth we shift attention to the ways it operates psychologically as a guiding story. The story tells us that scientists can use the pure and uncompromising quest of science both to seek ultimate reality and to help their fellow humans. The method becomes a kind oracle and the scientist a kind of hero. Many, perhaps most, scientists pursue their craft under the guiding idea that by doing so they are contributing to the greater storehouse of human understanding, thus making the world a better place. In a religious age, it might be called God's work, but even in an atheistic framework, this moral quest for secular truth retains a powerful numinosity. This belief operates psychologically as a driving force to motivate and justify scientific inquiry, even in the face of more troubling complications.

Cultural myths can be an incredible motivator for human beings, powerful enough to drive millions of humans to give their lives in war, as encapsulated in the noble maxim, "to die for one's country." If myth could give a human motivation to surrender its very life, why should we be surprised that myth could create a similarly emotionally charged motivation among scientists? Many humans would be willing to give their lives for what they believe to be the greater good—why should other humans not dedicate their lives to doing good through the pursuit of science? I am deeply sympathetic to such belief systems. I too want to believe that the work I am doing will make the world a better place. There is nothing inherently wrong with these mythic ideals; I follow them myself and sometimes wish a greater portion of humanity would do the same. The only condition for proceeding as such is that we must be willing to acknowledge our guiding ideals as myths, rather than facts. We want to believe the work we are doing will help, but we do not really know.

Harari writes that "many scientists do, in fact, act out of pure intellectual curiosity. However, only rarely do scientists dictate the scientific agenda" (2016, p. 273). The potential disjunction he proposes between the values of scientists and the larger agenda of science is alarming enough to beg further scrutiny. Belief in the purity and goodness of science may be a great motivator, and it may sometimes produce some truly wonderful results—but in itself, this belief will not dictate what should be studied, or how, or what will be done with the results. Those decisions are embedded in the larger cultural context of values in which the science takes place.

The ideal of scientific purity is an important guiding myth: the noble path of striving through robust and sometimes brutal means toward a truth that underlies our common understanding. This story contains important values, and science at its best often incorporates them. But such beliefs, when unquestioned, can also ultimately support interests and agendas that are completely at odds with the axioms they ostensibly pursue. When science is co-opted by any principle or interest outside of careful examination of the data, it can begin to corrupt the careful dedication to data from which scientific method draws its strength. In such an instance, the world that science asks us to imagine might begin to look very different, while still dubiously brandishing the brand of science. Potential corruptions of the purity of science may be manifold, but I will focus in the remainder of this section on just two: the social motivations for confirming a group consensus, and the role that money plays in the production and use of scientific knowledge.

Social considerations in the production of scientific knowledge

Recent neuropsychology has increasingly come to recognize the degree to which human behavior is grounded in interpersonal and social considerations (Cozolino, 2016; Porges, 2011; Schore, 2012; Siegel, 2012; Van Der Kolk, 2014). Even if we assume that most science is genuinely motivated by a mythology of pure science as indicated above, this noble motivation does not necessarily always or completely overcome the social factors that underlie all human group activities. Issues around belonging, shared belief systems, and above all social status and advancement, whether conscious or no, may subtly and innocently skew the results of scientific study in directions that a pure quest for truth would not.

First, let us acknowledge that social factors in science can often play a very positive role in the process of discovery. Cech (2001) discusses how important group dynamics in the laboratory were in the discovery of catalytic RNA: "several researchers in the laboratory ... were pursuing parallel yet distinct pathways. Had it just been me doing all the experiments and getting strange results, I might have suspected my own technical abilities or my judgment" (p. 13). Instead, his faith in his co-workers' abilities (and we presume vice versa) helped to create a psychological container for working through perplexing results toward an astounding discovery. A somewhat contrary example is offered by Watson (1968) in *The double helix*, which paints a picture of competition between scientists that ultimately drove the investigation into the structure of DNA toward it historic conclusion. But whether the dynamics lean more toward collaboration or competition, the social milieu in both cases was vital to their success. Wiesberg (1993) further argues that even in the case of a supposedly solitary scientist like Darwin, the historical record documents a rich network of friendships and correspondences with other scientists and intellectuals. This larger social milieu of relationships, ideas, and debates had demonstrably clear and powerful impact on the shaping of Darwin's thought.

But social factors in science can also lead to bad outcomes. Recall from Chapter 8 Solms and Turnbull's (2002) account of how Allan Hobson's new theory of dreams impacted the 1976 meeting of the American Psychiatric Association (APA). Hobson and his colleagues (1975) had just published their *activation synthesis* model of dreaming, which asserted that because dreaming seems to be initiated from activity in the brainstem, the forebrain does "the best of a bad job" of transforming the ensuing brain activity into a coherent episode. At the meeting in question, Hobson took the opportunity to employ this model in an attack on his mythic nemesis, Sigmund Freud, arguing that Freudian dream theory could not possibly be tenable in light of his recent research. Somewhat incredibly, the APA took a vote (that most scientific of procedures) to declare that Freudian dream theory was unscientific. Solms and Turnbull lament that in light of Freud's core tenet that dreams are the royal road to the unconscious, "this had serious implications for psychoanalysis in general" (2002, p. 190). Furthermore, an entire generation of scientific psychologists was now prone to dismiss dreams out of hand as meaningless noise, an epiphenomenon of activity in the brainstem.

And yet not even Hobson believed that dreams were meaningless, a position that he makes explicitly clear in his 2015 book *Psychodynamic neurology.* A number of elements in this story are quite disturbing. First of all, while there was strong evidence for REM sleep being initiated by the brainstem, there is no reason why this could not be framed differently as brainstem trigger for a higher and more complex cerebral function. Just because the heart is needed to pump fresh blood to the brain does not mean that the higher functions of the brain are only noise created by the heart. Yet the data on brainstem activation was treated with exactly that logic. Hobson, of course, had every right to interpret the data as he pleased and offer a speculative model about dreams and meaning—but only if we keep in mind that the model was completely speculative. He looked at some good data and used it to spin a story about the complex phenomena of dreams and meaning in the human psyche. And then the fatal error: this speculative story was presented as scientific truth, and because some good data was incorporated in the beginning of the story, the entire APA was willing to mistake the fictional conclusion for legitimate science. Legitimate science, as I understand it, would humbly recognize the sheer complexity of the phenomena in question and set out to spend the next several decades continuing to explore this and other models from a variety of perspectives. Instead, the APA took a vote— essentially reducing scientific psychology to a storytelling contest between Hobson and Freud, the latter of whom, being long dead, was unable to defend himself. There are other problems here of course: the unfounded certainty that REM and dreaming are same thing, and the larger epistemological conundrum of how brain function and consciousness are related. But most disturbing of all is to see a topic of such importance reduced to a popularity contest by group of people who had convinced themselves this exercise was somehow scientific.

Bohm and Peat (2000/1987) discuss at length the promises and perils of social factors in the world of science. While their terminology does not make mention of mythology outright, they do focus on a related conception of the tacit infrastructure of ideas that underlies a given scientific field. In their view, this tacit infrastructure is used as a basis for general coherence and consensus, and as such any challenges to it, however sound from the perspective of pure science, may meet steep resistance. Creative discovery in science, they argue, is often stymied because of the

> unconscious defense of ideas which are of fundamental significance and which are assumed to be necessary to the mind's habitual state of comfortable equilibrium. As a result, there is instead a strong disposition to impose familiar ideas, even when there is evidence that they may be false.... If several people are involved, collusion will follow, as they mutually support each other in their false responses. This often takes place in subtle ways that are extremely difficult to notice.
>
> (p. 50)

It is worth emphasizing that this "collusion" is framed as a primarily unconscious social process of keeping the present belief system stable. The drive to do so comes to inhabit the language of a given field itself, encouraging some models and possibilities while discounting others out of hand. Bohm and Peat argue that these issues of communication and language are fundamental to how scientists perceive the world. As such, scientists are continually in a process of "internal dialog with the whole structure of their particular discipline.... Motivations, questions, and attitudes arise out of the dialogs, so that all scientific research, in the end, arises out of a whole subcultural matrix of science" (p. 67). Furthermore, these factors become imbedded in the institutions that both train scientists and facilitate scientific research. They become fundamental tenants of the local culture.

It is only natural that humans want to belong. Lewis, Amini, and Lannon's (2001) *A general theory of love* argues that humans are inherently social and that acceptance by the tribe is a profound psychological need with tangible physiological consequences. The entire field of evolutionary psychology seems to trend in this direction as well, emphasizing humanity's long history in small hunter–gatherer groups where belonging was literally a matter of life and death (see also Barnes & Murray, 2012; Cozolino, 2016; Goodwyn, 2012; Porges, 2011). From this premise, we can easily imagine a renegade scientist entering the field might have a strong desire to belong to the professional community she is joining. This might not always be the case—it is possible to get such needs met in communities entirely outside of the workplace—but it would nevertheless be a motivating factor much of the time. The need to belong includes not only being tolerated by one's peers, but also being seen and appreciated for the contributions one can make. It may also involve forming specific peer alliances to help cement that belonging. All of this could subtly push a scientist toward group consensus, or agreement with allies, that pure data might dispute. It can take tremendous courage to go out on a limb and suggest a theoretical framework, model, or even confounding data that contradicts the favorites ideas, opinions, and general mythology of the group. An individual might face mockery, ostracization, even humiliation from an intolerant social group. Of course, ideally this would never happen. But it strikes me as wishful thinking to believe that scientific communities would never fall prey to these common human dynamics.

The leads directly to a second complicating factor: that of social status and social standing. Here I am specifically speaking of power dynamics within a social group. Inevitably, some scientists will come to have more power and prestige within their institutions (and in the larger field beyond the institution) than others. Power is a complicating factor in all relationships, and so we should expect, at least some of the time, for it to play the same role in scientific communities. Social standing has real consequences in terms of what a person can achieve professionally, as well as their financial prospects (more on this in the next section). And while we might expect most scientists to hold themselves to high ethical standards in this regard, the possibility of subtle unconscious behaviors may yet play a part. The desire to defeat a rival might predispose one to read that rival's work with extra skepticism, or to speak of that work in the larger community with greater disparagement than the work really deserves. Equally problematic, those with lower social status may feel inclined to tell their superiors what they want to hear—to agree with their ideas, to celebrate their work, to confirm their biases—because doing so might curry favor and thus advancement. It might be both ethical and noble to speak out against the establishment—but realistically speaking it might also spell real trouble for a young scientist's career. Of course, the history of science is full of stories of creative minds who did just that: took a stand for a new way of looking at the world despite a consensus to the contrary. What enables this sort of courage is itself a worthy subject for study. But however much we celebrate it, we cannot realistically expect such courage will always be present, or always successful.

As a final complicating factor arising in the social sphere, the question of ideological bias bears mentioning. By this I mean deep-seated and perhaps emotionally charged beliefs that do not necessarily have much to do with science in its purest expression. As the last chapter's discussion of ontological imagination argued, such belief systems, whether intellectual, political, metaphysical, or religious, can have a real effect in terms of what kinds of ideas and possibilities science can entertain, and to what ends. Take for example a young man who had a wounding experience with a fundamentalist religion; someone who was rejected by his community and also possibly his family for being different or thinking differently. I suspect that for a great many young people who have these experiences, religion as a whole becomes the enemy, and the world of science becomes a sort of ontic refuge. In some cases, science versus religion may become identified with a larger mythic pattern of truth versus falsehood, or even good versus evil. Such a move essentially transforms science itself into a quasi-religious entity, an irony that is often lost in the mythic quest to defeat the forces of darkness and liberate humankind into the light of (mythic) reason. So deeply emotional are such convictions I doubt anything I write here could sway them. And yet it seems plain as day to me that science and religion deal in such entirely different realms of human concern that they could not possibly become so opposed except by a category error: either mistaking religion for science or science for religion. I agree with celebrated biologist Stephen Jay Gould (1998) that "the lack of conflict between science and religion arises from a lack of overlap between their respective domains" (p. 271), with science being concerned with the empirical and religion with the ethical and spiritual aspects of human experience.

Of course, the recent wedding of certain fundamentalist religious groups to anti-science political movements such as climate denial is hugely problematic and potentially disastrous. This is a political problem in its own right that will be addressed briefly in the final chapter. But such anti-science movements cannot be identified with religion as a whole simply because they do not provide a representative sample of the phenomenon of religion. Pope Francis' (2015) passionate invective about the need for humanity to address climate change is just one powerful example of religion supporting science.

Nevertheless, the conflation of science with atheist myths and metaphysics remains a corruption of pure science, which simply seeks to understand those aspects of the universe that we know how to measure. I wholeheartedly respect atheism and scientific materialism as mythic belief systems, and would certainly fight for the right of anyone to believe in such stories. We all need stories to make meaning of our lives; myth and story is part of our deepest being. What I object to is mistaking these stories for science itself. They are not and cannot be, and to say otherwise sows seeds of confusion into what science really is, and why it must be respected.

Myths and metaphors of the brain

John G. Daugman (2001) has written a wonderful and concise essay reviewing brain metaphors throughout history. In it, he draws attention to the way the evolution of these images has reflected the technological progress of the age.

> The water technology of antiquity (fountains pumps, water clocks) underlies ... the Greek pneumatic concept of the soul (pneuma) and the Roman physician Galen's theory of the four humours; the clockwork mechanisms proliferating during the Enlightenment are ticking with seminal influence inside Le Mettrie's L'Homme machine (1748); Victorian pressurized steam engines and hydraulic machines are churning underneath Freud's hydraulic construction of the unconscious and its libidinal economy; the arrival of the telegraph network provided Helmholtz with his basic neural metaphor, as did reverberating relay circuits and solenoids for Hebb's theory of memory; and so on.
>
> (p. 24)

Daugman links the changing of metaphors in science to the changing of paradigms; new conceptions of the brain are both inspired by and give rise to new images to help contain them. Furthermore, he asserts that it is only arrogance that would lead us to believe that our current metaphors are somehow the final "correct" images that can at last be taken literally. "In this historical framework, surely it would be folly for us to regard the recent computer bewitchment of theoretical work in psychology and neuroscience an entirely different kind of breakthrough in the history of ideas" (p. 24). Describing our contemporary computer models as a form of bewitchment is particularly biting coming from Daugman, who is himself an accomplished computer scientist and one of the creators of the iris-scanning identification technologies now being used around the world.

His criticism is not for the computer metaphor itself as much as for a culture that has increasingly come to take it literally. This had become so widespread by the dawn of the twenty-first century that Daugman suggests that it

> begins to appear less like an innovate leap and more like a bandwagon phenomenon ... the irresistible temptation to announce a "computational theory of X" where X could be anything from the gill-withdrawal of aplysia ... to the hemispheric lateralization of the entire brain ... typically reveals more about the sociological diffusion of slogans than about any proven or natural connection between X and computation.
>
> (2001, p. 32)

While many have rushed to participate in the literalization of the computer metaphor, Daugman reminds us that there was also great enthusiasm for the hydraulic metaphor during Freud's influential tenure. Nor is the computer metaphor particularly robust even by modern standards. "Where syllogisms and symbols are concerned, people are terrible at computation, and ... any current implementation of computation is terrible at doing what people do or simulating what they are like" (p. 33). These words are now over 15 years old, and yet for all the amazing developments in computer technology, this fundamental difference remains: computers have become much better at imitating humans, but not at actually demonstrating human-like consciousness themselves. In theory, that day may yet come, but in the meantime, it remains firmly in the realm of fantasy.

Raymond Tallis (2011) has also been fiercely critical of the cultural tendency to take the computer metaphor of the brain too literally. Like Daugman, he believes it was inspired in part by the new ideas and images that technological progress inspired: "That this metaphor installed itself in the heart of psychology in the second half of the twentieth century was in part the result of huge advances in computer technology and the development of microprocessors" (p. 193). But Tallis' criticisms of this development are far more extensive than Daugman's—he sees it as a complete misunderstanding of what it means to be human. The sorts of events that take place in computers "do not amount to genuine understanding.... Symbols are symbols only to someone who understands that they are symbols, events in computers considered in isolation from conscious human beings do not even amount to the processing of symbols" (p. 186). Up to this point in history, computers don't actually understand anything by their information processing. The meaning that those informational processes might contain is only enabled by conscious human beings who program those meanings and by other human beings who receive them. As with the writing of a novel, the meaning is not somehow *in* the book itself; rather the book serves as a medium of transmission from one conscious mind to another. Computers, for all their sophistication, at present still serve the same function of relaying information between conscious subjects, rather than exhibiting any consciousness themselves. In 2017, any assertion that computers might be more than non-conscious information processors, however compelling, invariably remains an act of imagination. Scientifically and philosophically speaking, computers that currently exist outside of the imagination are mindless, non-conscious processing machines. If that bridge is ever crossed, it will likely represent paradigm shifts across the board, with our understanding of brains, computers, and consciousness re-imagined entirely.

In the meantime, Tallis is particularly critical of some modern attempts to equate the concepts of information and consciousness. This proceeds by "narrowing the conception of consciousness or awareness to that of information, and widening that of information way beyond the engineering sense that gives it respectability, and not acknowledging (or noticing) either of these moves" (2011, p. 202). This creates the possibility of understanding consciousness as information processing in the brain, despite the fact that there is no other known context where information processing gives rise to consciousness. Tallis goes on to describe a growing scientific trend to describe all events in nature and the cosmos as information exchanges, a move which he considers absurd: "Sun-bathing, for example, is information bathing" (p. 203). The information-processing brain then becomes a cultural metaphor for what it means to be a person, despite the fact that we really still know very little about how the brain works. "When you personify the brain and bits of brain then it is easy to 'brainify' people" (p. 187)—that is, to reduce their complex personhood to whatever crushingly narrow mechanistic model is being proposed. His scathing argument concludes that through sloppy thinking and a rush to consensus around incomplete models, humanity itself becomes degraded.

To exemplify this point, let us consider the recent phenomenon of driverless cars that will soon be hitting the market. These automated machines will only be considered safe if they can actively sense what is going on in their environment and move their mechanical bodies accordingly. Yet despite this stimulus response most people would not consider driverless cars conscious beings. We could further upgrade these cars in several ways: we could give them complex algorithms for semi-scripted conversations with their passengers, or even programs where they might learn and integrate new knowledge through these exchanges, in order to have more "personalized" conversations. We could give them complex self-sensors that read into the internal state of their processes and (perhaps arbitrarily) affect the artifice of their persona when interacting with humans, giving them a basis to talk about their "feelings." We could give them programs to seek out their own fuel sources like a living organism. We could even give them the capability to replicate themselves, and write programs for them to do so by interfacing with other driverless cars in order to design new models based on shared data on efficiency—the genesis of a new car-being, as it were. But did any of these upgrades give the cars the gift of consciousness? At what point do these programs become a conscious experience? What is the specific step that would transform complex information processing into an actual first-person phenomenological experience? If we say this is impossible for entities made of metal and circuits, then what is it specifically about the biological substrate of our brains that creates consciousness, as opposed to mere processing of complex information? The idea of conscious computers might make more sense in the context of panpsychism, but panpsychism too is anathema to traditional materialist accounts of the brain. This conundrum of the "hard" problem of consciousness will be further addressed below. For now, suffice to say, the computer metaphor of the brain appears to be significantly limited in explaining the full spectrum of our humanity.

The cultural myth that brains are computers has further dovetailed with older trends in Western thought to laud logic, reason, and rationalism above all other forms of thought and consciousness. That is, rather than appreciate reason as a wonderful if limited gift of the human psyche, reason tends to be elevated above other ways of valuing and understanding: aesthetic, imaginative, intuitive, emotional, somatic, and so on. We might call it the myth of the Great Rational Overlord. This worship of reason has translated in much neuroscience literature as praise for the prefrontal cortex. Though he is by no means alone in this valuation, Dietrich's (2015) transient hypofrontal theory (THT) is an excellent example of this kind of bias. Essentially, THT considers the prefrontal cortex to be the apex of brain evolution on planet earth because of its apparent role in executive functions such as reasoning, planning, decision making, and the like. Because altered states of consciousness, including dreaming, visionary experiences, and psychedelic experiences are marked by decreased activity in the prefrontal cortex, THT concludes that these must be "lower" forms of consciousness, because they make use of supposedly "less evolved" neural real estate. Thus, the Western bias toward the rational ego becomes a self-fulfilling prophecy. The data does not demand such an interpretation; the underlying cultural premise, rather than the results, shapes the theory.

In the first place, the notion that the brain should be understood as a series of hierarchical relations between higher and lower functions already reflects a set of cultural values around social hierarchy and power. But even if such a formulation could be demonstrated with some objectivity, the idea that executive function alone is the pinnacle of evolution seems a bit arbitrary. What good would that executive function be without the massive sensory integration that the temporal and parietal lobes provide in making sense of the world? What good would it be without an excellent somatosensory cortex to allow for nuanced embodied interactions, or a sophisticated limbic system to enliven it with useful emotional values? What about the creative insights of the association cortices and the emotional wisdom and potential unconscious wisdom spilling over from the dreaming centers of the brain? For that matter, what about Broca's area and Wernicke's area—which appear to give the great prefrontal cortex access to language itself? The point is not to raise any of these other brain centers up above the executive centers, but to point out that each offers riches, and the loss of any one of them would be a tremendous blow to human being.

Dietrich's valuation is especially ironic given his emphasis on the limited solution space that the prefrontal cortex provides. In theory there are all manner of things that the PFC is not well suited to comprehend. Why then would access to other states of consciousness be seen as anything but a potential gift? Should we not want access to the richest and fullest range of perceptions, experiences, and understandings available to us? Rationality and reason are wonderful, but why would we not want to access and appreciate even more? Of course there are concerns about discernment and integration of such states of consciousness. We would not, for example, want to take our dreams and visions too literally. But it has been a running theme throughout this discourse that taking things too literally appears to be a real problem even for dedicated rationalists, whether they laud the prefrontal cortex as the pinnacle of cosmic evolution or not.

The problem here, as with the computer model above, is that the metaphor ceases to be a useful analogy and instead becomes confused with objective reality. There is nothing inherently wrong with any of these models and metaphors for the brain. Some of them might prove quite useful in devising experiments and gathering data. A computer, a hydraulic system, a rational overlord—these are mythic frameworks for study, and in all likelihood different scientists will find different uses for each. The point is only this: *the myth or metaphor that organizes the study will most likely also be the myth or metaphor that the study confirms.* When this happens, it is not the confirmation of a theory, but the reiteration of a premise.

Having taken some time to deconstruct the literalized metaphors of the past, it is worth taking a look to what sorts of models might be on the horizon. One promising move is a shift toward understanding brains as parts of larger dynamic systems, rather than isolated information processors. Dan Siegel (2012) and many of his colleagues have been for some years developing an approach to neurobiology that emphasized human relationships as fundamental to understanding brain function. Others (Clark, 2009; Noë, 2009; Thompson, 2007) have taken interest in even broader models of brain-world dynamics that draw on ecological models as a primary metaphors. Alva Noë writes

> The locus of consciousness is the dynamic life of the whole, environmentally plugged-in person.... It is only when we take this holistic perspective on the active life of the person or animal that we can begin to make sense of the brain's contribution to conscious experience.
>
> (2009, p. xiii)

This sort of dynamic, ecological, systems-oriented model is a huge shift away from the twentieth-century image of a computer processing information in relative isolation. Such metaphors are further bolstered and expanded by the advent of complexity theory. Walter Freeman (2000) argues that the machine metaphors of the past are no longer tenable: "brains are not 'like' any artificial machine. If anything, they are 'like' natural self-organizing processes such as stars and hurricanes" (p. 4). I find this quote particularly delightful because, despite being based in sound mathematic and scientific models, it still manages to require a great imaginative leap. A hundred years ago, to say the brain was like the sun might have seemed hopelessly romantic.

Myths and mysteries of consciousness

Freeman's use of highly complex natural systems like hurricanes and stars as metaphors for the brain raises anew the question of how any material process should be supposed to give rise to phenomenal consciousness. The advent of complexity science has offered a new potential explanation to this problem, as summarized by Siegel (2017), "the consciousness that gives rise to subjective experience may be an emergent property of our complex minds" (p. 203). That is to say that just as hurricanes and stars (not to mention insect colonies and economies) show emergent levels of organization that cannot be predicted by their individual parts, so to do our billions of interacting neurons somehow give rise to phenomenal conscious experience. And yet, as attractive as this new model may be, it does not fully address the core criticisms of materialist accounts of consciousness that Chalmers (2002) and so many others raise (see Kelly, Crabtree, & Marshall, 2015; Koch, 2012; Nagel, 2015; Tallis, 2011). First there is a failure of explanation as to why the interactions of matter at any level of complexity would become a conscious experience. Second, if the degree of complexity in the interactions of matter is indeed the missing ingredient in the creation of consciousness, then are we not left with the logical conclusion that hurricanes, stars, economies, and beehives are also conscious entities? Such an assertion might sound absurd at first to minds raised in materialist cultures, but science has yet to produce an answer that is both satisfactory and verifiable. This is why Chalmers named this conundrum the "hard problem" of consciousness.

What I find most fascinating about the materialist myth is that it seems to hold such sway over so many scientists, despite a lack evidence to support it on scientific grounds. In the words of Noë, "after decades of concerted effort on the part of neuroscientists, psychologists, and philosophers, one proposition about how the brain makes us conscious ... has emerged unchallenged: we don't have a clue" (Noë, 2009, p. xi). Not only has this myth not been verified by science, it cannot even be rightly called a recent development. Writings attributed to Hippocrates around 400 BCE declare: "men ought to know that from nothing but the brain comes joys, delights, laughter and sports, and sorrows, griefs, despondency, and lamentations" (trans. 1923, p. 175). Tallis (2011) traces versions of the materialist idea back even further to the Pre-Socratics Pythagoras and Empedocles. If a majority of neuroscientists believe the brain must somehow create consciousness, it is not because any recent discovery has supported the idea, but rather because social, cultural, and other factors have given the myth fresh appeal.

Now intellectual honesty on my part demands that I must be open to the possibility that materialist accounts of consciousness are indeed true and will someday be discovered. I must also admit that they may be true even if science never finds a way to prove them—it may simply be the way the universe works. That I find this scenario implausible and perhaps a bit absurd may be a failure of imagination on my part. Where I will not compromise is that this myth is currently not only unproven by contemporary science, but at present seems to be un-provable. The choice to believe in this myth is like the choice to believe in any myth. Perhaps it will help move science along. Perhaps it will give some individuals and groups a sense of meaning and belonging. These are all excellent reasons to believe in myth. Myths can enrich our lives so long as they do not fall into the errors of fundamentalism.

Even the ostensibly most extreme form of this myth, *eliminative materialism*, may have a beneficial role to play. In brief summary, this is the position that mental experiences as described by common-sense psychological language should be viewed as illusory constructs, and neuroscience should abandon these ideas in terms of deeper physiological explanations (Ramsey, 2016). Taken literally, this is the kind of reductionism that eliminates any and all meaning from the concept of humanity. But viewed as a mythic framework, eliminative materialism can potentially function as a brilliant methodological approach, insofar as it asks scientists to check their basic cultural understandings at the door and see what might arise in their place. It is a myth that foregrounds the hidden variables behind what we see and calls for brutally empty clarity of consciousness in attempting to uncover them. Why shouldn't such an approach sometimes be employed, and why wouldn't it sometimes bring great returns? Unfortunately, eliminative materialism as myth and method is then carried out of the laboratory and mistaken for some sort of philosophical principle or literal truth, suggesting that psychological and cultural phenomena have no reality and must essentially be destroyed for science to progress. A similar move is too often made with Ockham's razor: a tool that may be quite useful in deriving simple explanations is mistaken as some sort of metaphysical maxim. It is a potentially useful methodological approach to pursue the simplest explanation, but as fruitful as such an approach may be, it cannot possible negate the simple fact that sometimes the more complex explanation is indeed the one that best fits the circumstances. Both eliminative materialism and Ockham's razor are stories about how science should be done. In that regard, they may be very useful indeed. But taken as absolute literal truths they are nonsensical and potentially quite destructive.

Perhaps the most outspoken scientific critic of the material account of consciousness is Raymond Tallis. Tallis is a clinical specialist in treating epilepsy and the author of some 200 papers on the brain. His *Aping mankind* (2011) is an exhaustive argument against materialism that goes on for hundreds of pages to demolish the idea as being both philosophically and scientifically absurd. Among the first of his many arguments is a criticism of the over-reliance on fMRI and other scanning technologies, which in his view produce incomplete data sets that are in turn widely mistaken for the whole. Tallis reminds us that fMRI measures blood flow, not brain activity per se; that even this is complicated by a significant time lag of 2–10 seconds which makes it difficult to discern where blood flow may be servicing more than one group of neurons; and that fMRI can only detect neural activity on the scale of millions, precluding potentially important contributions by smaller clusters. "In short, pretty well everything relevant to a given response at a given time might be invisible to an fMRI scan" (p. 76). These criticisms are mirrored by Dobbs (2005), who argues that these scans fail to recognize the networked or distributed nature of brain function and at worse may be seen as a new kind of phrenology. Such arguments are alarming and perhaps dispiriting to followers of neuroscience, but I believe they also serve as a humbling corrective. It is one thing to acknowledge that we have much to learn from scanning the brain; it is quite another to declare that brain scans have told us everything we need to know.

But Tallis' critique of materialist mythos in neuroscience goes much deeper than incomplete data. He further argues that our language has a natural animistic tendency to personify objects. When this personification happens to the brain we are easily fooled into forgetting that we are speaking of a material object that in itself exhibits nothing resembling a conscious mind. This linguistic mistake

> Enhances the apparent explanatory power of descriptive accounts of the brain, and indeed, enables the mind-brain barrier to be overcome *without any work being done*. By smuggling consciousness into the matter of the brain via the computer analogy, we make a materialist account of consciousness seem plausible.
>
> (2001, pp. 186–187; italics in the original)

In defiance of what he considers unconscious linguistic trickery, Tallis boldly insists that any kind of neural account of consciousness is a fundamental contradiction in terms. There is absolutely nothing about neurons in themselves, or the interactions of neurons, that could ever begin to account the creation of a conscious experience. "To seek the fabric of contemporary humanity within the brain is as mistaken as to trying to detect the sound of a gust through a billion leaved wood by applying a stethoscope to isolated seeds" (p. 11). He is asserting that such a move is both absurdly reductionist and a colossal category error. And given that this is a case of mistaken thinking, no degree of increased technical resolution into the structure of brain matter will make a difference, for it will still be matter, and not consciousness itself, that is being studied. Mapping out every movement of every subatomic particle in the brain would no more address consciousness than "a complete printout of his genome" would be able to tell you "what it is like to be with your friend" (p. 84). The one is an abstracted model of matter, the other a deeply human experience that cannot be explained without presupposing consciousness to begin with. Tallis' arguments continue in a dizzying array of biting invective, and for the sake of concluding, this very brief review will have to suffice. In the end, he may be proven wrong; but those who oppose him have their work cut out.

So what are ontologically curious neuroscientists and psychologists to do? While materialism seems deeply engrained in the zeitgeist as a whole, an increasing number of minds are beginning to take these problems seriously. Some, such as Chalmers (2002) have begun to mount serious arguments for panpsychism, the notion that consciousness is a property of the universe itself rather than the brain. Tallis (2011) rejects panpsychism along with materialism, and instead joins Nagel (2015) in choosing to outline the problem without offering a solution, ultimately calling for both humility and creativity in the years ahead. In this latter injunction, I wholeheartedly agree.

It can be painful sometimes to admit our myths are only myths, and yet myth is part and parcel of what we are. Faced with the unknown, we do what humans have done for millennia: gather round the fire with our fellows and tell stories beneath a canopy of stars.

Chapter 11

Conclusion

Facing Proteus

Homer tells us that following the events of the Trojan War, Menelaus, King of Sparta, becomes stranded with his men on the isle of Pharos off the coast of Egypt. There he is befriended by Eidothea ("image of the Goddess"), who tells him of her father Proteus, an ancient sea god who might both help Menelaus get home and tell him the fate of his friends in distant lands. To get these answers, Menelaus must seize Proteus when he comes out of the sea and onto the dry land to sleep, and then hold him tight despite the frightening fact that this ancient god has the power to assume the form of any living thing—even water and fire itself. Only if Menelaus can hold the wily shapeshifter through these terrifying transformations will Proteus reveal his true nature as an oracle and truth-teller, and help Menelaus get home.

The King and his men spend the next morning hiding in ditches under seal-skins reeking of fish, comforted only by the drops of ambrosia Eidothea provides. When the sun is high and the moment comes, they seize Proteus and hold him, even through the embodiment of a ferocious dragon and the shapeless element of water. Somehow Menelaus and his companions hold on, and in time Proteus resumes his true shape and sits down to talk with them. In the end, he gives them the answers they seek.

The terrain covered in the preceding chapters is vast. We've chased imagination through the long sweep of Western history, into the unfathomable complexity of the brain, and back out into philosophical questions about knowledge and being that rarely brook simple answers. Imagination has changed shape again and again, from one century to the next, from one branch of brain science to another. Long before the details of this study were conceived, I had first imagined it as a project of confronting Proteus. It is not only myself as author who has played the role of Menelaus, struggling to hold the ancient sea god as he changes shape. You the reader have been on this journey of myriad forms, struggling to contain the object of inquiry even as it transmutes itself from one kind of understanding to another. To grasp the essence of imagination, we have wrestled with the archetypal shapeshifter. But daunting as such a prospect may sound, Menelaus has but one task in the end: to hold on.

As we come at last the conclusion, not having faltered in our grip, even as imagination took a dozen, 100, 10,000 forms, the myth tells us that in the end the Old Man of the Sea will turn a new face toward us, and offer us the truth. What is it that we have truly come to seek, that will bring us home?

Seeking synthesis

Traditionally, the humanities differ from the sciences in that they look to the complex wholes of what it means to be human rather than the constituent parts. Thus, to understand the neurobiological correlates of imagination in humanistic terms, some sort of synthesis is inevitably required. But in bringing the pieces of mental imagery, perception, narrative, memory, and creativity together, the entire discussion is inevitably pulled back into much bigger and more confounding questions: the nature of perception, the limits of knowledge, the deep role of storytelling in human experience, and the mystery of consciousness itself. Reductionism may work well enough as myth and method in the laboratory, but it fails to satisfy the deeper questions of what it means to be human.

Pursuing a holistic account of imagination ultimately carries the discussion back to an exploration of the ontological and epistemological ground from which scientific inquiry itself must begin. Foregrounding the neurobiological correlates of mental images and narratives raised the possibility that most human experience and activity is organized by images and narratives. Because science is performed and understood by humans, images and narratives are presumably at work in practice of science as well. Following this through to its natural conclusion, I have ultimately argued that the role of imagination in producing neuroscientific knowledge is considerable.

In investigating a topic as tantalizing as the neuroscience of imagination it is natural to seek a grand synthesis, something that puts the pieces together in a neat, easily understood package; a heuristic for the non-specialist. I think that in so doing, what we are really looking for is a new story to be told. The neurobiology discussed in Part III is incredibly complex. Each of those chapters probably could have been extended by dozens (if not hundreds) of pages in order to fully explore the physiological nuances, theoretical arguments, and considerable disagreements within the field. To be accurate here means to allow for a staggering degree of complexity, perhaps so much so that we begin to doubt if the human mind can really contain it, much less grasp the vast implications. As Jung said, "anyone who knows the abysses of physiology will become dizzy at the thought of them" (1960a/1947, p. 326 [§620]). Some scientists, faced with these abysses, have come to doubt if the human brain is actually capable of understanding the human brain. That last point is contentious and the answer remains to be seen. But in the meantime, our recourse is to theories and stories. We take the data and weave fictions to use as maps to help us navigate being human.

The imaginative metaphor that I came to over and over again in the course of the research is that of a *reality simulator*. This is admittedly an extension of the computer metaphor for the brain, albeit one based more on science fiction than fact. And yet virtual reality seems to become more real each day; the staggering capacity of modern computers to generate richly detailed visual worlds has almost certainly added to our imaginative lexicon for mind and consciousness. This metaphor has drawbacks: in addition to remaining tied to the conception of humans as machines or computers, the "simulation" of reality connotes that something less than real is being created, a copy of the thing rather than the thing itself (an interesting parallel to Plato's ideal forms versus the pale reflection of the phenomenal world). "Virtual" reality has similar connotations, suggesting something convincingly real that in actuality is not. Speaking in terms of simulated or virtual reality subtly continues the unfortunate trend of discounting the unmeasurable phenomenal world of consciousness as somehow unreal, thus gently pushing us back into the trap of materialism. This too easily becomes an unconscious assumption and we forget to consider in what ways that material reality is itself being imaginatively constructed by each of us in turn. The maps of the world our minds assemble may be only approximations of the physical world beyond, but existentially speaking, they are the very heart of human reality.

I expect there will be objections to this conclusion. Some may say that despite my promise to respect science on its own terms, I have collapsed science into imagination. I would counter that on the contrary, this model is a corrective to a pervasive tendency to collapse imagination into science. What is intended in this offering is a nuanced compromise: imagination and science as partners in making meaning of the world. Imagination lies at the heart of our human experience, while science reaches beyond to discover what is true about the broader reality we share. Some, no doubt, will nevertheless prefer to remain in conflict.

More than in any other branch of science, it seems the neurosciences are destined to clash with the humanities around these issues. Because neuroscience aims to map out the physiological correlates of our experiences, it all too easily encroaches into the territory of human meaning. This clash may be inevitable. For many neuroscientists, studying the brain is as close as we will ever come to mapping the soul. Although I thoroughly agree with Tallis, Chalmers, and Nagel that there is no real scientific basis for the widespread belief that the brain somehow creates consciousness, I must also concede that our brains are clearly deeply important to our human-ness. Issues of

mind are debatable, but there is abundant evidence that the brain is responsible for both sensory perception and embodied action: it directly mediates
the ways we perceive and interact with our environment. If the goal of the
humanities is to understand what it means to be human, we can hardly
ignore these facts.

In this regard, neuroscience repeatedly forces the question of how these
two great spheres of human knowledge will relate to each other. Traditionally, the humanities have been tasked with looking to the larger picture,
what we would today describe as the complex wholes of human experience, which reductive science, particularly in the wake of complexity
theory, cannot adequately address. As Holton puts it, "it has always been,
and must always be, the job of the humanist to construct and disseminate
a meaningful picture of the world" (1996, p. 52). And Kuhn has pointed
out that although science may turn to philosophy to help generate new
ideas in times of crisis, "generally scientists have not needed or wanted to
be philosophers" (1996/1962, p. 88). This is not to say that scientists
cannot be humanists and vice versa—I am myself an interloper, a humanist
attempting to build a bridge to a worldview not my own. But if such cross-
disciplinary engagements are going to be mutually beneficial, they must
first and foremost be grounded in mutual respect. We must approach each
other with humility, offering the gifts of knowledge our own domains
bring, without insisting that the other adopt our ways. It is the difference
between colonization and community-building. In this endeavor confusion
should be expected and tolerated. We will not agree on everything. We can
each have our piece of the truth without insisting that it be the whole.

Anything less, in my judgment, is a collapse back into power struggle, a
tribal war of stories. I would never want to live in a world where the soldiers of scientism have won the war and stripped the soul from the world.
Truth be told, I would rather not be in conflict with them at all. We can
struggle to have power over each other, as we have for millennia, or we
can strive to love one another. I do not know which is the safer bet for
success, but I do know which will make a better world.

Concluding remarks in defense of science

From the beginning I have been transparent in my advocacy for the liberation of imagination in the human psyche, and my desire to push back against
an overbearing scientism at work in the world. Doing so has inevitably
meant criticizing the excesses of science and deconstructing some elements of
scientific culture. In this I imagined myself defending the underdog.

What a shock then, in the course of this project, to witness what appears
to be an astounding reversal of American culture on these matters. Anti-
science movements are on the rise, reflected by a Presidential administration in the United States that, as of this writing, refuses to acknowledge the

existential threat of human-created climate change. Equally disturbing, 2016 saw the rise of the "fake news" phenomenon—the propagation of completely fabricated stories masquerading as objective news reporting—designed to mislead the people and sway elections based on misinformation and outright lies. This alone is a terrifying development, as a democracy can only function if the citizenry have access to accurate information in order to make their decisions. To make matters even worse, the current administration almost immediately took the term "fake news" and rhetorically repurposed it to rebuff any journalism that paints the administration in an unfavorable light. Not only has the disinformation campaign of legitimate "fake news" been largely ignored, but some of the most respectable journalistic establishments in the country are being discredited by the government itself. While it may be fair to point out that some of these news organizations are more biased than others, the phenomenon of bias is a far cry from the deliberate fabrication of outright falsehoods. In the last 18 months, it seems as though Western civilization has suddenly come into danger of losing touch with the basic ground of reality that we all share. The *Oxford English dictionary* not only added the word "post-truth" last year—but declared it the word of the year in 2016 (Wang, 2016).

These profoundly disturbing developments add a new ethical consideration to the project of defending imagination and critiquing science. I consider the related phenomena of anti-science, fake news, and post-truth to be a clear and direct threat to the foundations of human civilization. Together they represent an opposite extreme to scientism: the shadow of imagination and tribal mythos run wild without a common ground to stand on. For just as surely as science without imagination strips the soul from the world, imagination without science threatens to strip the ground out from under our feet.

Science makes maps of the world using extremely high standards for shared systems of measurement. Both the robust and sometimes merciless methods of science and its insistence on broad consensus among those who make the measurements are among the most effective tools human beings have created for securing our place in the world. To point out that there are many things science cannot measure—or to inquire into the role imagination inevitably plays in shaping the research or filling in the gaps—in no way disparages the validity of the underlying collective measurement. In advocating for imagination, I am looking to enrich and expand the human world, not undermine the ground on which it is built.

I will use climate change as a primary example both because it presents a case of unusually clear consensus among scientists and because it represents an existential threat to humankind (not to mention many other sentient species). With regards to consensus, an astounding 97 percent of scientists agree that human activity has accelerated global warming with dangerous and perhaps cataclysmic consequences (Cook et al., 2016). Now as argued in Chapter 10, at some point the public dialog around this issue becomes a matter of stories about climate change—this is inevitable. But the role of science is to create a measurable and verifiable ground for those stories to point back to. This may not amount to absolute certainty, but it does provide the most sophisticated models and the most rigorous testing at our disposal. The deniers of climate change need to do more than just provide an alternative narrative—they need to back it up with equally robust evidence if they want to describe their position as scientific. And while there should always be room for skepticism and doubt in science, agnosticism runs aground when it comes to existential threats demanding immediate action. If 97 doctors recommended a life-saving surgery to prevent a slow, painful death, and three doctors said, "well I am not sure, let's wait and see"—who among us would not take the calculated risk of the surgery? Perhaps in ten years or 100 years a new paradigm shift in climate science will show us that we were wrong about global warming after all—but common sense and common decency compels us to recognize that for now, no robust models exist to support the denial story as anything but fantasy.

There are phenomena that can be measured and phenomena that cannot. Science is the business of measuring the measurable, and as such can only be convincingly refuted by contrary measurement. Similarly, the proposition that "Hillary Clinton ran a pedophilia ring out of a pizza shop in Washington, DC" is verifiably false—anyone claiming to the contrary would have quite a bit of work to do in justifying their methodology. This might seem so obvious as to be absurd in a piece of academic writing, and yet American culture as a whole seems to be seriously struggling with these issues, with potentially disastrous consequences. Obvious and absurd or no, the ivory tower must take notice.

At the same time, I stand my ground that what science cannot measure it cannot speak to—at least not scientifically. Science cannot, for example, speak to the existence of God. It cannot even speak to the existence of the "supernatural"—because, by definition, the supernatural would be beyond nature and thus beyond measurement. Scientists and non-scientists alike are welcome to believe in stories that declare God and the supernatural as nothing but human inventions—they have every right to do so. I would fight to the bitter end for their right to believe in such stories. But they cannot with integrity call these stories science.

Furthermore, it is worth soberly considering the degree to which anti-religious sentiments among scientists may have contributed to anti-science movements. Science, as I understand it, has no real business attacking religion except on specific matters of measurable phenomenon. When ideologues like Sam Harris (2004) and Richard Dawkins (2008) attack religion broadly, they are playing the role of priests, not scientists. While these thought-leaders are welcome to weave their own atheist mythologies and base them in part on scientific stories, they distort and misrepresent science by even suggesting that scientific method, in itself, supports their unverifiable beliefs. Tragically, by perpetuating the myth that science and religion are opposed, they create enemies to science who might otherwise be open-minded to reviewing the evidence. Thus it is not only misguided politicians who abuse imagination—scientists are sometimes guilty as well. But here again we've come to the question of conflict—and I do not believe conflict will ultimately lead us anywhere we want to go.

I am myself a great lover of science. And the principle source of my love is that science has allowed me to imagine this world in such richer detail than I would have ever come to on my own. Perhaps my favorite class during my freshman tenure at Berkeley was a course on plant biology. Over the course of 16 weeks, we dove deep into the structure of plant cells and the extraordinary biochemistry that drove the growth of roots and branches—a breathtakingly detailed and sophisticated map of "the force that through the green fuse drives the flower" (Thomas, 1938). As the semester progressed, the lush Berkeley campus took on a numinous aura as the miraculous complexity of the surrounding flora enriched my vision. The technical biochemical details have long since faded from memory, but that vision of a vegetative world surging with intricate hidden life will remain for a lifetime. So it was first studying physics in high school, and experiencing the wonderment of secret and sometimes strange laws, invisibly governing the universe. Or when I first began to study neuroplasticity as a young man, and began to imagine how I too might change.

Science has not only given humanity unprecedented technological power. It has also given us a material world that is richer, deeper, and more beautiful. Thank goodness, then, that we also have the gift of imagination, through which we can actually enter into that world and inhabit it.

Sitting with the shapeshifter

Inherent in the formulation of "facing Proteus" is a conflict: the face-off, as it were, between hero and god. A Jungian framework could quickly yield the interpretation of the ego facing the unconscious. Jungian thought is often prone to using ocean metaphors to refer to the unconscious, and Proteus is a sea god, an immortal being from the depths, one who literally lives beneath the sea and emerges briefly onto solid ground, only when the sun is high. Proteus is a shapeshifter, an archetypal image of transformation—but he is also an oracle, a wise seer, a being "who never lies" (Homer, trans. 1996, p. 136). He is transformation, but he is also the deeper truth at the heart of that transformation, the wisdom that comes from enduring complexity and change. In focusing on the moment of conflict between hero and immortal and fixating on the spectacle of shapeshifting, many other parts of the story are forgotten. The actual struggle lasts only a few lines in Homer's original text, while the myth itself is comprised of over a dozen stanzas.

I am most struck that on either side of this brief conflict is a story of desperation and mercy, perhaps even empathy. Menelaus and his men are not only stranded on Pharos—they are in danger of starvation, scattered about the island with their fishhooks, "slowly dying of hunger" (Homer, trans. 2013, p. 47). Menelaus may be a brave hero, but in this tale he is in a place of tremendous vulnerability, marooned by angry gods and unable to help the men he leads. Mercy first comes in the form of Eidothea "the glistening one" (Homer, trans. 1996, p. 137). Menalaus comes upon the goddess while walking alone on the seashore and claims "I touched her heart, when she saw me" (Homer, trans. 2013, p. 47). Eidothea offers to help the helpless King, and asks for nothing in return. She is under no obligation to tell Menelaus about her father's oracular powers, nor the means to coerce him, much less to aid the mortals in the endeavor. She does so out of voluntary mercy and kindness. Not only does she provide disguises so they may lie in wait, she even gives them sweet ambrosia under their nostrils so they are not sickened by the stench of the seal-skins. In this latter point, the Goddess is tending not only to their survival, but to their comfort as well.

After the famous wrestling match we see a further expression of this tenderness in Proteus. Having resumed the principle shape for which he otherwise named, the Old Man of the Sea, Proteus shows a surprising degree of emotional intelligence. He warns Menelaus that he should be careful what he asks for: "Son of Atreus, why do you ask me that? Why do you need to know? Why probe my mind? You won't stay dry-eyed long, I warn you, once you have heard the whole story" (Homer, trans. 1996, p. 140). And indeed, once Menelaus learns of the death of his friend Ajax, and the treacherous betrayal and murder of his brother Agamemnon, the hero collapses in grief. "So Proteus said, and his story crushed my heart. I knelt down in the sand and wept. I'd no desire to go on living and see the rising light of day" (p. 141). But again, the Old Man of the Sea shows empathy and mercy, instructing Menelaus not to lose himself in sorrow, but to set his spirits instead upon the return voyage home.

This striking theme of immortal generosity and care is all the more apparent when contrasted to the actual solution Proteus gives to the dilemma of being marooned. Menelaus is indeed here as punishment for his hubris, and the only way to escape is to return to Egypt and make sac-rifices to the offended Gods. Likewise, the Old Man's account of the hero Ajax, friend to Menelaus, claims he was drowned by a wrathful Poseidon for declaring himself above the Gods. There is no tolerance for hubris in this world, and the Gods owe mortal men nothing. Yet Eidothea and Proteus offer the stranded soldiers mercy, empathy, and guidance.

The suffering of Menelaus in this tale is great. First he suffers becoming marooned, lost, starving, and helpless. Then he must endure a wrestling match with a God. And then he learns that both his friend and brother have died. If holding the shapeshifter means enduring change, Menelaus is eventually forced to confront change on a deeper level—a loss so great he despairs for his own life. This is a tale then not only of a shapeshifting god or the hero that comes to wrestle with him, but about the vicissitudes of making our way through a changing, sometime violent and brutal world.

That the world can change, and that we can change, has been a running theme throughout this volume. From Kant's notion of imaginative synthesis within the human mind to a modern neurobiology that entangles mental images and beliefs with the very act of perception; from Kuhnian paradigm shifts to miraculous tales of neuroplasticity—recognizing imagination at work at the deepest levels of our human world suggests just how radically things can change. This is both promising and disconcerting. In Homer's myth, it is a tale of endurance, loss, and grief, but it is also a tale of mercy and empathy. Above all it is a story of finding one's way home.

The conflict over what is real has probably been with humanity since we first learned to tell stories. We may scoff at the prehistoric fantasy of warring tribes before the dawn of civilization, fighting over totems—but with the advent of fake news in 2016, I wonder how far we have really come. This book inevitably invites its own form of conflict—by pushing back against scientism it constellates an enemy. In advocating for imagination the work pushes against strict rationalism, and by lifting up the humanities it risks diminishing the sciences. The constellation of these polarities may be inevitable, but this need not mean the ensuing conflicts must be perpetual. One of the principle gifts in recognizing image and story at the core of our worldviews is the gentle reminder that we need not take them too literally. Ideas are wonderful and important, but they are not concrete things. Our ideas about the real are sources of meaning and purpose. They are not worth hate and hurt and violence.

I am comforted that in this myth of change and loss, mercy and empathy figure so prominently. As much as we may wish to control the world, it will continue to change. However much power we acquire, the strongest among us will never be immune to powerlessness. We will all become lost from time to time, and we will all lose people that we love. Change is inevitable. We can be in conflict over what we think is real—or we can learn to love each other amid the flux and uncertainty.

Menelaus may be the hero of the tale, but we need not identify with him exclusively. Proteus too is inside us, a part of what makes us human. He reminds us that we are capable of transformation, wisdom, and yes, even empathy for those who attack us and try to hold us down. He will sit with us and guide us when we are lost, lift us out of our grief, and tell us how to find our way to where we belong. As an archetypal image of imagination, he reminds us what is possible, and returns us to our own hearts.

I wrestled with the Old Man of the Sea for many months. When at last I sat by his side and put my question to him, his answer was surprisingly simple:

> *Imagination makes this world.*
> *Let love be your guide,*
> *As you make your way through it.*

References

Abram, D. (1996). *The spell of the sensuous.* New York, NY: Vintage Books.

Abrams, M. H. (1953). *The mirror and the lamp: Romantic theory and the critical tradition.* New York, NY: Oxford University Press.

Agnati, L. F., Guidolin, D., Battistin, L., Pagnoni, G., & Fuxe, K. (2013, May). The neurobiology of imagination: Possible role of interaction-dominant dynamics and default mode network. *Frontiers in Psychology, 4*(269), 1–17.

Andreasen, N. (2005). *The creative brain: The science of genius.* New York, NY: Plume.

Andreasen, N. C., O'Leary, D. S., Cizadlo, T., Arndt, S., Rezai, K., Watkins, G. L., Ponto, L. L., & Hichwa, R. D. (1995). Remembering the past: Two facets of episodic memory explored with positron emission tomography. *American Journal of Psychiatry, 152*(11), 1576–1585.

Aquinas, T. (1945). *Basic writings of Thomas Aquinas* (Vol. 1) (A. C. Pegis, Trans.). New York, NY: Random House. (Original work published 1265–1274).

Aristotle. (1968). *Aristotle's de anima* (D. W. Hamlyn, Trans.). New York, NY: Oxford University Press.

Aristotle. (2007). *Aristotle on memory and recollection* (D. Bloch, Trans.). Boston, MA: Brill.

Arnaud, P. (2013). The powerful impact of mental imagery in changing emotion. In D. Hermans, B. Rime, & B. Mesquita (Eds.), *Changing emotions* (pp. 187–194). New York, NY: Psychology Press.

Aserinsky, E., & Kleitman, N. (1953). Regularly occurring period of eye motility and concomitant phenomena during sleep. *Science, 118*(3062), 273–274.

Barnes, M. E., & Murray, D. J. (2012). Evolutionary psychology. In R. W. Rieber (Ed.), *Encyclopedia of the history of psychological theories* (Vol. 1, pp. 399–438). New York, NY: Springer. Retrieved from Gale Virtual Reference Library.

Barrett, D. (2001). *The committee of sleep.* New York, NY: Crown.

Barrett, D. (2007). An evolutionary theory of dreams and problem solving. In D. Barrett & P. McNamara (Eds.), *The new science of dreams* (Vol. 3, pp. 133–153). Westport, CT: Praeger.

Begley, S. (2007). *Train your mind change your brain: How a new science reveals our extraordinary potentials to transform ourselves.* New York, NY: Ballantine Books.

Bekoff, M. (2010). *The animal manifesto.* Novato, CA: New World Library.

Bennet, M. R., & Hacker, P. M. S. (2003). *Philosophical foundations of neuroscience*. Malden, MA: Blackwell.

Benvenuti, A., & Davenport, J. L. (2011). The new archaic: A neurophenomenological approach to religious ways of knowing. In B. M. Stafford (Ed.), *Bridging the humanities-neuroscience divide: A field guide to a new meta-field* (pp. 204–238). Chicago, IL: University of Chicago Press.

Bernstein, B. J. (1985). *Beyond objectivism and relativism: Science, hermeneutics, and praxis*. Philadelphia, PA: University of Pennsylvania Press.

Berrios, G. (2010) Preface. In Y. A. Haskell (Ed.), *Diseases of the imagination and imaginary disease in the early modern era* (pp. ix–xxiii). Turnhout, Belgium: Brepols.

Blackmore, S. (2006). *Conversations on consciousness*. New York, NY: Oxford University Press.

Bohm, D., & Peat, D. (2000). *Science, order, and creativity* (2nd ed.). New York, NY: Routledge. (Original work published 1987)

Boorstin, J. (1992). *The creators: A history of the heroes of the imagination*. New York, NY: Vintage Books.

Bowra, M. C. (1950). *The romantic imagination*. New York, NY: Oxford University Press.

Bradshaw, G. (2009). *Elephants on the edge: What animals teach us about humanity*. New Haven, CT: Yale University Press.

Brown, A. D., Addis, D. R., Romano, T. A., Marmar, C. R., Bryant, R. A., Hirst, W., & Schacter, D. L. (2014). Episodic and semantic components of autobiographical memories and imagined future events in post-traumatic stress disorder. *Memory, 22*(6), 595–604.

Buckner, R. L., Andrews-Hanna, J. R., & Schacter, D. L. (2008). The brain's default network: anatomy, function, and relevance to disease. *Annals of the New York Academy of Sciences, 1124*, 1–38.

Buckner, R. L., & Carroll, D. C. (2007). Self-projection and the brain. *TRENDS in Cognitive Sciences, 11*(2).

Bulkeley, K., & Hurd, R. (2014). Introduction. In R. Hurd & K. Bulkeley (Eds.), *Lucid dreaming: New perspectives on consciousness in sleep* (Vol. 1, pp. xiii–xxxii). Santa Barbara, CA: Praeger.

Bundy, M. W. (1927). *The theory of imagination in classical and medieval thought*. Urbana, IL: University of Illinois Press.

Cambray, J. (2009). *Synchronicity: Nature and psyche in an interconnected universe*. College Station, TX: Texas A&M University Press.

Cameron, J. (1992). *The complete artist's way*. New York, NY: Tarcher/Penguin.

Campbell, J. (1968). *The Hero With a Thousand Faces*. Princeton. NJ: Princeton University Press.

Carson, S. (2010). *Your creative brain*. San Francisco, CA: Jossey-Bass.

Castoriadis, C. (1987). *The imaginary institution of society*. Cambridge, MA: The MIT Press. (Original work published 1975.)

Cech, T. R. (2001). Overturning the dogma: Catalytic RNA. In K. H. Pfenninger & V. Shubik (Eds.), *The origins of creativity* (pp. 5–17). New York, NY: Oxford University Press.

Chalmers, D. J. (Ed.). (2002). *Philosophy of mind: Classical and contemporary readings*. New York, NY: Oxford University Press.

Cheetham, T. (2015). *Imaginal love: The meanings of imagination in Henry Corbin and James Hillman.* Thompson, CT: Spring Publications.

Chodorow, J. (1997). *Jung on active imagination.* Princeton, NJ: Princeton University Press.

Clark, A. (2009). *Supersizing the mind: Embodiment, action, and cognitive extension.* Oxford, UK: Oxford University Press.

Clarke, A. C. (1967). Hazards of prophecy: The failure of imagination. In *Profiles of the future: An enquiry into the limits of the possible* (pp. 14–36). New York, NY: Bantam Books.

Cloos, M., Weßlau, C., Steil, R., & Höfling, V. (2016, June). Latent classes of dysregulated behaviors relate to negative mental images. *Journal of Psychopathological Behavior Assessment, 39*(2), 1–10.

Cocking, J. (1991). *Imagination: A study in the history of ideas.* P. Murray (Ed.). New York, NY: Routledge.

Coleridge, S. T. (1906). *Biographia literaria.* G. Watson (Ed.). London, UK: Dent. (Original work published 1817.)

Cook, J., Oreskes, N., Doran, D. T., Anderegg, W. R. L., Verheggen, B., Maibach, E. D., Carlton, J., Lewandowsky, S., Skuce, A. G., Green, S. A, Nuccitelli, D., Jacobs, P., Richardson, M., Winkler, B., Painting, R., & Rice, K. (2016). Consensus on consensus: A synthesis of consensus estimates on human-caused global warming. *Environmental Research Letters, 11*(4). Retrieved from http://iopscience.iop.org/article/10.1088/1748–9326/11/4/048002#artAbst.

Corbin, H. (1972). Mundus imaginalis or the imaginary and the imaginal. *Spring Journal,* 1–19.

Cozolino, L. (2006). *The neuroscience of human relationships.* New York, NY: Norton.

Cozolino, L. (2016). *Why therapy works: Using our minds to change our brains.* New York, NY: Norton.

Crabtree, A. (1993). *From Mesmer to Freud: Magnetic sleep and the roots of psychological healing.* New Haven, CT: Yale University Press.

Crandall, S., Cruikshank, S. J., & Connors, B. W. (2015, May). A corticothalamic switch: Controlling the thalamus with dynamic synapses. *Neuron, 86*(3), 768–782.

Croce, B. (1972). *Aesthetic* (15th print ed.). New York, NY: Noonday Press. (Original work published 1902.)

Cron, L. (2012). *Wired for story.* Berkeley, CA: 10 Speed Press.

Csikszentmihalyi, M. (1996). *Creativity: Flow and the psychology of discovery & invention.* New York, NY: HarperCollins.

Cushman, P. (1996). *Constructing the self, constructing America.* Boston, MA: Da Capo Press.

Damasio, A. (1999). *The feeling of what happens.* New York, NY: Harcourt.

Damasio, A. (2001). Some notes on brain, imagination, and creativity. In K. H. Pfenninger & V. Shubik (Eds.), *The origins of creativity* (pp. 59–68). New York, NY: Oxford University Press.

Dang-Vu, T. T., Schabus, M., Desseilles, M., Schwartz, S., & Maquet, P. (2007). Neuroimaging of REM sleep and dreaming. In D. Barrett & P. McNamara (Eds.), *The new science of dreams* (Vol. 1, pp. 95–114). Westport, CT: Praeger.

Dark matter, dark energy. (n.d.). Retrieved from https://science.nasa.gov/astrophysics/focus-areas/what-is-dark-energy.

Darwin, C. (2005a). The descent of man and selections in relation to sex. In *The Darwin compendium*. New York, NY: Barnes & Noble. (Original work published 1871.)

Darwin, C. (2005b). The expression of the emotions in animal and man. In *The Darwin compendium*. New York, NY: Barnes & Noble. (Original work published 1872.)

Daston, L. (2005). Fear and loathing of the imagination in science. *Daedalus, 134*(4), 16–30.

Daugman J. (2001). Brain metaphor and brain theory. In W. Bechtel (Ed.), *Philosophy and the neurosciences* (pp. 23–36). Oxford, UK: Blackwell.

Davis, R. H. (2005). *Jung, Freud, and Hillman: Three depth psychologies in context*. Westport, CT: Praeger.

Dawkins, R. (2008). *The god delusion*. New York, NY: Mariner Books.

Dawkins, R. (2012). *The magic of reality: How we know what's really true*. New York, NY: Free Press.

Debus, D. (2014). "Mental time travel": Remembering the past, imagining the future, and the particularity of events. *Review of Philosophy and Psychology, 5*(3), 333–350.

Dement, W., & Kleitman, N. (1957). Cyclic variations in EEG during sleep and their relations to eye movements, body motility and dreaming. *Electroencephalography and Clinical Neurophysiology, 9*(4), 673–690.

Denzin, N. K., & Giardina, M. D. (Eds.). (2008). *Qualitative inquiry and the politics of evidence*. Walnut Creek, CA: Left Coast Press.

Denzin, N. K., & Lincoln, Y. S. (Eds.). (2011). *The Sage handbook of qualitative research* (4th ed.). Thousand Oaks, CA: Sage.

Dewey, L. (1997). The aesthetic in experience. In S. L. Feagin & P. Maybard (Eds.), *Aesthetics* (pp. 45–55). New York, NY: Oxford University Press. (Original work published 1934.)

Dietrich, A. (2004). The cognitive neuroscience of creativity. *Psychonomic Bulletin and Review, 11*(6), 1011–1026.

Dietrich, A. (2007). Who is afraid of a cognitive neuroscience of creativity? *Methods, 42*(1), 22–27.

Dietrich, A. (2015). *How creativity happens in the brain*. New York, NY: Palgrave Macmillan.

Dietrich, A., & Haider, H. (2017). A neurocognitive framework for human creative thought. *Frontiers in Psychology, 7*(2078), 1–7.

Dilthey, W. (1976a). Goethe's poetical imagination. In H. P. Rickman (Ed. & Trans.), *Dilthey: Selected writings* (pp. 98–104). New York, NY: Cambridge University Press. (Original work published 1877.)

Dilthey, W. (1976b). The great poetry of imagination. In H. P. Rickman (Ed. & Trans.), *Dilthey: Selected writings*. New York, NY: Cambridge University Press. (No Date given for original publication.)

Dobbs, B. J. T. (1975). *The foundations of Newton's alchemy*. New York, NY: Cambridge University Press.

Dobbs, B. J. T. (1991). *The Janus face of genius: The role of alchemy in Newton's thought*. New York, NY: Cambridge University Press.

Dobbs, D. (2005). Fact or phrenology? *Scientific American Mind, 16*(1), 24–31.

Doidge, N. (2007). *The brain that changes itself*. New York, NY: Penguin.

Dongaonkar, B., Hupbach, A., Gomez, R., & Nadel, L. (2013). Effect of psychological stress on episodic memory updating. *Psychopharmacology, 226*(4), 769–777.

Downing, C. (1981). *The goddess: Mythological images of the feminine.* New York, NY: Crossroad.

Downing, C. (2000). Sigmund Freud's mythology of soul. In D. Slattery & L. Corbett (Eds.), *Depth psychology: Meditations in the field* (pp. 59–72). Einsiedeln, Switzerland: Daimon.

Downing, C. (2006). Bruno Bettelheim: A wounded healer. In *Gleanings* (pp. 101–109). New York, NY: iUniverse. (Original work published 1997.)

Dry, S. (2014). *The Newton papers.* New York, NY: Oxford University Press.

Eagleman, D. M. (2009). Brain time. Retrieved from www.edge.org/conversation/brain-time.

Egan, K. (n. d.). A very short history of imagination. Unpublished manuscript. Vancouver, British Columbia: Imaginative Education Research Group, Faculty of Education, Simon Fraser University. Retrieved from http://ierg.ca/wp-content/uploads/2014/04/History-of-Imagination.pdf.

Einstein, A. (1954). A mathematician's mind. In *Ideas and opinions.* (S. Bargman, Trans.). New York, NY: Three Rivers Press. (Original work published 1945.)

Einstein, A. (2009). *On cosmic religion with other opinions and aphorisms.* Mineola, NY: Dover. (Original work published 1931.)

Eliade, M. (1963). *Myth and reality.* New York, NY: Harper & Row.

Ellenberger, H. (1970). *The discovery of the unconscious.* New York, NY: Basic Books.

Engell, J. (1981). *The creative imagination: Enlightenment to romanticism.* Cambridge, MA: Harvard University Press.

Ethington, P. J. (2011). Sociovisual perspective: Vision and the forms of the human past. In B. M. Stafford (Ed.), *Bridging the humanities-neuroscience divide: A field guide to a new meta-field* (pp. 123–152). Chicago, IL: University of Chicago Press.

Falchier, A., Cappe, C., Barone, P., & Schroeder, C. E. (2012). Sensory convergence in low-level cortices. In B. E. Stein (Ed.), *The new handbook of multisensory processing* (pp. 67–80). Cambridge, MA: MIT Press.

Federmeier, K. D., Segal, J. B., Lombrozo, T., & Kutas, M. (2000). Brain responses to nouns, verbs, and class ambiguous words in context. *Brain, 123*(12), 2552–2566.

Feyerabend, P. (2010). *Against method* (4th ed.). New York, NY: Verso. (Original work published in 1975.)

Ficino, M. (2005). In W. J. Hanegraaff, A. Faivre, R. van den Broek, & J.-P. Brach (Eds.), *Dictionary of gnosis and Western esotericism* (Vol. 1, pp. 360–367). Retrieved from Gale Virtual Reference Library.

Francis. (2015). *On care for our common home.* Boston, MA: Pauline Books & Media.

Franks, N. R. (1989). Army ants: A collective intelligence. *American Scientist, 77*(2), 138–145.

Freeman, W. J. (2000). *Neurodynamics: An exploration in mesoscopic brain dynamics.* London, UK: Springer.

Frewen, P., & Lanius, R. (2015). *Healing the traumatized self: Consciousness, neuroscience, treatment.* New York, NY: Norton.

Funkenstein, A. (1986). *Theology and the scientific imagination: From the Middle Ages to the seventeenth century.* Princeton, NJ: Princeton University Press.

Gabora, L., & Ranjan, A. (2013). How insight emerges in a distributed, content-addressable memory. In O. Vartanian, S. Bristol, & J. C. Kaufman (Eds.), *Neuroscience of creativity* (pp. 19–44). Cambridge, MA: MIT Press.

Gadamer, H.-G. (1977). *Philosophical hermeneutics.* (D. E. Linge, Trans.). Berkeley, CA: University of California Press. (Original work published 1966.)

Gadamer, H.-G. (2004). *Truth and method* (2nd ed.). (J. Weinsheimer & D. G. Marshall, Trans.). New York, NY: Continuum. (Original work published 1975.)

Gardner, H. (1983). *Frames of mind: The theory of multiple intelligences.* New York, NY: Basic Books.

Gardner, H. (1999). *Intelligence reframed: Multiple intelligences for the 21st century.* New York, NY: Basic Books.

Gardner, M. (1957). *Fads and fallacies in the name of science.* New York, NY: Dover.

Giamatti, A. B. (1968). Proteus unbound: Some versions of the sea god in the Renaissance. In P. Demetz, T. Greene, & L. Nelson (Eds.), *The disciplines of criticism.* New Haven, CT: Yale University Press.

Gilbert, E. (2015). *Big magic: Creative living beyond fear.* New York, NY: Riverhead Books.

Ginot, E. (2015). *The neuropsychology of the unconscious.* New York, NY: Norton.

Goldstein, B. E. (Ed.). (2001). *Blackwell handbook of perception.* Malden, MA: Blackwell.

Golinski, J. (1998). *Making natural knowledge: Constructivism and the history of science.* New York, NY: Cambridge University Press.

Goodwyn, E. (2012). *The neurobiology of the gods.* New York, NY: Routledge.

Gould, S. J. (1998). *Leonardo's mountain of clams and the diet of worms: Essays on natural history.* New York, NY: Harmony Books.

Gould, S. J. (2003). *The hedgehog, the fox, and the magister's pox.* New York, NY: Harmony Books.

Grandin, T., & Johnson, C. (2006). *Animals in translation. Using the mysteries of autism to decode animal behavior.* San Diego, CA: Harcourt.

Gray, R. T. (2011). Introduction. In R. T. Gray, N. Halmi, G. J. Handwerk, M. Rosenthal, & K. Vieweg (Eds.), *Inventions of the imagination: Romanticism and beyond* (pp. 3–16). Seattle, WA: University of Washington Press.

Graziosi, B. (2013). Petrarch paints the gods. In *The gods of Olympus: A history* (pp. 185–194). London: Profile Books.

Griffin, D. R. (1981). *The question of animal awareness, revised and expanded edition.* Los Altos, CA: William Kaufmann.

Hackett, T. A. (2012). Multisensory convergence in the thalamus. In B. E. Stein (Ed.). *The new handbook of multisensory processing* (pp. 49–66). Cambridge, MA: MIT Press.

Haig, B. D. (2010). Scientific method. In N. J. Salkind (Ed.), *Encyclopedia of research design* (Vol. 3, pp. 1325–1329). Retrieved from Gale Virtual Reference Library.

Harari, Y. N. (2016). *Sapiens: A brief history of humankind.* New York, NY: HarperCollins.

Harper, W., & Schulte, O. (2005). Scientific method. In D. M. Borchert (Ed.), *Encyclopedia of philosophy* (2nd ed., Vol. 8, pp. 682–688). Retrieved from Gale Virtual Reference Library.

Harris, S. (2004). *The end of faith*. New York, NY: Norton.

Hartmann, E. (1998). *Dreams & nightmares: The new theory on the origins and meanings of dreams*. New York, NY: Plenum Trade.

Hartmann, E. (2007). The nature and functions of dreaming. In D. Barrett & P. McNamara (Eds.), *The new science of dreams* (Vol. 3, pp. 171–192). Westport, CT: Praeger.

Hasson, U. (2008). Neurocinematics: The neuroscience of film. *Projections*, 2(1), 1–26

Hasson, U., Ghazanfar, A. A., Galantucci, B., Garrod, S., & Keysers, C. (2012). Brain-to-brain coupling: A mechanism for creating and sharing a social world. *Trends in Cognitive Science*, 16(2), 114–121.

Hedley, D. (2016). *The iconic imagination*. New York, NY: Bloomsbury.

Helmholtz, H. V. (1896). *Vorträge und reden*. Brunswick, Germany: Friedrich Viewig und Sohn.

Hillman, J. (1972). *The myth of analysis*. New York, NY: HarperCollins.

Hillman, J. (1976). *Re-visioning psychology*. New York, NY: HarperCollins.

Hillman, J. (1979a). Image sense. *Spring*, 130–143.

Hillman, J. (1979b). *The dream and the underworld*. New York, NY: HarperCollins.

Hillman, J. (1983). *Archetypal psychology: A brief account*. Dallas, TX: Spring Publications.

Hillman, J. (1992). *The thought of the heart and the soul of the world*. Putnam, CT: Spring Publications.

Hillman, J. (1994). *Healing fiction*. Putnam, CT: Spring. (Original published 1983.)

Hillman, J. (2005). Peaks and vales. In G. Slater (Ed.), *Senex and Puer* (pp. 67–90). Putnam, CO: Spring. (Original work published in 1975.)

Hippocrates (1923). *Hippocrates* (Vol. 2). G. P. Gould (Ed.). (W. H. S. Jones, Trans.). Cambridge, MA: Harvard University Press.

Hobson, J. A. (1988). *The dreaming brain*. New York, NY: Basic Books.

Hobson, J. A. (2002). *Dreaming: A very short introduction*. New York, NY: Oxford University Press.

Hobson, J. A. (2015). *Psychodynamic neurology: Dreams, consciousness, and virtual reality*. Boca Raton, FL: CRC Press.

Hobson, J. A., & McCarley, R. (1977). The brain as a dream state generator: An activation synthesis hypothesis of the dream process. *American Journal of Psychiatry*, 134(12), 1335–1348.

Hobson, J. A., McCarley, R., & Wyzinki, P. (1975). Sleep cycle oscillation: Reciprocal discharge by two brainstem neuronal groups. *Science*, 189(4196), 55–58.

Holton, G. (1996). *Einstein, history & other passions*. Cambridge, MA: Harvard University Press.

Homer. (1996). *The Odyssey*. (R. Fagle, Trans.). New York, NY: Penguin.

Homer. (2013). *The Odyssey*. (S. Mitchell, Trans.). New York, NY: Simon & Schuster.

Horrigan, B. J. (Ed.). (2003). *Voices of integrative medicine*. Saint Louis, MO: Churchill Livingstone.

Howe, K. R. (2008). Isolating science from the humanities. In N. K. Denzin (Ed.), *Qualitative inquiry and the politics of evidence* (pp. 97–118). Walnut Creek, CA: Left Coast Press.

Hume, D. (1978). *A treatise on human nature* (2nd ed.). Oxford, UK: Oxford University Press. (Original work published 1888.)

Hupbach, A., Gomez, R., & Nadel, L. (2009). Episodic memory reconsolidation: Updating or source confusion? *Memory, 17*(5), 502–510.

Ihde, D. (2009). *Postphenomenology and technoscience: The Peking University lectures.* New York, NY: State University of New York Press.

Ingham, P. C. (2015). *The medieval new: Ambivalence in an age of innovation.* Philadelphia, PA: Pennsylvania University Press.

Jacobs, N. S., Allen, T. A., Nguyen, N., & Fortin, N. J. (2013). Critical role for the hippocampus in memory for elapsed time. *The Journal of Neuroscience, 33*(34), 13888–13893.

Jeste, D., & Meeks, T. (2009). Neurobiology of wisdom: A literature overview. *Archives of General Psychiatry, 66*(4), 355–365.

Johnson, R. (1986). *Inner work.* New York, NY: HarperCollins.

Jung, C. G. (1954a). Analytical psychology and education. In H. Read, M. Fordham, G. Adler, & W. McGuire (Eds.), *The collected works of C. G. Jung* (R. F. C. Hull, Trans.) (Vol. 17, pp. 63–132). New York, NY: Princeton University Press. (Original work published 1946.)

Jung, C. G. (1954b). The aims of psychotherapy. In H. Read, M. Fordham, G. Adler, & W. McGuire (Eds.), *The collected works of C. G. Jung* (R. F. C. Hull, Trans.) (Vol. 16, 2nd ed., pp. 36–52). Princeton, NJ: Princeton University Press. (Original work published 1931.)

Jung, C. G. (1954c). The practical use of dream-analysis. In H. Read, M. Fordham, G. Adler, & W. McGuire (Eds.), *The collected works of C. G. Jung* (R. F. C. Hull, Trans.) (Vol. 16, 2nd ed., pp. 139–162). New York, NY: Princeton University Press. (Original work published 1934.)

Jung, C. G. (1954d). The psychology of the transference. In H. Read, M. Fordham, G. Adler, & W. McGuire (Eds.), *The collected works of C. G. Jung* (R. F. C. Hull, Trans.) (Vol. 16, 2nd ed., pp. 163–323). Princeton, NJ: Princeton University Press. (Original work published 1946.)

Jung, C. G. (1958). Psychological commentary on "The Tibetan book of the great liberation." In H. Read, M. Fordham, G. Adler, & W. McGuire (Eds.), *The collected works of C. G. Jung* (R. F. C. Hull, Trans.) (Vol. 11, pp. 475–508). Princeton, NJ: Princeton University Press.

Jung, C. G. (1960a). The nature of the psyche. In H. Read, M. Fordham, G. Adler, & W. McGuire (Eds.), *The collected works of C. G. Jung* (R. F. C. Hull, Trans.) (Vol. 8, pp. 159–324). Princeton, NJ: Princeton University Press (Original work published 1947.)

Jung, C. G. (1960b). Spirit and life. In H. Read, M. Fordham, G. Adler, & W. McGuire (Eds.), *The collected works of C. G. Jung* (R. F. C. Hull, Trans.) (Vol. 8, pp. 159–324). Princeton, NJ: Princeton University Press (Original work published 1926.)

Jung, C. G. (1964). The role of the unconscious. In H. Read, M. Fordham, G. Adler, & W. McGuire (Eds.), *The collected works of C. G. Jung* (R. F. C. Hull, Trans.) (Vol. 10, pp. 3–28). Princeton, NJ: Princeton University Press: Princeton, NJ. (Original work published 1918.)

Jung, C. G. (1966a). The practical use of dream analysis. In H. Read, M. Fordham, G. Adler, & W. McGuire (Eds.), *The collected works of C. G. Jung* (R. F. C. Hull, Trans.) (Vol. 16, 2nd ed., pp. 139–162). Princeton, NJ: Princeton University Press. (Original work published 1934.)

Jung, C. G. (1966b). The structure of the unconscious. In H. Read, M. Fordham, G. Adler, & W. McGuire (Eds.), *The collected works of C. G. Jung* (R. F. C. Hull, Trans.) (Vol. 7, pp. 269–304). Princeton, NJ: Princeton University Press. (Original work published 1916.)

Jung, C. G. (1967). Commentary on "the secret of the golden flower." In H. Read, M. Fordham, G. Adler, & W. McGuire (Eds.), *The collected works of C. G. Jung* (R. F. C. Hull, Trans.) (Vol. 13, pp. 1–56). Princeton, NJ: Princeton University Press. (Original work published 1929.)

Jung, C. G. (1968). Gnostic symbols of the self. In H. Read, M. Fordham, G. Adler, & W. McGuire (Eds.), *The collected works of C. G. Jung* (R. F. C. Hull, Trans.) (Vol. 9.2, 2nd ed., pp. 194–221). Princeton, NJ: Princeton University Press. (Original work published 1951.)

Jung, C. G. (1969a). On the nature of dreams. In H. Read, M. Fordham, G. Adler, & W. McGuire (Eds.), *The collected works of C. G. Jung* (R. F. C. Hull, Trans.) (Vol. 8, 2nd ed., pp. 281–300). Princeton, NJ: Princeton University Press. (Original work published 1945.)

Jung, C. G. (1969b). The transcendent function. In H. Read, M. Fordham, G. Adler, & W. McGuire (Eds.), *The collected works of C. G. Jung* (R. F. C. Hull, Trans.) (Vol. 8, 2nd ed, pp. 67–91). Princeton, NJ: Princeton University Press. (Original work published 1957.)

Jung, C. G. (1970). Mysterium coniunctionis. In H. Read, M. Fordham, G. Adler, & W. McGuire (Eds.), *The collected works of C. G. Jung* (R. F. C. Hull, Trans.) (Vol. 14, 2nd ed.). Princeton, NJ: Princeton University Press. (Original work published 1955.)

Jung, C. G. (1971). Psychological Types. In H. Read, M. Fordham, G. Adler, & W. McGuire (Eds.), *The collected works of C. G. Jung* (R. F. C. Hull, Trans.) (Vol. 6). Princeton, NJ: Princeton University Press. (Original work published 1921.)

Jung, C. G. (1976). *The visions seminars, book two.* New York, NY: Spring Publications. (Original lecture given May 4, 1932.)

Jung, C. G. (1989). *Memories, dreams, reflections.* A. Jaffe (Ed.). (R. Winston & C. Winston, Trans.). New York, NY: Vintage Books. (Original work published 1961.)

Jung, R. E., & Haier, R. J. (2013). Creativity and intelligence: Brain networks that link and differentiate the expression of genius. In O. Vartanian, S. Bristol, & J. C. Kaufman (Eds.), *Neuroscience of creativity* (pp. 233–254). Cambridge, MA: MIT Press.

Kandel, E. R. (2006). *In search of memory.* New York, NY: Norton.

Kant, I. (1958). *Critique of pure reason.* (N. K. Smith, Trans.). New York, NY: Modern Library. (Original work published 1781.)

Karnes, M. (2011). *Imagination, meditation, and cognition in the middle ages.* Chicago, IL: University of Chicago Press.

Kaufman, A. B., Kornilov, S. A., Bristol, A. S., Tan, M., & Grigorenko, E. L. (2010). The neurobiological foundation for creative cognition. In J. C. Kaufman

& R. J. Sternberg (Eds.), *The Cambridge handbook of creativity* (pp. 216–232). New York, NY: Cambridge University Press.

Kaufman, J. C., & Beghetto, R. A. (2009). Beyond big and little: The four-C model of creativity. *Review of General Psychology, 13*(1), 1–12.

Kaufman, S. B. (2013, August 19). The real neuroscience of creativity [Web log post]. Retrieved from http://blogs.scientificAmerican.com/beautiful-minds/the-real-neuroscience-of-creativity/.

Kaufman, S. B., & Gregoire, C. (2015). *Wired to create: Unraveling the mysteries of the creative mind*. New York, NY: Tarcher Perigee.

Kaufman, W. (1992). Nietzsche as the first great (depth) psychologist. In S. Koch & D. E. Leary (Eds.), *A century of psychology as science* (pp. 911–920). Washington, DC: American Psychological Association. (Original work published 1985.)

Kearney, R. (1988). *The wake of imagination: Toward a post-modern culture*. New York, NY: Routledge.

Kearney, R. (1998). *The poetics of imagining: Modern to post-modern*. New York, NY: Fordham University Press. (Original work published 1991.)

Kelly, E. F., Crabtree, A., & Marshall, P. (Eds.). (2015). *Beyond physicalism: Toward reconciliation of science and spirituality*. Lanham, MD: Rowman & Littlefield.

Kelly, E. F., & Presti, D. E. (2015). A psychobiological perspective on "transmission" models. In E. F. Kelly, A. Crabtree, & P. Marshall (Eds.), *Beyond physicalism: Toward reconciliation of science and spirituality* (pp. 115–155). Lanham, MD: Rowman & Littlefield.

Kerr, C. E. (2008). Dualism redux in recent neuroscience: "Theory of mind" and "embodied simulation" hypothesis in light of historical debates about perception, cognition, and mind. *Review of General Psychology, 12*(2), 205–214.

Kind, A. (1997). *The workings of the imagination* (Order No. 9803482). Available from ProQuest Dissertations & Theses Global. (304327360). Retrieved from http://pgi.idm.oclc.org/login?url=http://search.proquest.com.pgi.idm.oclc.org/docview/304327360?accountid=45402.

Kind, A. (2016). Introduction: Exploring imagination. In A. Kind (Ed.), *The Routledge handbook of philosophy of imagination* (pp. 1–12). New York, NY: Routledge.

Kind, A., & Kung, P. (Eds.). (2016). *Knowledge through imagination*. New York, NY: Oxford University Press.

Koch, C. (2012). *Consciousness: Confessions of a romantic reductionist*. Cambridge, MA: MIT Press.

Koons, R. C., & Bealer, G. (2010). *The waning of materialism*. Oxford, UK: Oxford University Press.

Korzybski, A. (2010). *Selections from science and sanity: An introduction to non-Aristotelian systems and general semantics* (2nd ed.). L. Strate (Ed.). Fort Worth, TX: Institute of General Semantics. (Original work published 1948.)

Kosslyn, S. M., Ganis, G., & Thompson, W. L. (2001). Neural foundations of imagery. *Nature Reviews: Neuroscience, 2*(9), 635–642.

Kosslyn, S. M., Thompson, W. L., & Ganis, G. (2006). *The case for mental imagery*. New York, NY: Oxford University Press.

Kradin, R. (2008). *The placebo response and the power of unconscious healing*. New York, NY: Routledge.

Kraemer, D. (2005). Evil and suffering, Judaic doctrines of. In J. Neusner, A. J. Avery-Peck, & W. S. Green (Eds.), *The encyclopedia of Judaism* (Vol. 1., 2nd ed., pp. 778–784). Retrieved from Gale Virtual Reference Library.

Kristeller, P. O. (2006). Ficino, Marsilio (1433–1499). In D. M. Borchert (Ed.), *Encyclopedia of philosophy* (Vol. 3, 2nd ed., pp. 620–626). Detroit, MI: MacmillanReference.

Kugler, P. (2005). *Raids on the unthinkable: Freudian and Jungian psychoanalysis.* New Orleans, LA: Spring Journal Books.

Kuhn, T. (1996). *The structure of scientific revolutions* (3rd ed.). Chicago, IL: University of Chicago Press. (Original work published 1962.)

Kunzendorf, R. G. (2007). "Symbolic" images in dreams and daydreams. In D. Barret & P. McNamara (Eds.), *The new science of dreams* (Vol. 3, pp. 155–170). Westport, CT: Praeger.

LaBerge, S. (1990). Lucid dreaming: Psychophysiological studies of consciousness during REM sleep. In R. R. Bootzen, J. F. Kihlstrom, & D. L. Schacter (Eds.), *Sleep and cognition* (pp. 109–126). Washington, DC: American Psychological Association.

LaBerge, S. (2007). Lucid dreaming. In D. Barret & P. McNamara (Eds.), *The new science of dreams* (Vol. 2, pp. 307–328). Westport, CT: Praeger.

LeDoux, J. (2002). *The synaptic self: How our brains become who we are.* New York, NY: Penguin.

Le Goff, J. (1985). *The Medieval imagination.* (A. Goldman, Trans.). Chicago IL: University of Chicago Press.

Lewin, R. (1999). *Complexity: Life at the edge of chaos.* Chicago, IL: University of Chicago Press.

Lewis, T., Amini, F., & Lannon, R. (2001). *A general theory of love.* New York, NY: Vintage.

Llinas, R. (2001). *I of the vortex.* Cambridge, MA: MIT Press.

Lloyd, R. (2015, February). Is there really a war on science? *Scientific American.* [web]. Retrieved from: www.scientificAmerican.com/article/is-there-really-a-war-on-science/.

Locke, J. (1693). *Some thoughts concerning education.* Retrieved from https://legacy.fordham.edu/halsall/mod/1692locke-education.asp.

Madill, A. (2008). Realism. In L. M. Given (Ed.), *The Sage encyclopedia of qualitative research methods* (Vol. 2, pp. 731–735). Thousand Oaks, CA: Sage.

Maquet P., Peters, J. M., Aerts J., Delfiore, G., Degueldre, C., Luxen, A., & Franck, G. (1996). Functional neuroanatomy of human rapid-eye-movement sleep and dreaming. *Nature, 12*(383), 163–166.

Mar, R. A. (2004). The neuropsychology of narrative: Story comprehension, story production, and their interrelation. *Neuropsychologia, 42*(10), 1414–1434.

Mar, R. A., & Oatley, K. (2008). The function of fiction is the abstraction and simulation of social experience. *Perspectives on Psychological Science, 3*(3), 173–192.

Mchaffie, J. G., Fuentes-Santamaria, V., Alvarado, J. C., Farias, A. L. F., Gutierrez-Ospina, G., & Stein, B. E. (2012). Anatomical features of the intrinsic circuitry underlying multisensory integration in the superior colliculus. In B. E. Stein (Ed.), *The new handbook of multisensory processing* (pp. 31–48). Cambridge, MA: MIT Press.

McGilchrist, I. (2009). *The master and his emissary: The divided brain and the making of the Western world.* New Haven, CT: Yale University Press.

Mehl-Madrona, L. (2015). *Remapping your mind: The neuroscience of self-transformation through story.* Rochester, VT: Bear.

Merchant, C. (1980). *The death of nature: Women, ecology and the scientific revolution.* San Francisco, CA: Harper.

Meredith, M. A. (2012). Multisensory convergence: Where it all begins. In B. E. Stein (Ed.), *The new handbook of multisensory processing* (pp. 3–12). Cambridge, MA: MIT Press.

Mitchell, M. (2009). *Complexity: A guided tour.* New York, NY: Oxford University Press.

Montaigne de, M. (1993). *Essays.* (J. M. Cohen, Trans). Irvine, CA: Xist. (Original work published 1580.)

Moore, M. E. (2010). *Imagination and the mind's ear* (Doctoral dissertation). Available from ProQuest Dissertations and Theses database (UMI No. 3423241).

Moore, T. (1982). *The planets within: The astrological psychology of Marsilio Ficino.* Great Barrington, MA: Lindisfarne Books.

Morosini, P. (2010). *Seven keys to imagination.* Tarrytown, NY: Marshall Cavendish.

Morris, B. (1981). *The reenchanment of the world.* Ithaca, NY: Cornell University Press.

Murray, P. (1991). Editor's introduction. In P. Murray (Ed.), *Imagination: A study in the history of ideas* (pp. vii–xvi). New York, NY: Routledge.

Muzur, A., Pace-Schott, E. F., & Hobson J. A. (2002). The prefrontal cortex in sleep. *Trends In Cognitive Science,* (6), 475–481.

Nagel, T. (2015). *Mind and cosmos: Why the materialist neo-Darwinian conception of nature is almost certainly false.* New York, NY: Oxford University Press.

Newberg, A., & Waldman, M. R. (2009). *How god changes your brain.* New York, NY: Ballantine Books.

Nicholas of Cusa. (1978). Trialogus de possest. In J. Hopkins (Ed.), *A concise introduction to the philosophy of Nicholas of Cusa.* Minneapolis, MN: University of Minnesota Press. (Original work spublished in 1460.)

Nickles, T. (2005). Positivism. In M. C. Horwitz (Ed.), *New dictionary of the history of ideas* (Vol. 5, pp. 1852–1857). Detroit, MI: Scribner.

Nietzsche, F. (1967). *Ecce homo.* W. Kaufman (Ed. & Trans). New York, NY: Vintage Books. (Original work published 1908.)

Nietzsche, F. (1974). *The gay science.* W. Kaufman (Ed. & Trans). New York, NY: Vintage Books. (Original work published 1882.)

Nietzsche, F. (1997). *Beyond good and evil.* (H. Zimmern, Trans.). Mineloa, NY: Dover. (Original work published 1886.)

Noë, A. (2009). *Out of our heads: Why you are not your brain, and other lessons from the biology of consciousness.* New York, NY: Hill & Wang.

Noordzij, M. L., & Postma, A. (2012). Language of space: A comparison between blind and sighted individuals. In V. Gyselinck & F. Pazzaglia (Eds.), *From mental imagery to spatial cognition and language* (pp. 162–176). London, UK: Psychology Press.

Nofzinger, E. A., Mintun, M. A., Wiseman, M., Kupfer, D. J., & Moore, R. Y. (1997). Forebrain activation in REM sleep: An FDG PET study. *Brain Research,* 770(1–2), 192–201.

Oakes, G. (2005). Dilthey, Wilhelm. In L. Jones (Ed.), *Encyclopedia of religion* (2nd ed., Vol. 4, pp. 2352–2353). Retrieved from Gale Virtual Reference Library.

O'Craven, K. M., & Kanwisher, N. (2000). Mental imagery of faces and places actives corresponding stimulus-specific brain regions. *Journal of Cognitive Neuroscience, 12*(6), 1013–1023.

Okasha, S. (2002). *Philosophy of science: A very short introduction.* New York, NY: Oxford University Press.

Olson, R. (2015). *Houston, we have a narrative: Why science needs story.* Chicago, IL: University of Chicago Press.

Pace-Schott, E. (2007). The frontal lobes and dreaming. In D. Barret & P. McNamara (Eds.), *The new science of dreams* (Vol. 1, pp. 115–154). Westport, CT: Praeger.

Pagel, J. F. (2014). Archaeology, anthropology, and dreaming. In *Dream science: Exploring the forms of consciousness* (pp. 1–20). Retrieved from Gale Virtual Reference Library.

Panksepp, J. (1998). *Affective neuroscience: The foundations of human and animal emotions.* New York, NY: Oxford University Press.

Paris, G. (2007). *Wisdom of the psyche: Depth psychology after neuroscience.* New York, NY: Routledge.

Passmore, J. (1967). Logical positivism. In P. Edwards (Ed.), *The encyclopedia of philosophy* (Vol. 5, pp. 52–57). New York, NY: Free Press.

Patton, K. (2009). Ancient Asklepieia: Institutional incubation and the hope of healing. In S. Aizenstat & R. Bosnak (Eds.), *Imagination & medicine: The future of healing in an age of neuroscience* (pp. 3–34). New Orleans, LA: Spring Journal Books.

Payne, M. (2006). *Narrative therapy* (2nd ed.). Thousand Oaks, CA: Sage.

Peasley-Miklus, C. E., & Panayiutou, G. (2016). Alexithymia predicts arousal-based processing deficits and discordance between emotion response systems during emotional imagery. *Emotion, 16*(2), 164–174.

Pfenninger, K. H. (2001). The evolving brain. In K. H. Pfenninger & V. Shubik (Eds.), *The origins of creativity* (pp. 89–97). New York, NY: Oxford University Press.

Pico Della Mirandola (1945). *Of being and unity.* V. M. Hamm (Trans. & Ed.). Milwaukee, WI: Marquette University Press. (Original work published 1519.)

Pinker, S. (2002). *The blank slate: The modern denial of human nature.* New York, NY: Viking.

Pinker, S. (2013). Science is not your enemy. *The New Republic.* Retrieved from https://newrepublic.com/article/114127/science-not-enemy-humanities.

Plait, P. (2009, April 6). Science is imagination [Web log post]. Retrieved from http://blogs.discovermagazine.com/badastronomy/2009/04/06/science-is-imagination/#.WUKlEcmQy8o.

Plato. (1968). *The republic of Plato.* (A. Bloom, Trans.). New York, NY: Basic Books.

Plato. (2000). *Timaeus.* (D. J. Zeyl, Trans.). Indianapolis, IN: Hackett.

Porges, S. W. (2011). *The polyvagal theory.* New York, NY: Norton.

Presti, D. E. (2016). *Foundational concepts in neuroscience.* New York, NY: Norton.

Pulvermuller, F., Lutzenberger, W., & Preiss, H. (1999). Nouns and verbs in the intact brain: Evidence from event-related potentials and high-frequency cortical responses. *Cerebral Cortex, 9*(5), 297–506.

Putnam, H. (1990). *Realism with a human face.* Cambridge, MA: Harvard University Press.

Radel, R., Davranche, K., Fournier, M., & Dietrich, A. (2015, January). The role of (dis)inhibition in creativity: Decreased inhibition improves idea generation. *Cognition, 134,* 110–120.

Raichle, M. E., Macleod, A. M., Snyder, A. Z., Powers W. J., Gusnard, D. A., & Shulman, G. L. (2001). Inaugural article: A default mode of brain function. *Proceedings of the Natural Academy of Sciences, 98*(2), 676–692. Retrieved from http://plato.stanford.edu/archives/win2014/entries/hermeneutics.

Ramsey, W. (2016, Winter). Eliminative materialism. In Edward N. Zalta (Ed.), *The Stanford encyclopedia of philosophy.* Retrieved from https://plato.stanford.edu/archives/win2016/entries/materialism-eliminative/.

Reas, E. (2013, February). Your brain has two clocks. *Scientific American.* Retrieved from www.scientificAmerican.com/article/your-brain-has-two-clocks/#.

Renaissance Platonism. (2005). In E. I. Bleiberg, J. A. Evans, K. M. Figg, P. M. Soergel, & J. B. Friedman (Eds.), *Arts and humanities through the eras* (Vol. 4, pp. 232–238). Retrieved from Gale Virtual Reference Library.

Ribeiro, S. (2004). An evolutionary theory of sleep and dreams. *MultiCiencia, 3,* 1–20.

Richardson, A. (2011). Defaulting to fiction: Neuroscience rediscovers the romantic imagination. *Poetics Today, 32*(4), 663–692.

Rickman, H. P. (Ed.). (1976). *Dilthey: Selected writings.* Cambridge, MA: Cambridge University Press.

Robinson, D. (1976). *An intellectual history of psychology.* Madison, WI: University of Wisconsin Press.

Rowland, S. (2012). Ariadne's thread and the bloodsucking ghosts. In D. P. Slattery & J. L. Selig (Eds.), *The soul does not specialize: Revaluing the humanities and the polyvalent imagination* (pp. 25–36). Carpinteria, CA: Mandorla Books.

Rubin, D. C. (2006). The basic systems model of epistemic memory. *Perspectives on Psychological Science, 1*(4), 277–311.

Russell, B. (1945). *History of Western philosophy.* London: Allen and Unwin.

Russell, D. (2013). *The life and ideas of James Hillman, volume I: The making of a psychologist.* New York, NY: Helios Press.

Sartre, J.-P. (2004). *The imaginary: A phenomenological psychology of the imagination.* J. Weber (Trans. & Ed.). New York, NY: Routledge. (Original work published 1940.)

Schacter, D. L., Addis, D. R., & Buckner, R. L. (2007, September). Remembering the past to imagine the future: The prospective brain. *Nature Reviews: Neuroscience 8*(9), 657–661.

Schelling, F. W. J. (1978). *System of transcendental idealism.* (P. Heath, Trans.). Charlottesville, VA: University of Virginia Press. (Original work published 1800.)

Schipperges, H. (1995). *Hildegarde of Bingen: Healing and the nature of the cosmos.* (J. Broadwin, Trans). Princeton, NJ: Markus Wiener.

Schore, A. N. (2012). *The science of the art of psychotherapy.* New York, NY: Norton.

Shafir, T., Stephan, F., Atkinson, A. P., Scott, A., & Zubieta, J.-K. (2013). Emotional regulation through execution, observation, and imagery of emotional movements. *Brain and Cognition, 82*(2), 219–227.

Shamdasani, S. (2003). *Jung and the making of modern psychology*. New York, NY: Cambridge University Press.

Shein-Idelson, M., Ondracek, J. M., Liaw, H.-P., Reiter, S., & Laurent, G. (2016, April). Slow waves, sharp waves, ripples, and REM in sleeping dragons. *Science, 352* (6285), 590–595.

Shelley, P. B. (1965). *A defense of poetry*. J. E. Jordan (Ed.). Indianapolis, IN: Bobbs-Merrill. (Original work published 1840.)

Shepard, A. D. R. (2014). *The poetics of phantasia: Imagination in ancient aesthetics*. New York, NY: Bloomsbury.

Shulman, H. (1997). *Living at the edge of chaos: Complex systems in culture and psyche*. Einsiedeln, Switzerland: Daimon.

Siegel, D. (2012). *The pocket guide to interpersonal neurobiology*. New York, NY: Norton.

Siegel, D. (2017). *Mind: A journey to the heart of being human*. New York, NY: Norton.

Sipiora, M. (2012). Psychology is unthinkable without the humanities. In D. P. Slattery & J. L. Selig (Eds.), *The soul does not specialize: Revaluing the humanities and the polyvalent imagination* (pp. 99–112). Carpinteria, CA: Mandorla Books.

Slingerland, E., & Collard, M. (Eds.). (2011). *Creating consilience: Integrating the sciences and the humanities*. New York, NY: Oxford University Press.

Smith, C. M. (2007). *Jung and shamanism in dialogue*. New York, NY: Paulist Press.

Solms, M. (1997). *The neuropsychology of dreams*. Mahwah, NJ: Lawrence Erlbaum.

Solms, M., & Turnbull, O. (2002). *The brain and the inner world*. New York, NY: Other Press.

Sperry, R. W. (1974). Lateral specialization in the surgically separated hemispheres. In F. Schmitt & F. Worden (Eds.), *Third neurosciences study program* (Vol. 3, pp. 5–19). Cambridge, MA: MIT Press.

Spreng, R. N., Mar, R. A., & Kim, A. S. N. (2008). The common neural basis of autobiographical memory, prospection, navigation, theory of mind, and the default mode: A quantitative meta-analysis. *Journal of Cognitive Neuroscience, 21*(3), 489–510.

Stein, B. A. (2012). Introduction. In B. E. Stein (Ed.), *The new handbook of multisensory processing* (pp. xi–xvi). Cambridge, MA: MIT Press.

Steiner, R. (1911). *Mystics of the Renaissance and their relationship to modern thought*. New York, NY: Putnam.

Stent, G. S. (2001). Meaning in art and science. In K. H. Pfenninger & V. Shubik (Eds.), *The origins of creativity* (pp. 31–42). New York, NY: Oxford University Press.

Sternberg, E. M. (2009). Can believing make you well? A decade later. In S. Aizenstat & R. Bosnak (Eds.), *Imagination & medicine: The future of healing in an age of neuroscience* (pp. 79–106). New Orleans, LA: Spring Journal Books.

Stumbrys, T., & Erlacher, D. (2014). The science of lucid dream induction. In R. Hurd & K. Bulkeley (Eds.), *Lucid dreaming: New perspectives on consciousness in sleep* (Vol. 1, pp. 77–102). Santa Barbara, CA: Praeger.

Suess, Z., & Rahman, R. (2015, July). Mental imagery of emotions: Electrophysio-logical evidence. *NeuroImage, 114*, 147–157.

Sumner, P., Vivian-Griffiths, S., Boivin, J., Williams. A., Venetis, C. A., Davies, A., Ogden, J., Whelan, L., Hughes, B., Dalton, B., Boy, F., & Chambers, C. D. (2014). The association between exaggeration in health related science news and academic press releases: Retrospective observational study. *BMJ, 349*, 7015.

Tallis, R. (2011). *Aping mankind: Neuromania, Darwinitis, and the misrepresenta-tion of humanity*. Durham, UK: Acumen.

Tarnas, R. (1991). *The passion of the Western mind: Understanding the ideas that have shaped our world view*. New York, NY: Ballantine Books.

Theocharis, T., & Psimopoulos, M. (1987). Where science has gone wrong. *Nature, 329*(6140), 595–598.

Thomas, D. (1938). The force that through the green fuse drives the flower. Retrieved from www.poets.org/poetsorg/poem/force-through-green-fuse-drives-flower.

Thompson, E. (2007). *Mind in life: Biology, phenomenology, and the science of mind*. Cambridge, MA: Harvard University Press.

Trinkaus, C. (1986). Marcilio Ficino and the ideal of human autonomy. In K. Eisenbichler & O. Z. Pugliese (Eds.), *Ficino and Renaissance Neoplatonism* (pp. 142–148). Ottawa, Canada: Dovehouse.

Tyndall, J. (2015). *Essays on the use and limit of imagination in science*. London, UK: Forgotten Books. (Original work published 1870.)

Uddin, L. Q. (2016). *The salience network of the human brain*. Cambridge, MA: Academic Press.

Van Der Kolk, B. (2014). *The body keeps the score: Brain, mind, and body in the healing of trauma*. New York, NY: Viking.

Varela, F., & Shear, J. (Eds.). (1999). *The view from within: First-person approaches to the study of consciousness*. Thorverton, UK: Imprint Academic.

Vartanian, O., Bristol, S., & Kaufman, J. C. (2013). *Neuroscience of creativity*. Cambridge, MA: MIT Press.

Velmans, M. (1999). Intersubjective science. In J. Shear & F. Varela (Eds.), *The view from within: First person approaches to the study of consciousness* (pp. 299–306). Thorverton, UK: Imprint Academic.

Vishkontas, V., & Miller, B. L. (2013). Art and dementia: How degeneration of some brain regions can lead to new creative impulses. In O. Vartanian, S. Bristol, & J. C. Kaufman (Eds.), *Neuroscience of creativity* (pp. 115–132). Cambridge, MA: MIT Press.

Von Franz, M.-L. (1997). *Alchemical active imagination: Revised edition*. Boulder, CO: Shambhala. (Original work published 1979.)

Voss, U., Holzmann, R., Tuin, I., & Hobson, A. J. (2009, September 1). Lucid dreaming: A state of consciousness with features of both waking and non-lucid dreaming. *Sleep, 32*(9), 1191–1200.

Voss, U., & Voss, G. (2014). A neurobiological model of lucid dreaming. In R. Hurd & K. Bulkeley (Eds.), *Lucid dreaming: New perspectives on consciousness in sleep* (Vol. 1, pp. 23–36). Santa Barbara, CA: Praeger.

Waldrop, M. (1992). *Complexity: The emerging science at the edge of order and chaos*. New York, NY: Simon and Schuster.

Wallas, G. (1926). *The art of thought*. New York, NY: Harcourt Brace.

Wang, A. B. (2016). "Post-truth" named word of the years by Oxford Dictionaries. [Web log]. Retrieved from www.washingtonpost.com/news/the-fix/wp/2016/11/16/post-truth-named-2016-word-of-the-year-by-oxford-dictionaries/?utm_term=.4a4ec7d260b3.

Ward, A. M. (2016). A critical evaluation of the validity of episodic future thinking: A clinical neuropsychology perspective. *Neuropsychology, 30*(8), 887–905.

Warnock, M. (1976). *Imagination.* Berkeley, CA: University of California Press.

Watkins, M. (1984). *Waking dreams.* Putnam, CT: Spring Publications. (Original work published 1976.)

Watson, J. D. (1968). *The double helix: A personal account of the discovery of the structure of DNA.* New York, NY: Atheneum.

Watts, A. (1957). *The way of zen.* New York, NY: Mentor Books.

Weisberg, R. W. (1993). *Creativity: Beyond the myth of genius.* New York, NY: Freeman.

Westman, R. S. (1977). Magical reform and astronomical reform: The Yates thesis reconsidered. In R. S. Westman & J. E. MacGuire (Eds.), *Hermeticism and the scientific revolution.* Los Angeles, CA: William Andrews Clark Memorial Library.

Wichert, S., Wolf, O. T., & Schwabe, L. (2013). Updating of episodic memories depends on the strength of new learning after memory reactivation. *Behavioral Neuroscience, 127*(3), 331–338.

Wieland-Robbescheuten, J. (2006). Prophets of the Hebrew Bible. In E. M. Dowling & W. G. Scarlett (Eds.), *Encyclopedia of religious and spiritual development* (pp. 354–356). Retrieved from Gale Virtual Reference Library.

Wilkinson, M. (2006). *Coming into mind: The mind-brain relationship: A Jungian perspective.* New York, NY: Routledge.

Wilson, E. O. (1998). *Consilience: The unity of knowledge.* New York, NY: Knopf.

Wilson, R. A. (1990). *Quantum psychology.* Tempe, AZ: New Falcon.

Wilson, R. A. (1997). *The new inquisition.* Tempe, AZ: New Falcon.

Wilson, R. A. (2005). *Email to the universe.* Tempe, AZ: New Falcon.

Witherington, D. C. (2011). Taking emergence seriously: The centrality of circular causality for dynamic systems approaches to development. *Human Development, 2011*(54), 66–92.

Wolfson, E. (1994). *Through a speculum that shines: Vision and imagination in Medieval Jewish mysticism.* Princeton, NJ: Princeton University Press.

Wordsworth, W. (1926). *The prelude or growth of a poet's mind.* Oxford, UK: Oxford University Press. (Original work published 1850)

Yu, C. K. (2001). Neuroanatomical correlates of dreaming: The supramarginal gyrus controversy (dream work). *Neuropsychoanalysis, 3*(1), 47–59.

Zak, P. J. (2015). Why inspiring stories make us react: The neuroscience of narrative. *Cerebrum, 2.* Retrieved from www.dana.org/Cerebrum/2015/Why_Inspiring_Stories_Make_Us_React__The_Neuroscience_of_Narrative/.

Zimmer, H. D. (2012). Visual imagery in the brain: Modality specific and spatial, but perhaps without space. In V. Gyselinck & F. Pazzaglia (Eds.), *From mental imagery to spatial cognition and language* (pp. 43–74). London, UK: Psychology Press.

Zunshine, L. (2006). *Why we read fiction: Theory of mind and the novel.* Columbus, OH: Ohio State University Press.

Zweig, A (2006). Goethe, Johann Wolfgang von (1749–1832). In D. M. Borchert (Ed.), *Encyclopedia of philosophy* (2nd ed., Vol. 4, pp. 140–144). Retrieved from Gale Virtual Reference Library. (Original work published 1967.)

Index

Cambray, Joseph 34
Campbell, Joseph 92, 101, 109, 161
Carson, Sherry 160, 164
Castoriadis, Cornelius 83
causality 96; bidirectional 36; circular
  34; pluralistic model of 34
Cech, Thomas 194–5, 219
central executive network (CEN) 158,
  167, 172
Charcot, Jean-Martin 89
Chodorow, Joan 99
Christian meditation 53
Christian monotheism 59
Christian Patriarchs 53
Christ, Jesus 95
Clarke, Arthur C. 204
climate change 223; global warming
  236–7; human-created 236
Clinton, Hillary 106, 237
Cocking, John 54, 60, 70
co-created belief 207
cognitive revolution 41
cognitive science 145
Coleridge, Samuel Taylor 72–3, 76, 84,
  101
collective primordial images 96–8
collective unconscious 81, 84, 96–7;
  concept of 96–8
colorblind 124
common-sense psychological language
  229
community organizing, practice of 15
complex system, science of 31–5, 148,
  228
conscious awareness 95–6, 134–5,
  167–8, 182, 210
consciousness: hard problem of 229; of
  human scientists 198; mystery of
  233; myths and mysteries of 228–31;
  notion of 34; phenomenon of 4, 83;
  theories of 7, 225
conscious personality 94, 96
conscious union, with a poetic cosmos
  69–70
constructive imagination 66
"Copernican Revolution" of
  philosophy 66, 90
Copernicus 200, 202
Corbin, Henry 7, 54, 101, 102–4;
  hatred of idolatry and
  fundamentalism 103; imaginal
  cosmology 103
core consciousness 130–1

cortical arousal 176–8
cosmic imagination 49, 73, 79, 170,
  187, 227
cosmic religion 205
Cozolino, Louis 142–4, 147, 149–50
creative arts 10, 15, 56, 59, 100, 174;
  practice of 15
creative cognition, phenomenon of 164,
  166–7
creative imagination: and art of making
  models 193–5; Creative imagination
  (1981) 69; failure of 194–5;
  formulation of 190; interpretation of
  192; in scientific method 190–3
creative production 162–7; "aha"
  moments 163; classical model of 163;
  conscious–unconscious dialog in 163;
  working out of 163
creative science 189, 190–5, 202
creative unconscious 167–8, 171, 173,
  181, 184
creativity, neuroscience of 4; and
  continuity in dreaming and waking
  consciousness 174–6; creative
  production 162–7; defined 160–2;
  dream and 160, 173–4; free
  association and 169–71; incubation
  and insight 171–3; monolithic
  conception of 164; theory of 181;
  thinking outside the box 166;
  unconscious 167–8, 184; usefulness,
  aspects of 161; "whole brain"
  account of 162, 164, 181
Crick, Francis 168, 193–4, 205
critical philosophy 90
Croce, Benedetto 64
cultural belief system 32, 216
cultural imperialism 30
cultural myths 197, 216–17, 226

Damasio, Antonio 130–1, 165, 167;
  assessment of unconscious mind 168;
  self-awareness, theory of 130
dark ages, characterization of 56
dark energy 196
dark matter 196
Darwin, Charles 130; theory of natural
  selection 25
Daston, Lorraine 12, 26, 78, 79, 187
Daugman, John G. 223–4
da Vinci, Leonardo 58
Dawkins, Richard 29, 102, 237
daydreaming, importance of 172, 175

Printed in the United States
By Bookmasters